RIVER · RUNNERS
OF THE GRAND CANYON

RIVER RUNNERS

OF THE GRAND CANYON

by David Lavender

GRAND CANYON NATURAL HISTORY ASSOCIATION

For my steadfast and reliable word processor

M I L D R E D

Paperbound edition published by Grand Canyon Natural History Association, Grand Canyon, Arizona
ISBN 0-938216-23-6

Clothbound edition published by the University of Arizona Press, Tucson Arizona
ISBN 0-8165-0940-9

Library of Congress Number: 85-70524

Editorial: Sandra Scott, Margaret Stephan
Production: Sandra Scott, Margaret Stephan
Book design: Christina Watkins
Typography: Business Graphics, Albuquerque, New Mexico
Lithography: Classic Printers, Prescott, Arizona

Cover Illustration: Ellsworth Kolb and his brother Emery made the first motion pictures of the Colorado canyons during a reckless, trouble-filled trip in 1911.

Contents

4   A Preface In Two Parts

12   *Chapter One,* POWELL'S TRAILBLAZERS

22   *Chapter Two,* THE PERSISTENT ENGINEER

34   *Chapter Three,* NEW TECHNIQUES

44   *Chapter Four,* FREE-LANCING THE HARD WAY

58   *Chapter Five,* DAM SITES

66   *Chapter Six,* THE OPPORTUNISTS

78   *Chapter Seven,* FOR THE SAKE OF FAME

86   *Chapter Eight,* BUZZ

96   *Chapter Nine,* BOATS FOR HIRE

106   *Chapter Ten,* AGAINST THE GRAIN

116   *Chapter Eleven,* THUNDER ON THE WATER

128   Epilogue, And Now

134   Acknowledgments

136   Bibliography

142   Index

146   Photography Credits

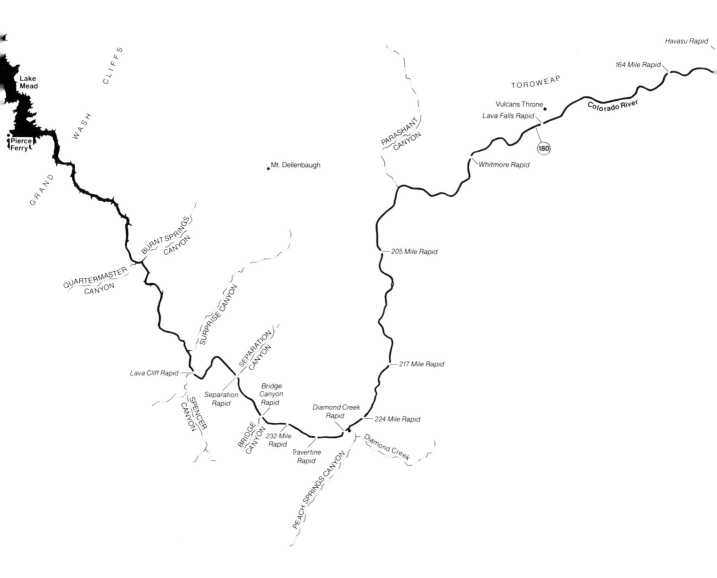

SCALE—MILES

0   5   10   15   20

Havasu Rapid

164 Mile Rapid

TOROWEAP

Lake
Mead

W A S H   C L I F F S

Vulcans Throne

Lava Falls Rapid

Co lo rado River

180

Pierce
Ferry

PARASHANT
CANYON

Whitmore Rapid

G R A N D

• Mt. Dellenbaugh

BURNT SPRINGS
CANYON

205 Mile Rapid

QUARTERMASTER
CANYON

SURPRISE CANYON

217 Mile Rapid

SEPARATION
CANYON

Lava Cliff Rapid

*Bridge
Canyon
Rapid*

*Diamond Creek
Rapid*

224 Mile Rapid

SPENCER
CANYON

*Separation
Rapid*

*232 Mile
Rapid*

Diamond Creek

BRIDGE
CANYON

*Travertine
Rapid*

PEACH SPRINGS CANYON

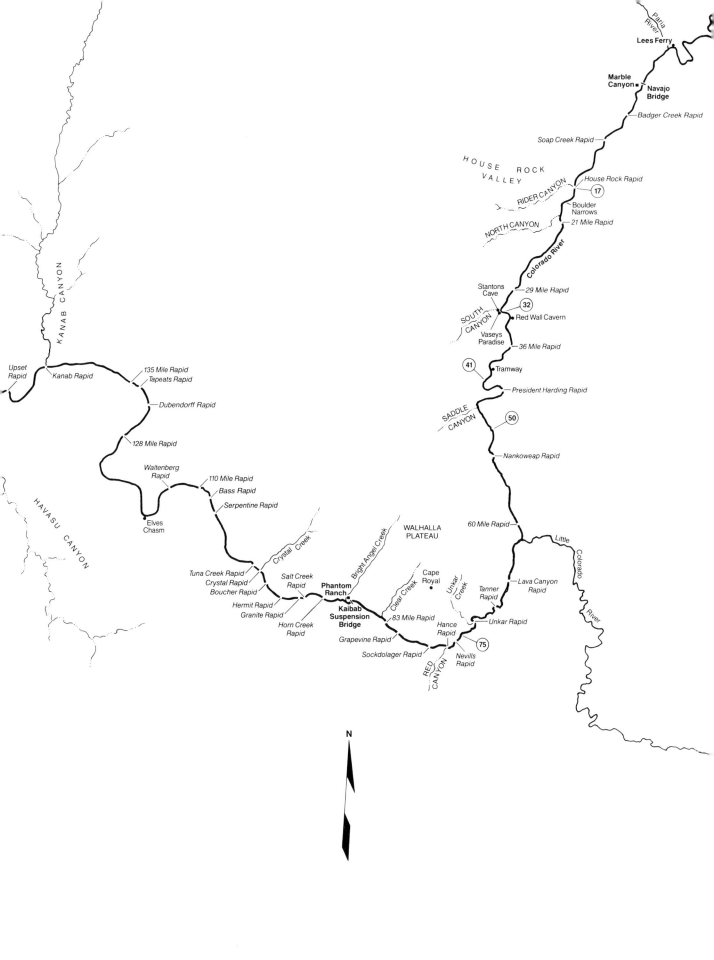

Paria River

Lees Ferry

Marble Canyon

Navajo Bridge

Badger Creek Rapid

Soap Creek Rapid

HOUSE ROCK VALLEY

RIDER CANYON

House Rock Rapid

(17)

Boulder Narrows

NORTH CANYON

21 Mile Rapid

Colorado River

29 Mile Rapid

Stantons Cave

(32)

Red Wall Cavern

SOUTH CANYON

Vaseys Paradise

36 Mile Rapid

(41)

Tramway

President Harding Rapid

SADDLE CANYON

(50)

Nankoweap Rapid

60 Mile Rapid

Little Colorado River

KANAB CANYON

Upset Rapid

Kanab Rapid

135 Mile Rapid

Tapeats Rapid

Dubendorff Rapid

128 Mile Rapid

Waltenberg Rapid

110 Mile Rapid

Bass Rapid

Serpentine Rapid

Elves Chasm

HAVASU CANYON

Crystal Creek

Tuna Creek Rapid

Crystal Rapid

Boucher Rapid

Salt Creek Rapid

Hermit Rapid

Granite Rapid

Horn Creek Rapid

Phantom Ranch

Kaibab Suspension Bridge

Bright Angel Creek

WALHALLA PLATEAU

Clear Creek

Cape Royal

Unkar Creek

Lava Canyon Rapid

Tanner Rapid

83 Mile Rapid

Grapevine Rapid

Sockdolager Rapid

RED CANYON

Hance Rapid

Nevills Rapid

Unkar Rapid

(75)

N

A Preface In Two Parts

1. *Crazy Water*

The river is placid here, but for several minutes the roar of water ahead of the neoprene rafts has been growing louder, pulsing between the cliffs. Then suddenly the flat surface drops out of sight, its place taken by coils of spray tossed upward by whatever lies below.

The boatmen pull ashore, tie up, and with the passengers following worm through the tamarisk and scramble across a hillside littered with boulders to the head of the falls. A big one, rated up toward eight on the scale of difficulty river runners have developed over the years to evaluate rough water. The guides study it carefully, looking for whatever changes may have occurred since last they traversed it — changes caused either by shifts in the position of hazardous boulders or, more generally, by differences in the volume of water.

Back in the boats, each oarsman rows into the middle of the current. As he nears the brink, he lets his craft drift sideways while he stands for a last look at what lies ahead. Almost invariably the accelerating water gathers into a broad, smooth "V", or tongue, that licks hungrily down into the masses of churned water below. There is no turning back now, but there are opportunities for last-second adjustments. By pivoting quickly with his oars, the boatman can shift his course enough to gain the exact spot he had selected earlier, from the bank, as the best one for entering the maelstrom. Once in the turmoil he guides himself by checking on markers — bushes, distinctive rocks, or even transverse waves in the rapid — that he memorized during his study.

The run takes less than a minute. On rare occasions a boat flips — turns over — but nearly always the passengers, buoyed by their life jackets, are able to

4

hang onto it and ride through unscathed. Far more often the boat reaches the bottom of the rapid still upright, the passengers still aboard. Some of the rafts shipped only a few cupfuls of water during the run, while others in the same group filled to the brim. Whatever the case, the passengers are exhilarated. They have had an adventure, but, curiously, most of them know very little about why the rapids that provide the adventure happen to be where they are.

One facile explanation has it that rough water occurs when boulders fall from the canyon walls into a swift current. Certainly masses of rock now and then do slump off the cliffs; the light-colored spots on some precipices are clear remnants of such happenings. In Cataract Canyon, just below the junction of the Green and Colorado rivers, boulder falls have indeed caused rapids. Seldom in the Grand Canyon, however. With few exceptions (the giant boulders in Boulder Narrows and Harding rapids, for example) the tumbling rocks seldom have enough momentum to roll across the talus slopes at the foot of the cliffs into the river. When they do reach the water, they generally cause nothing more than a little fretting.

Riverside walls composed of very hard rock, as in the Upper Granite Gorge of the Grand Canyon, hold the river to a narrow span and with their jaggedness create turbulence. "Ledges of rock jut into the stream," John Wesley Powell noted during his pioneering run through the gorge in 1869, "their tops sometimes just below the surface, sometimes rising a few or many feet above; the island ledges and island pinnacles and island towers break the swift course of the stream into chutes and eddies and whirlpools." And then he adds almost casually, "We soon reach a place where a creek comes in from the left, and, just below, the channel is choked with boulders, which have washed down this lateral channel and formed a dam, over which there is a fall . . ."

Right there is the key. Most rapids in the Grand Canyon are formed by tremendous outwashes of boulders from side streams. These deltas, or boulder fans as they are sometimes called, often reach entirely across the channel and extend downstream, in the water and on the banks, for a quarter of a mile or more. They are very beautiful, for they are made up of masses of water-polished stone of many colors and sizes that have been hewn from thousands of feet of strata of different composition — souvenirs of hundreds of millions of years of geologic history.

There is a paradox here. Some of the boulders in the mass are as big as small houses, and the river is unable to move them out of the way, rage at them though it will. Yet they have been brought down through lateral channels that are either dry during normal times or, at the most, contain only small creeks. How can this be?

Powell's explanation on entering Marble Gorge contains a hint, though not a very clear one. "We have learned to observe closely the texture of the rock. In softer strata we have a quiet river, in harder we find rapids and falls. Below us are the limestones and hard sandstones which we found in Cataract Canyon. This bodes toil and danger." To put the matter another way, soft strata erode easily into small fragments that gradually wash away as sediment. The canyon broadens; side streams flow more gently. Hard stone, on the other hand, forms cliffs. Drainage channels from the rim are narrow and steep. When occasional cloudbursts pour down them, the water attains awesome power. George Simmons and David Gaskill of the United States Geological Survey have translated the abstraction into mathematics. "If the speed of a body of water is doubled then its ability to transport is increased by 2 cubed, or 8 times; if the speed is trebled, the transporting power is increased by a factor of 27."

Consider the experience Robert Brewster Stanton and a small party of surveyors encountered in 1889 while climbing a side gulch out of Marble Canyon during a heavy summer rain:

> It seemed to us as if the whole edge of the canyon [i.e., of the side gulch] had begun to move. Little streams rapidly growing into torrents came over the hard top stratum from every crevice and fell on the softer slope below. In a moment they changed into streams of mud . . . undermining huge loose blocks of the harder strata. . . . As the larger blocks plunged ahead of the stream, they crashed against other blocks lodged on the slopes, and, bursting with an explosion like dynamite, broke into pieces, while the fragments flew into the air, and as the whole conglomerate mass of water, mud, and flying rocks came down the slopes to where we were, it looked as if nothing could prevent us from being buried.

Such avalanches lodge in the bottom of the side gully and, if the storm continues, are swept on into the river. There they back the water up into still pools, some a mile long. Soon, of course, the river finds ways through the blockade. The currents converge on the openings, creating the V-shaped tongues described earlier, and then plunge on into the looser masses of boulders that make up the lower part of the delta.

Any jagged rock in fast water is a threat. Still worse is a giant-size "hole" created when part of the river rushes across the top of a huge boulder and drops down its backside like a waterfall. The plunge blasts a pit into other swirls that have been sweeping around the lower parts of the boulder. The resulting compression forces the water up into a vast standing wave, sometimes fifteen feet high, on the down side of the hole. Its crest, exploding at intervals into bursts of spray, often curls back upstream, to drop thunderously into the vortex it borders.

Motor-driven, flexible rafts that drive fast and straight into the hole and the standing wave beyond it can generally break through the barrier, though the raft may be folded back almost into a right angle during the process. Wooden boats — the material all early runners used — are less supple. If one of them hits at the crest of a standing wave at an angle, topples back, turns sideways perhaps, and is churned around and around until finally the current spits it out — well, it is better to have figured out in advance a course that will enable one to avoid the hole without cracking up on the boulders that flank it.

Sometimes the deltas that create rapids also squeeze the current against the cliff on the opposite side of the river. The cliff's unyielding faces and projecting snouts drive powerful reflex waves back into the channel, often at angles that can catch a boat sideways and roll it over in a twinkling. Nor is internal wildness the only problem. Often strong eddies flow backwards between the central storm of rough water and the shore. The "shear line" dividing the eddy from the downward flowing currents can be abrupt and powerful; an oar-powered raft caught inside the eddy often has trouble breaking out. Then there is downstream turbulence, particularly noticeable at times of high water. The accelerating currents in the rapid, both those on the surface and deep down, intermingle at different velocities. Air captured in the rapid by spray increases the turmoil. The churning gathers into clots beneath the surface and often will travel hundreds of yards before breaking upward in whirlpools strong enough to spin a boat completely around and sometimes even tip one over. At other times huge "boils" erupt like bubbles in a kettle of thick, heated soup.

There are about one hundred and fifty rapids in the Grand Canyon above the farthest extensions of Lake Mead. (The count varies somewhat with the level of the river.) Their total length is roughly twenty-five miles, or nine percent of the canyon's length. In those twenty-five miles the river drops eleven hundred feet, or approximately half of the total descent from Lees Ferry at the head of the canyon to the Grand Wash Cliffs at its foot. So the Colorado is by no means all foam and thunder. There are marvelous stretches of silence, where the iridescent water, gleaming with braids of light and shadow, glides like rippling silk. In places the walls rise directly from the water, their bases beautifully sculptured and polished by tens of thousands of years of silt-laden currents. In other places, where the strata are soft, the cliffs draw back from the river, revealing tier upon tier of creased and colored rock, one of the greatest geologic storybooks on earth.

This overwhelming majesty is generally what one remembers after the excitement of the running of the rapids has faded. Still, boatmen and boatwomen, following the beat of many drums, have spent more than a century learning first how to ride the complex torrent and then developing the equipment needed to bring the adventure within reach of thousands of outdoor enthusiasts each year. Their triumphs and mishaps, their connivings, comedies and tragedies are the burden of the pages that follow.

It is an American epic. Fittingly, two legendary heroes, one Indian and one white, set its tone and, in the fashion of all enduring myths, give meaning to its otherwise haphazard events.

2. *Folk Heroes*

Shortly after the Hopi Indians emerged from the underworld through the sipapu — a spring in the top of a big yellow dome of travertine in the canyon of the Little Colorado River still marks the place — a part of them settled on Navajo Mountain. It was not a good spot. The springs were small, the clouds patchy, the corn stunted.

The melancholy of the situation drove a young man named Tiyo to sorrowful wanderings along the cliffs bordering the San Juan River and, further down, the Colorado where it flowed into a huge gorge his people called Picicva. So much water! Where did it go? Why did the gorge never fill?

Over the protests of his family Tiyo decided to learn. Reluctantly his father helped him cut a hollow cottonwood tree so large that the outstretched arms of both men barely encompassed it. They removed a section from its trunk, plugged the ends, and waterproofed the improvised boat with piñon gum. A small knothole would serve the navigator as a lookout.

While Tiyo's mother and sisters prepared food for the journey, his father made five special prayer sticks, *pahos*, to serve as credentials, and also gave him a wand to use in steering his craft. Off he went. He used his wand for pushing

away from rocks as well as for steering. As recounted by J. Walter Fewkes in the
Journal of American Ethnology and Archeology, 1894:

> Spray splashed through the opening, and this he caught in his
> basin when he wished to drink . . . and he was also provided with
> a plug to close the hole when he neared the roaring water. He
> floated over smooth waters and swift rushing torrents, plunged
> down cataracts, and for many days spun through wild whirlpools,
> where black rocks protruded their heads like angry bears.

On reaching the sea he began a series of adventures with Spiderwoman, the
Sun, and the Snake People. Versions vary, but in all of them he learned about
the Snake god and about the ceremonies and songs that were necessary for
bringing rain to his people. He also met a beautiful maiden he took back to
Navajo Mountain with him to be his wife.

In due time his wife gave birth to a family of snakes. The proud grandfather
showed them to the community, but the snakes bit the little children. A flight
resulted that eventually ended at the present Hopi towns on the southern slopes
of Black Mesa. Later Tiyo's family also reached the area — again there are
different versions — and were given shelter there.

Purportedly the story explains the origin of the Snake clan among the Hopis
and of rain-bringing ceremonies conducted every other year in certain of the
mesa-top villages. The point here is not the ceremony itself — it is far too
complex for summarizing — but the way in which it embodies basic Hopi
concepts about man's place on the earth.

Every object, animate or inanimate, the Hopi believe, is inhabited by a
spirit. If propitiated properly, many of these spirits will carry messages about the
needs of the tribe to the great deities of nature, one of whom is the serpent that
controls life-maintaining fluids — blood, sap, water. It is the duty of the Snake
clan's priests and their associates to establish, as Tiyo taught them to do, the
necessary communication with the vital god by means of captured rattlesnakes
and other snakes. That is to say, the Hopi seek to attain harmony and well-being
by bringing about a oneness between man and the forces of nature. And it was
Picicva, the Grand Canyon, that led Tiyo, the Snake Hero, to this truth.

Americans are too objective, too scientific, to create nature myths to explain
themselves. Yet the canyon is spawning a legend for them, too. This is the tale
of James White. Like many modern folk stories, it deals with an actual person
involved in a presumably actual event. (George Washington and the cherry tree.)
In the process it plumbs enough basic instincts that it also reveals, in true
mythological fashion, fundamental national attitudes.

James White was a prospector. Shortly before the Civil War, he appeared in
Colorado, found nothing and drifted on to Nevada. There, on the outbreak of
hostilities, he enlisted in the Union Army. Throughout most of 1862 he was
stationed at Fort Yuma beside the lower Colorado River. There he surely heard
about the excitement resulting from gold discoveries made farther upstream
during the same period at La Paz, Arizona, and in El Dorado Canyon, Nevada.

After the war, White wandered east as far as Kansas, where he obtained a
job driving a stagecoach on the Santa Fe Trail. His cronies were Joe Goodfellow,

George Strole, and Charles Baker. Baker had also prospected in Colorado before the war. Deciding to give the area another fling, the quartet stole some Indian horses and headed for the San Juan River. Along the way White quarreled with and wounded Goodfellow, forcing him to drop out of the expedition. The others followed the San Juan toward its junction with the Colorado and then cut north, hoping, White said later, to come to the Grand River (now the upper Colorado), which drained rich mineral ground in the central Rockies.

Indians ambushed them. Baker was killed but Strole and White escaped. Afraid to turn back yet unable to take their horses down the plunging side gulch in which they had been surprised, the two survivors fled afoot, taking with them an ax, their guns, some rope, and ten pounds of flour. On reaching the river they built a raft of — shades of Tiyo! — three cottonwood logs. Each log was eight inches in diameter and ten feet long. Later they enlarged it — to no avail. Though they had smooth water at first, they soon ran into a rough stretch. Both George Strole and their dab of flour, White reported later, were washed into the torrent and disappeared.

For fourteen days, twelve to fourteen hours each day, he floated through the canyon. At night he tied the raft to streamside rocks or bushes and slept on it, for if he lost it he would be doomed. He ate mesquite beans and lizards; when those failed he chewed up his leather knife scabbard. After his raft broke apart, he managed to build another. He did not try to climb out of the canyon for fear of being captured in the desert by Indians. Though he had trouble with whirlpools and eddies, he recalled only one rapid as exceptionally violent. Early in September 1867 he was plucked out of the river, dazed, sun-blistered, and emaciated, at the Mormon steamboat landing at Callville, Nevada, now buried under the water of Lake Mead.

His story spread rapidly. One version appeared in the *Transactions* of the St. Louis Academy of Sciences for 1868. Yet White never tried to capitalize on the fame. After a brief stint of carrying mail on horseback along the lower river, he moved north to the vicinity of Fort Bridger, Wyoming, where he landed a job cutting ties for the Union Pacific Railroad, then building west.

At Fort Bridger he possibly encountered John Wesley Powell, who stopped by the post during the winter of 1868 to collect supplies for his Rocky Mountain exploring expedition, then camped a hundred miles off to the southeast on the lower White River in Colorado. It has been conjectured that James White's tale convinced Powell that the Colorado could be run. Powell mentioned no such incident in his later reports, possibly for fear of losing his status as the Colorado River's first explorer — or possibly because the alleged conversation never took place.

For more than a century White's tale has been attacked fiercely. Could a lone man have floated as far as he claimed, in the time he stated, on a primitive raft through several (not one) exceptionally violent rapids? What of his mistakes in geography? Of certain descriptions that don't fit the Grand Canyon? Where did he actually enter the river? Had his party been bound for the gold mines of El Dorado Canyon when dissension broke out, during which Strole and he, not Indians, killed Baker? Indeed, did White kill Strole as well and then invent an "Indian" attack far to the north to divert suspicion?

It is as irrelevant to detail the controversy here as it is to describe the Snake ceremonials that Tiyo brought back to the Hopis. The ingredient that has kept both tales alive for so many years is not made up of facts but of the way they mirror basic instincts. Both involve the river as a symbol of life's journey into the unknown. And both reveal characteristic national attitudes.

The Hopi seek to placate and become one with nature. Not so most technologically minded Americans. They strive to conquer. White's adventure epitomizes the difference. A humble, semi-literate frontiersman, he won his battle against incalculable odds by using qualities Americans valued: physical bravery, endurance, and luck — the pioneers never undervalued luck. And so, whatever the literal truth of his canyon experience may have been, White's story persists. Thrills, spills, and ultimately, conquest.

Thesis and antithesis; out of the dialectic a new synthesis may yet emerge: in the middle way, to misquote Thoreau, lies the salvation of the world. At least more and more river runners think so.

David Lavender
4771 Thacher Road
Ojai, California 93023

One

POWELL'S TRAILBLAZERS

When one-armed Major John Wesley Powell and his eight weary boatmen reached the site of Lees Ferry, where river runners begin their Grand Canyon trips today, they had been on the water, some of it very rough water, for seventy-two days. May 24 to August 4, 1869. From southern Wyoming to northern Arizona.

What next? They did not know. The sightings they took with their sextants showed they were still hundreds of miles from their destination. Immediately ahead, strata of hard limestone were appearing, and they had learned earlier that such rock boded, in Powell's words, "toil and danger."

The worst was that no real unity of purpose held them together. Powell, obsessed with ambition, was the only potential explorer among them, and his qualifications, from an academic standpoint, were meager. The son of a Methodist circuit rider, he had grown up in a series of drab Midwestern towns. The courses in natural science he had taken in various small colleges had not satisfied his questing mind, and he had never stayed put long enough to get a degree, educating himself instead by reading voraciously and collecting specimens while rambling through the Midwestern countryside, sometimes by boat. The Civil War was disastrous for him. As a second lieutenant, he lost his right arm during the battle of Shiloh. Although he could have been mustered out then, he fought grimly on as an artillery major until exhaustion forced him to resign on January 2, 1865.

Rested, he got jobs teaching geology at small Illinois colleges. During the summers of 1867 and 1868 he led students on field trips through the Colorado Rockies. They were in part family affairs. His wife Emma and his brother-in-law Almon Thompson went along, as did his moody, ox-strong younger brother

These trips gave Powell the idea of following the Colorado River through the last considerable piece of unexplored territory in the United States.

Walter, a former Army captain unbalanced by several months in a Confederate military prison. The family hoped strenuous outdoor living might stabilize him.

These trips gave Powell the idea of following the Colorado River through the last considerable piece of unexplored territory in the United States. He picked the nucleus of his party not from among scientists — qualified ones might not have subordinated themselves to an unknown leader — but from the packers, hunters, and guides who had outfitted his field trips.

Their leader was Jack Sumner, aged twenty-eight in 1868 and owner of a small Indian trading post. Assisting Sumner were Oramel Howland, thirty-five, who supported his love affair with the outdoors by working as a part-time printer in Denver; Oramel's younger brother, twenty-five-year-old Seneca Howland; and Bill Dunn and Billy Hawkins, both in their twenties. All five had served as enlisted men in the Union Army. They had disliked its discipline and were predisposed to turn sullen whenever Major Powell, who was thirty-four in 1868, chose to impose similar restrictions on them.

Powell spent part of the winter of 1868-69 seasoning himself and his brother Walter by camping with the five mountaineers in northwestern Colorado. (His wife was there, too.) In March he went East to raise money. Thin pickings. He obtained an army order allowing him to draw ten months' rations for twelve men at any western fort. Some of this order he commuted to cash. He borrowed instruments from the Smithsonian Institution, talked small sums out of a few Illinois sponsoring organizations, added savings of his own, and prevailed on the new Union Pacific Railroad to transport to Green River, Wyoming, a principal tributary of the Colorado, his equipment and the four boats he had ordered specially built in Chicago.

Stout boats. Three were double-ribbed with oak and had double posts at stern and stem. They weighed close to half a ton each and were buoyed by watertight compartments fore and aft. Twenty-one feet long, four feet of beam, and twenty-two inches deep, they could carry two thousand pounds of cargo. Their bottoms were rounded. Two cross seats in the middle accommodated a pair of oarsmen, one behind the other. Powell supposed that one of the oarsmen (or a third member if the boat carried a passenger) could use a heavy sweep oar protruding over the stern to help steer the craft in fast water.

The fourth boat, built of pine and sixteen feet long, was considerably lighter. Powell called it the *Emma Dean* (his wife's maiden name) and planned to lead the way in it. Whenever he heard the roar of rapids ahead, he would halt, scout out the situation, and use flags to signal the next move to the following boats.

He rendezvoused at Green River with seven men — Walter, the five mountaineers, and George Bradley, a soldier somewhat familiar with boats whom he had managed to pluck out of the Army at Fort Bridger, Wyoming, during the preceding winter. Seven men were not enough to handle the four big craft. (The one-armed Major of course could not row.) Powell must have known this in Washington, where he could have found eager young scientists to help with observations as well as rowing, or in Chicago, where experienced lakemen were available. But perhaps he couldn't afford transportation or was jealous of sharing credit with other scientists. Anyway he did not fill out the crew until he reached Green River. There he hired two wanderers who chanced by — a florid-faced

13

Englishman, Frank Goodman, and a nineteen-year-old, unemployed teamster, Andy Hall.

During the winter Powell had decided that he would have to stay in the canyons for ten months if he were to understand them thoroughly. He had come to terms with his five original mountaineers — Sumner, Hawkins, Dunn, and the Howland brothers — on that assumption. If he succeeded in winning federal backing for the trip he would pay them $1000 each for their time in the canyons. Otherwise he would give them $25 a month. He would also allow them to trap and pan for gold when those pursuits did not interfere with their other work. Well, he'd not gotten federal backing. The five agreed to go anyway, hoping, Sumner later implied, for rich pickings of gold and fur in the virgin territory. Presumably hope and $25 a month also suited Bradley, Goodman, and Hall. Walter Powell went along because his brother told him to.

As the untrained boatmen neared the Uinta Mountains, through which the Green slices on its way south to join the Colorado, they encountered rapids. At first the crew enjoyed running them. But the way they did it! They sat with their backs to the bows, the normal position for oarsmen, and rowed blindly backward at full speed, thinking they could keep better control of the boats if they went faster than the current. The man at the sweep oar peered ahead through the spray, trying to see obstacles and shouting directions — "Right! Left!" In spite of that they crashed into boulders and ran into angling waves, heavy with silt, that threatened to swamp them. Realizing the danger without sensing the remedy — that knowledge would come to river runners years later — Powell decided to avoid big rapids rather than risk a wreck that would cost the party a boatload of food, instruments, and clothing.

Sometimes they would land at the head of a rapid, unload the cargo, tote it sack by sack through brush and over boulders to the bottom of the rough water, and then run the boat down empty. More often they lined the boat, sometimes with part of its cargo, but generally empty. The process involved working the craft down close to the bank by lines affixed to bow and stern. Generally a man stayed in the boat and held it off the rocks with an oar. Others waded beside it, slipping, floundering, falling as they helped boost it over obstructions until they reached a point where it could be reloaded and launched. When cliffs blocked these procedures, climbers took the bow line to the bottom of the rapid and braced for a shock. The others eased the boat downstream as far as possible with the stern line and then let it go, counting on those below to bring the plunging craft up short with the bow line. If these devices were not possible, the half-ton boats had to be lifted from the water and portaged past the obstruction, often on skids of driftwood.

The first wreck came in Lodore Canyon, two weeks out of Green River. Because of a mix-up in signals, the Howland brothers and Frank Goodman let their boat, the *No Name*, wallow into what has become known as Disaster Falls. The craft hit a rock and broke in two, with a loss of considerable food and clothing. A few days later a gust of wind blew embers from a cooking fire into the dry brush around their camp. More clothing and several cooking utensils were destroyed. The only replacement was three hundred pounds of flour that Powell managed to obtain from the Uinta Ute Agency, forty miles up the Uinta River from the Green.

At the agency Frank Goodman quit. Now there were nine men in three

14

boats, and during the ensuing days in Desolation and Cataract canyons they became, of necessity, seasoned rivermen. The *Emma Dean* swamped, throwing Powell and his two oarsmen overboard. Another boat broke loose while being lined but was recovered in an eddy. They were constantly patching battered planking and sawing new oars out of driftwood to replace broken ones. They often slept in blowing sand and were everlastingly wet from sudden thunderstorms, spray, or wading beside the boats. The sun broiled them, their shoes were in shreds, and they were frequently hungry in spite of the occasional killing of a beaver or mountain sheep. Ten months in here? The prospect no longer looked like El Dorado.

In that state of mind they passed the mouth of the Paria (Lees Ferry) and plunged into Marble Gorge, the first section of the Grand Canyon. It is a difficult sixty-five-mile stretch, and a beautiful one, especially between miles 22 and 35, where massive cliffs of Redwall limestone, glowing rose-colored in the sunlight, rise abruptly from the water. Powell caught the contrast in one crowded paragraph of his official report.

> The limestone of this canyon is often polished and makes a beautiful marble. [Actually, marble is metamorphic limestone. There is none in Marble Gorge, as Powell probably knew, but the thought of a canyon composed of classic marble made for romantic reading.] Sometimes the rocks are of many colors — white, gray, pink, and purple, with saffron tints. It is with very great labor that we make progress, meeting with many obstructions, running rapids, letting down our boats and cargos around bad places. We camp at night, just after a hard portage, under an overhanging wall, glad to find shelter from the rain. We have to search some time to find a few sticks of driftwood, just sufficient to boil a cup of coffee.

In spite of the difficulties, they reached the mouth of the Little Colorado River without an upset. They paused there for two days in a hot, miserable camp, plagued with insects, while Powell climbed the walls for a view from the top, collected geologic specimens, and made observations. What little food remained was all but inedible, but light loads, he wrote optimistically, would make for easy portages. And then comes the most frequently quoted passage in his official account.

> We are three quarters of a mile in the depths of the earth . . . pigmies *[sic]*, running up and down the sands, or lost among the boulders. . . . What falls there are, we know not; what rocks beset the channel, we know not; what walls rise over the river, we know not. Ah, well! . . . The men talk as cheerfully as ever; jests are bandied about freely this morning; but to me the cheer is somber and the jests are ghastly.

George Bradley, writing in his diary at the actual time of the events puts things differently. "The men are uneasy and discontented and eager to move on. If the Major does not do something soon I fear the consequences, but he is contented and seems to think that biscuit made of sour and musty flour and a few dried apples is ample to sustain a laboring man."

For a time after they started out again the temperature between the sun-reflecting walls rose to 115° Fahrenheit. Change came with sudden deluges of cold rain. Glumly they entered the jaws of Upper Granite Gorge — "black and narrow below, red and gray and flaring above." At times the current was so swift and the waves so high that the boats became unmanageable and the men simply hung on. Whirlpools spun them; reflex waves filled the compartments where the rowers sat. Oars were lost, men swept overboard. But they survived and on August 16 reached "a clear, beautiful creek," coming down from the north. They landed to rest and make new oars.

A couple of miles up the creek they found a suitable pine that had been washed down from the Kaibab Plateau. While the men sawed, Powell and perhaps Jack Sumner climbed around, looking. Though the Major does not say so, his geologic eyes were surely attracted by the region's transverse faults and twisted rock — schist and gneiss nearly two billion years old, striped with intrusive, zigzagging bands of pink granite and, occasionally, quartz. Such rock is far more likely than sandstone to contain gold and silver.

Powell named the stream Silver Creek, possibly because of its contrast with the muddy river. But Jack Sumner, who had joined the expedition to prospect, later told Robert Brewster Stanton, the second man to lead a group through the canyon, that the name came from chunks of silver "float" ore they found in the creek bed, washed down from — they had no time to search for the source.

Later, during the course of his lecturing, Powell's romantic flair led him to contrasting images. They had named an odorous, unpalatable stream far above the Grand Canyon the Dirty Devil. So "we concluded to name [this one] 'Bright Angel.'" Actually, though, it stayed Silver long enough to cause a sharp ripple in Grand Canyon history, as we shall see.

At Bright Angel they threw away the last of their rancid bacon and by mishap lost their baking powder, so that their only food for the rest of the trip would be unleavened bread, a little dried fruit, and coffee. Their state of mind was such that several of the rapids they encountered looked, each in its turn, the worst yet. But of all those watery upheavals the most dreadful, or so it appeared to their weary eyes, was the one they encountered shortly before noon on August 27.

But of all those watery upheavals the most dreadful, or so it appeared to their weary eyes, was the one they encountered shortly before noon on August 27.

Floods, roaring down lateral canyons whose mouths were directly opposite each other, had clogged the main channel with monumental boulders. The river raged. With sinking hearts the wayfarers scouted the bordering cliffs but found no footing that would let them portage or line the boats. They would have to run the maelstrom, Powell decided, including two more tumults they could see farther downstream. "Appalling," George Bradley told his diary, "the darkest day of the trip."

They camped for the night in the side canyon coming from the south. After supper Oramel Howland sought out Powell and said that he, his brother Seneca, and Bill Dunn were leaving. In the morning they would cross the river and try to climb out the north canyon, relying on rainwater collected in potholes to sustain them until they reached the Mormon settlements in the vicinity of St. George, Utah.

There is a dark side to this story that surfaces often enough to need mention. Its source is Robert Brewster Stanton, repeating, in a book called *Colorado River Controversies*, material he obtained from Jack Sumner and Billy

Hawkins many years after the events described. The two men say that the trouble began when Powell tongue lashed Oramel Howland for causing the wreck of the *No Name*. Then Howland sneered at Powell's stinginess in bringing down only three hundred pounds of flour from the Uinta Ute Agency. There was more trouble over the maps Howland was making. And Bill Dunn's falling into the river with Powell's expensive watch. The quick-tempered Major demanded payment. When that was not forthcoming, he ordered Dunn either to leave the party, a physical impossibility at that particular point, or pay board at the rate of a dollar a day. More snarling. More snapping. Even fisticuffs and a show of revolvers, which made Powell and his hulking brother back down. Smugly Sumner finishes, "Major Powell did not run the outfit in the same overbearing manner after that."

In that state of uneasy truce they reached what ever since has been known as Separation Rapid. There Dunn decided to obey orders and leave the party. The Howlands agreed to accompany him. At that Powell caved in and decided the whole group would have to quit the river. But no! Billy Hawkins — this is Billy reminiscing now — said that if Powell would give him and Andy Hall a boat, they would finish the run on their own. This stiffened Powell. He would continue. Sumner's version tallies except for the statement that it was his, Sumner's, determination that swung Powell back into line.

Robert Stanton, a contentious but not a foolish man, took all this seriously, partly because he had discovered that Powell's official account, written under pressure in 1874, did contain some exaggerations and misstatements. But Stanton seems not to have read the journals that George Bradley and Jack Sumner kept during the trip. Those diaries do contain some normal griping by ex-soldiers about the way the brass ran things. Neither, however, mentions a clash with Howland over the wreck of the *No Name* or the melodrama about the watch, natural things to dwell on if they had occurred.

If they did not occur, why did the two men invent them? Spleen perhaps. Though Powell gave the men the expedition's boats and what money he had at the end of the trip neither Hawkins nor Sumner felt he had received his due. The neglect festered, to find relief in wild tales to Stanton when the men were old and their memories faltering.

For whatever reason — exhaustion, fear of the rapids, animosity toward Powell — the Howlands and Dunn decided to pull out. Feeling their chances were negligible (he wrote later in his report), Powell tried to dissuade them. During the night he unwrapped his sextant and plotted their position by lunar observation. After correlating results with his maps, he concluded they were close to the end of the canyon. He wakened Howland and tried to talk him into continuing. He failed. The next morning Hawkins baked the remaining flour into unleavened biscuits and divided the tasteless lumps equally among the men. Bradley's and Sumner's diaries dwell on the sadness of the parting; there is no mention of ill will. Indeed, the departing trio helped take the boats across the river and boost two of them into position for the run — two because there wasn't enough manpower left to handle the battered *Emma Dean*.

While the departing trio watched, the river runners dived safely through the first of the rapids and then waited, hoping their success would encourage the others to follow in the *Emma Dean*. It did not. So on the six went to Lava Cliff Rapids. On the left Spencer Canyon had thrown a jumble of boulders into the stream. Just below the canyon mouth was a cliff too steep to allow lining. On the right a hundred-foot wall of granite topped by fifty more feet of jagged lava guarded the far side of the seething water. At the end of the wall was a rocky bench where boats could be landed and adjustments made for running the lower part of the cascade. The problem was to ease the boats past the cliff to the bench.

Bradley got into the first boat with an oar to use as a fender. Some of the others climbed to the top of the lava cliff and started lining him down but discovered they lacked enough rope, because of the heights. They tied up and went for another length. Bad judgment. The current beat the craft Bradley was in mercilessly back and forth against the cliff. He was about to cut the rope with his sheath knife when the stern post gave way and the mangled boat flew into the maelstrom. Walter Powell and Sumner, who had been waiting on the bench to help him land, scrambled after him along the rocky shore. Up at the head of the rapid, Major Powell, Hawkins, and Andy Hall jumped into the second boat and set out in pursuit. They rolled upside down. No life jackets, except for the Major. But luck — and Bradley's skill — served them well. Somehow, Powell wrote later, the lone boatman had managed to place the "great Scull" (sweep) oar into the stern rowlock of the heaving boat. Pulling with all his might, he turned the bow downstream. Keeping straight with the current, he plunged into and out of the thundering troughs until he reached the foot of the rapid. There a whirlpool brought him up short and he was able to fish Powell, Hawkins, and Hall out of the water as they floated by.

At noon on August 29, they left the canyon at the Grand Wash Cliffs. The next day they met three Mormon fishermen at the mouth of the Virgin River and sent for help. But no help ever reached Bill Dunn and the two Howlands. Shortly after struggling out of the canyon they were killed by Shivwits Indians who later said they had mistaken the three whites for prospectors who had violated one of their women.

Famous now, Powell obtained $10,000 from Congress, part for fleshing out the records of the first traverse and the rest for extending the surveys of the high plateau country west and north of the main canyon. Ten thousand dollars! That may have helped sour Hawkins and Sumner when they heard about it. In their minds they had helped Powell earn it but they never saw a cent of it.

Actually the sum was not enough for what Powell wanted to do. He spent the summer of 1870 in Utah setting up a supply system for his rowboats and making peace with the Shivwits Indians, so the surveyors could cross their land unharmed. Back East, he ordered three new boats. They were almost replicas of the first expedition's craft, heavy and clumsy and round-bottomed, though storage space was increased by a third watertight compartment placed between the two seats. He named his flagship *Emma Dean* after the boat that had been abandoned at Separation Rapid. He bolted an arm-chair onto the *Dean's* central compartment, hoping the extra elevation would give him a better view of his surroundings. It also increased the *Dean's* inherent, round-bottomed instability.

When he picked his crew, he invited only Jack Sumner of the original group to return. Did the rejection of the others indicate there had been ill feeling after all? Or did he hope to form a more cohesive group by choosing men dedicated to the common goal of scientific research? Be that as it may, he settled on academic types, either his own friends and relatives or friends and relatives of his brother-in-law, Professor Almon Thompson, who was to be in charge of the topographic work. Among Thompson's connections was seventeen-year-old Frederick Dellenbaugh, who was ambitious to be an artist. He could do sketches for the party. Standing outside of this closed circle but deemed necessary because of his skill was E.O. Beaman, a New York photographer. Beaman turned out to be neither a good outdoorsman nor a loyal employee.

High snow in the Rockies prevented Sumner from joining the expedition. To fill his place Powell chose a Utah teamster, Jack Hillers, a hard-working jewel who eventually took over the photographic work and became one of the great picture takers of the American West.

Nothing went as planned. Boats overturned, a man quit.

The expedition left Green River, Wyoming, on May 22, 1871. Nothing went as planned. Boats overturned, a man quit. Early in the descent Powell left the expedition for thirty-nine days to visit his pregnant wife, who was waiting in Salt Lake City until she could join him at the conclusion of the canyon runs. The supply system broke down. Half-starved, the explorers quickened their pace by hiding one of the boats, the *Cañonita,* near the head of Glen Canyon. That way more hands were available for strong-arming the remaining two craft across sandbars left exposed by low water.

The first segment of the run ended on October 23 at the mouth of the Paria. During the next several months, some of which Powell spent in Washington, the men ran surveys out of a base located near the Mormon town of Kanab, Utah. Three more of the party, including the photographer, Beaman, withdrew. After snow had left the high country, Almon Thompson, working superbly in convulsed, unexplored sandstone wastes, led a small group across country to Glen Canyon to retrieve the *Cañonita* and take it to the Paria, where John D. Lee, hiding out from federal authorities for his share in the Mountain Meadows Massacre of 1857, was starting to build his historic ferry. There they found that one of the boats that had been cached in the willows the previous October was in no condition to tackle the Grand Canyon. So only two craft and seven men — Powell sitting in his chair atop the middle compartment of the *Emma Dean* — took off on August 17, 1872, for the final run.

To Powell the river seemed higher than it had been in 1869, and heavy rains kept raising the level. How high? River historian Otis Marston, no admirer of Powell's, has concluded from descriptions and pictures taken by the expedition's new photographer, Jack Hillers, that the stream was nowhere near flood stage. These things are relative, however. The Major was facing more water than he had experienced before, and it alarmed him.

Friday and Saturday, August 30 and 31, were especially miserable. After spending Thursday night on broken granite ledges in pelting rain and bellowing thunder, the men discovered that both leaky boats needed patching. Dropping three hundred yards or so to a protected alcove, they began work, only to have the rising river drive them higher and higher, hauling boats and cargo up the

19

slippery walls as they went. The night was another soaker, and when the boats were lowered back into the water, they bucked so on the waves that they could scarcely be loaded — and the *Emma Dean* was still leaking. They fled the trap in spite of that, floundering heavily until they reached a narrow talus slope where they could pull the boat out of the water and complete the repairs.

When the Major's boat did flip, it was in a relatively tough rapid since identified as Serpentine, two days below Bright Angel Creek. All four passengers managed to climb onto the upside-down bottom, reach over to the gunwale on the far side, and, heaving back, pull it upright.

On September 7, 1872, they reached Kanab Creek, its mouth flooded by water backing in from the main stream. They rowed in for three hundred yards and there met a pack train which, by prearrangement, had brought supplies down a rough trail that prospectors had built to the river bank the year before. The packers had worrisome news. The Paiutes, the Shivwits band among them, were restive. Running into an ambush farther downstream might be risky.

Powell and Thompson talked the situation over. They were already wondering, according to Dellenbaugh's reminiscences, whether they could run Separation Rapids on this high water in their battered boats. The Indian threat added another negative element.

Rivals had also appeared. The year before, in 1871, the Army Corps of Engineers had ordered Lt. George M. Wheeler to conduct a topographic survey of the far Southwest. In the course of the work Wheeler decided to learn what the lower part of the Grand Canyon was really like by traveling *up* it. In September, accompanied by seven scientists, six boatmen, six soldiers, and fourteen Mohave Indians he made his way from Camp Mohave near present Needles to the Grand Wash Cliffs. After picking up fresh supplies there, the party plowed into the canyon dragging three rowboats with them.

For fifty-two miles they fought the fearsome rapids and rocks that Powell had dashed by two years before. Boats were swamped and records lost. Straining at the limits of endurance, the Indians clambered to the top of Lava Cliff, scene of Bradley's climatic run, and somehow surmounted that rapid. Aided by crew members struggling with oars, they ascended Separation as well. At one point the exhausted Mohaves threatened to revolt but were cowed. Rations were gone by October 19, when the party finally reached Diamond Creek, where a land trail led over the south rim of the canyon to Truxton Springs. Inordinately proud of what was essentially a useless accomplishment, the scientists walked out. The others turned the boats around, scooted back through the supposedly hair-raising rapids, and reached Camp Mohave, two hundred miles away, in five days — the upward journey had taken thirty-three.

All this was known to Powell and the others. They must have been aware, too, that comparisons would arise if they ran into trouble again at rapids Wheeler's party had both ascended and descended. Did Powell want to risk that kind of exposure?

Neither he nor Thompson ever said. But they did decide to leave the river at Kanab Canyon, scarcely halfway through Grand Canyon, and complete their survey from the rim. (Actually those investigations were never carried out.) Anticlimax. Powell sensed it acutely. He did not turn in an official report about any of his work in the canyons until 1874, and only because Congressman James Garfield pressured him by saying that until he did so he would receive no further appropriations for the expanded surveys he was directing from Washington. At that Powell reluctantly wrote what purported to be an account of the 1869 trip alone. When it suited him to introduce events and place names that actually related to the 1871-72 runs, he did so without acknowledgment. He used notes taken by the men of the second trip to flesh out several passages. But he never mentioned the second expedition itself or gave credit to its participants. The eliminations allowed him to present a unified account, filled with deeply sensitive descriptive passages, in which suspense rises steadily to a climax at Separation Rapid. Above all, it avoided imputations of incompleteness and of failure.

A cop-out? Not really. Even after the deceptions are acknowledged, the account remains one of the best ever written about a run down the Colorado River. This is as it should be, for despite his personality quirks and passion for self-aggrandizement, Powell was a true trailblazer both on the river and in his deep understanding of the arid West.

Two

THE PERSISTENT ENGINEER

. . . he knew from work with railroads already operating in the Rockies that the height of a cliff, whether two thousand feet or two hundred, had little effect on constructing a roadbed along its base.

In April 1889 engineer Robert Brewster Stanton signed a contract with Frank M. Brown, president of the newly incorporated Denver, Colorado Canyon, and Pacific Railroad Company, to survey a water-level train route from western Colorado to the deserts below the Grand Canyon, from which point the rails would swing west into the Los Angeles Basin. The project fitted Brown. Overweight and impatient, he was given to glimpsing the end of a scheme without worrying unduly about the problems along the way. This one, for instance. There was lots of coal in western Colorado, very little in Los Angeles. Connecting the two along a gentle grade already prepared by the Colorado River required only a willingness to risk the unknown — plus money, and that would flow in as soon as Stanton's survey demonstrated practicability. To lend still more credence to his arguments, Brown determined to lead the trip in person.

Stanton was physically trimmer than Brown. He wore a neat mustache and pointed Van Dyke beard. A childhood accident had crippled his left arm, so that, like Powell, he could neither row nor swim effectively. He believed Brown's idea was sound, for he knew from work with railroads already operating in the Rockies that the height of a cliff, whether two thousand feet or two hundred, had little effect on constructing a roadbed along its base. To make this truth apparent to laymen, he suggested that a photographer go along to supplement technical data with a visual record. The man chosen was Franklin A. Nims of Colorado Springs.

Hoping to avoid the heavy labor that Powell had encountered while lining and portaging his ponderous boats, Brown ordered five sleek craft about fifteen feet long. Pointed at both ends and built of thin strips of red cedar, they were round bottomed, narrow of beam, and weighed only one hundred and fifty pounds each when dry. He forgot about life preservers.

Take-off point was Green River, Utah (not to be confused with Powell's starting place, Green River, Wyoming). Sixteen men assembled there, including two inexperienced, ill-conditioned — but wealthy — Denver lawyers whom Brown wanted to impress. Stanton's long-time black servants, George Gibson and Henry Richards, were to act as cook and cook's helper. The rest were boatmen and surveyors, most notably John Hislop, who held a degree in civil engineering from McGill University, Montreal. Because men, food, and equipment overflowed the five small boats and a dory that Brown picked up in Green River, the group packed some of their clothing and much of their food into several watertight zinc boxes, each three feet square. These they lashed onto a raft hammered together out of driftwood. The cooks were to tow the clumsy scow behind the dory.

Cataract Canyon, which began four miles below the junction of the Green and Grand rivers, just about finished them. The first rapid split the raft into pieces and sent the zinc boxes careening into oblivion. Whirlpools, broken oars, and the loss of two boats held progress to a mile a day. When food ran out, Brown and the larger part of the group bolted ahead in three of the remaining craft, hoping to reach the new placer mining camps in Glen Canyon.

Stanton stayed behind with one small boat and four volunteers: the blacks, George Gibson and Henry Richards; big, muscular John Hislop; and boatman C.E. Potter. For six days of arduous surveying they ate only a little bread and thin coffee fortified with sugar and a few drops of evaporated milk. Just as they emerged from the lower end of Cataract Canyon they met three men towing a boatload of food upstream to them and learned that the others had gotten through.

On reaching the post office of Hite in Glen Canyon, one lawyer and two boatmen quit. In their place Brown hired a buckskin-clad prospector and trapper who was probably worth more, on the river, than all three deserters. He was Harry McDonald. He claimed to have fought in some of Custer's early campaigns and to have ridden with the Texas Rangers before wandering over to the Colorado River. An excellent carpenter, he soon put the party's four remaining craft back into shape.

His patience rebelling at the slow progress, Brown came up with an ill-considered notion. Let one boatload of surveyors finish running an accurate line to Lees Ferry. Brown, Stanton, Hislop, the photographer Nims, the remaining lawyer, the cooks, and the rest would go ahead in the other three boats to make a quick reconnaissance of the Grand Canyon. Brown could then take their reports and pictures to New York to show to potential investors.

On July 2, 1889, the scouts reached Lees Ferry, operated then by Warren M. Johnson on behalf of the Mormon church. Renting a horse from Johnson, Brown rode ninety miles to the little Mormon town of Kanab for a wagonload of fresh supplies. During his absence the second lawyer decided he'd had enough and dropped out. On July 9, the remaining eight men pointed their three heavily loaded, fifteen-foot boats into Marble Canyon.

They portaged around Badger Creek Rapids, eight miles below Lees Ferry, and halfway around Soap Creek Rapids, nearly four miles further on. They camped beside the middle of Soap, its din loud in their ears. As they watched the turmoil, Brown spoke to Stanton of his wife and children, who were traveling in Europe, and the next morning remarked that for the first time on the trip his sleep had been troubled by dreams of rapids.

At 6:23 A.M. — Stanton took notes on things like that — Brown started down Soap's tail waves. Harry McDonald was at the oars, rowing backward. Ahead was a ripple of rough water that Brown decided to scout from the bank before entering. He called his directions to McDonald, who swerved out of the riffle into a fast eddy. Exactly what happened is not clear. The torque between the main current and eddy may have rolled the boat over. Or underwater currents welling upward after the river's plunge through Soap Creek Rapid may have been responsible. McDonald's account suggests the latter: "We came to a large whirlpool or eddy, which was boiling furiously at the time, and just as we were well into it the water seemed to split and the boat was thrown one way and we another."

McDonald caught a rock, clambered out, and ran back along the shore. He could see Brown's head bobbing in the whirlpool. Though a powerful swimmer, the company president could not break free. When Stanton's boat came into sight, McDonald gestured and yelled. Divining what had happened, Stanton directed his oarsman, Peter Hansbrough, into the whirl. They were seconds too late. All they recovered was Brown's small, leather-bound notebook. Whether the owner's heart, already burdened by too much flesh, had failed or whether, as his companions later conjectured, his clothing had filled with silt and dragged him under is impossible to say.

The survivors spent two days searching the river bank. They retrieved the boat from an eddy but found no body. Grimly, Stanton determined to go ahead. John Hislop supported him and although the others were nervous because of the accident, they agreed to continue.

Four days of lining the boats and lugging the cargo over piles of boulders took them twelve miles deeper into Marble Canyon. On Sunday, July 15, they rested. On Monday they tackled Mile 25 Rapid, where the main hazard is the surge of the current against an overhanging cliff on the left side of the river. Running first, Harry McDonald and George Gibson, one of the cooks, skirted the obstacle handily and landed at the bottom to wait for the others. In spite of their example, Henry Richards, the other black, thought that he and Peter Hansbrough should line their boat through. Hansbrough talked him out of it.

The current seized the boat, drove it under the overhang, and pinned it against the rock. Shipping their oars, the two men tried to push loose with their hands. Unbalanced, the round-bottomed boat rolled over. No one saw Hansbrough again, though he was a good swimmer. Jumping into their own craft, McDonald and Gibson rowed after Richards, who was flailing strongly in the swift water, but before they could reach him, he sank. If the two men — and Brown — had been wearing life jackets, they probably would have lived.

Although the survivors found the wrecked boat and salvaged most of its cargo, Stanton finally admitted that he could not conduct a proper reconnaissance with five frightened men and three battered craft. They would have to escape from the gorge.

Six miles farther downstream they found a narrow slit — today's South Canyon — that looked as if it opened a way to the rim. They made camp at its mouth and then walked a short distance farther for a better view of two springs of cool, crystal water that gushed out of the Redwall limestone high overhead.

Powell had named the lush oasis Vaseys Paradise, for George Vasey, a friend of his in the United States Department of Agriculture. It spoke now to the men's low spirits. They picked ferns and flowers to carry back to camp, but the lift to their morale did not last. A thunderstorm crashed down. To escape it Stanton and Nims climbed forty feet up a cliff and huddled in a small cave, looking out at the blinding flashes of lightning and listening to demoniac thunder rolling through "what was, to us, death's canyon."

The next day they found a bigger cave above the highest watermark the river had left. Stanton determined to cache their material in it, for already he was planning to return. One wonders: did they notice, in the debris of what is now called Stanton's Cave, any figurines of animals made out of split, twined willow twigs? Archaeologists have since picked up several dozen of the effigies, left there as items of magic by prehistoric Indians, and have dated them by radiocarbon methods as being three to four thousand years old, the oldest human remnants in the Grand Canyon. But Stanton's people were working hard, lugging goods to the cache, and while they were at it their whole attention was seized by something puffed and white, like a bundle of laundry, floating down the river. Brown's body! one of them yelled — and maybe it was. McDonald and Hislop rushed one of the boats into the water and set out in pursuit, hoping to bring the president's remains back to Vaseys Paradise for fitting burial. Before they could overtake it, it swirled into rough water and disappeared. No, they probably would not have written about twig figurines even if they had seen one.

. . . their whole attention was seized by something puffed and white, like a bundle of laundry, floating down the river.

The cache completed, each man burdened himself with a single blanket and a little food, and they trudged single file along a difficult Indian trail leading up South Canyon. Near the top a landslide almost engulfed them. (See Preface, page 6). After it had roared by, they crawled up the final stretch and spent a wet, cold night beside a smoldering fire of sagebrush. The next day they found a rancher who guided them to Kanab.

By August, Stanton was in New York, urging the investors Brown had lined up not to lose faith. Reluctantly they authorized him to continue, but granted only niggardly funding. He must have known the sum was too little, but his determination was such that he agreed and afterwards dipped into his own pocket for about $12,500, a handsome sum in 1889.

From a boat company in Illinois he ordered three stout craft much like those Powell had used on his second trip. They were twenty-two feet long and four and a half of beam. Watertight compartments for storage and buoyancy were built into bow and stern and smaller ones ranged along the sides. There were two cross seats in the middle, separated not by another compartment as in Powell's boats, but by a simple frame of heavy boards. Each boat weighed about eight hundred and fifty pounds before being put into the water. To make sure the builders cut no corners, Stanton sent Harry McDonald to the boatyard to supervise construction.

Personnel consisted of twelve men. Four were veterans of the first effort — Stanton himself, McDonald, John Hislop, and the photographer, Franklin Nims. Nims's role had grown even more important, for to save time and money Stanton planned to survey only the most difficult stretches of the proposed line and to use photographs to indicate the nature of the rest of the terrain.

The boats, christened *Bonnie Jean*, *Water Lily*, and *Sweet Marie*, and the men went by train to Green River, Utah, and by wagon to Glen Canyon, where they arrived late in November. On December 10 they started out on exceptionally low water. As they were floating along a man hailed them from the bank, asking for tobacco. Landing, they met Jack Sumner of Powell's first expedition, who was prospecting in the nearby Henry Mountains. Stanton talked to him at length about the nature of the river below Marble Canyon, about Sumner's dissatisfaction with Powell, and about the heavily mineralized, silver-bearing rock near Bright Angel Creek.

After a bounteous Christmas feast on a table set outside the old stone fort at Lees Ferry, they plunged again into Marble Canyon. On December 31, they passed the eddy where Brown had died. "The whirls," Stanton noted in his diary that night, "came up and roared alongside in a dull, angery snarl." [His spellings.] A warning, perhaps.

The next day, the first of 1890, Hislop helped lug Nims's camera up a small pinnacle so that the photographer could get a sweeping view of a rapid they had just run. Today we would consider his equipment ungainly indeed — a big square box that had to be used on a tripod and focused under a little tent of black cloth. Film had to be loaded under the same cover. There was no shutter. The operator simply removed the cap from the lens, guessed at the exposure, and replaced the cap. But the camera did use dry film rather than early style, wet-collodion glass plates; after exposure the film could be sent outside for processing — a great saving of pictures, for there was no glass to break.

While concentrating on the apparatus, Nims forgot where he was, made a misstep, and fell twenty-two feet onto the boulders below. The others rushed to him. He was unconscious, blood oozing from his mouth and right ear. One leg was broken and there were probably additional injuries; the amateurs could not tell. They put splints on the leg and then, as their own shock wore off, looked at the future. Clearly they could not take Nims on through the canyon, though getting him out would be an ordeal. As for abandoning the trip, the thought seems not to have entered Stanton's mind. He himself would learn to handle the camera.

McDonald, ever resourceful, encased Nims's broken leg in a wooden box to protect it against rougher jars than splints could withstand. They spread a canvas between oars as a stretcher and smoothed the load in one of the boats to make a bed for the injured man. The next morning they started downstream, hunting an exit. Most of the time Nims was in a coma, unaware of a wild ride through one rapid or of being portaged, like the goods, around another. Toward evening they came to Rider Canyon, through which House Rock Creek empties into the main gorge. There they camped.

In the morning, Stanton, Hislop, and McDonald scouted Rider Canyon to learn whether it was passable. Rough going. Stanton had to be helped up one band of cliffs with a rope. At noon they reached the top, seventeen hundred feet higher than the river. Deciding the route was as good as anything they were likely to find, they separated. Hislop and McDonald returned to the river; Stanton cut across the Marble Platform toward Lees Ferry, to fetch Warren Johnson and a wagon. He expected to be back at the head of Rider Canyon by the following afternoon.

The next morning the ten able-bodied men in the main canyon divided into three sections. Two went ahead to pick the easiest way; they carried blankets for Nims and only lunches for everyone else, for they anticipated being back on the river by dark. The others, split four and four, took turns carrying the stretcher up the narrow canyon, sloshing now and then through muddy pools, the only drinking water they had. They cleared out one passage under a huge chockstone and pushed and pulled the stretcher through inch by inch. Farther on, similar boulders blocked them completely and they crept up the sidling walls. In places four of the men had to climb above the bearers and brace the stretcher with ropes while their companions eased the burden along the cliffs and around protruding rocks. One of them recalled later, a fall would have hurled Nims several hundred feet.

Exhausted and streaming with perspiration, they topped out late in the afternoon. No sign of Stanton. As snow began to fall, they wrapped Nims in blankets and built a fire close by, feeding it throughout the night by pulling up sagebrush and dry weeds. The only food left over from lunch was a little chocolate they dissolved in hot water and gave to Nims, sip by sip, whenever he roused briefly into consciousness.

At dawn three of the men went to the boats for provisions and bedding, for they feared an accident had befallen Stanton and they would have to carry Nims to Lees Ferry. By 9:30 A.M. the trio were back — and so was Stanton. The engineer had walked for twelve hours across the Marble Platform and had reached the ferry, with blistered feet, about midnight. After a few hours sleep, he had climbed into a wagon with Johnson and Johnson's small son and had started back. Marble Platform looks smooth but is not, and there were many side gullies to skirt. Darkness caught them short of their destination. They camped out in the same snow that was falling on the others and at daylight, after Johnson had knelt in the snow to pray, they resumed their journey, joining the Nims group just after 9:00 A.M.

For a week the photographer lay unconscious on the floor of the cookhouse at Lees Ferry. Just as he was waking and pleading for a doctor, a small party of Mormons came through, heading south. They agreed to take him to Winslow, Arizona, one hundred eighty-five miles away — a nine-day wagon trip — for $85. The doctor there found several broken and dislocated bones in addition to the injured leg and a slight fracture at the base of the skull. Patched up, he was sent to Denver for further treatment. On June 15, five and a half months after the fall, he at last discarded his crutches — and wrote bitterly that the company had paid none of his expenses "and cut my salary off January 1, 1890, the day of the accident." Still, a dozen men had devoted considerable energy to getting him out.

The remaining men had meanwhile resumed their surveying. They recovered the goods that had been cached by the first party and shortly afterwards, on Friday, January 17, spied a body left on top of a boulder by high water. Fragments of clothing showed that it was Peter Hansbrough. They took the remains ashore, buried them under a mesquite tree, and covered the shallow grave with "marble slabs." In his diary Stanton wrote, "I offered a short prayer. Not for poor Peter but a petition that we might be spared his fate, but if called upon to meet the same death, that we might be prepared to go."

Eight miles below the mouth of the Little Colorado River, they glimpsed something of the impact that another railroad, the Atlantic & Pacific (later the

Santa Fe), was having on the countryside. Its completion through Arizona in 1883 had stirred first prospectors and then tourists into visiting the South Rim of the Grand Canyon. By making old Indian trails passable for pack stock, the miners had ventured into the bottom of the canyon and had found traces of gold, silver, copper, and asbestos. Seth Tanner developed one trail down from the vicinity of today's Desert View; John Hance improved another that dropped over the rim near today's Moran Point. Finding they could guide tourists more profitably than they could pack ore out of the canyon, they began building lodges near the rim and rough camps in sheltered spots within the gorge. The latter work was just getting underway when Stanton's party went through.

First they encountered, near the foot of Tanner Trail, a prospector, Felix Lantier, who agreed to carry out the negatives Stanton had exposed up to that point and send them to Denver for developing. What Lantier said about mineral prospects in the vicinity sent McDonald and some of the others clambering around the cliffs scouting for veins until Stanton ordered them on.

Eight miles downstream they laboriously lined the boats through thundering Hance Rapid and entered the dark, narrow throat of Upper Granite Gorge. There they encountered Sockdolager Rapid, so boxed by cliffs that normally there is no shoreline along which men can walk. Even the cautious Powell had had to run the furious stretch. The men of his second expedition, buffeted by high water, called it a real "sockdolager," and the name stuck. When Stanton's party came along, the unusually low water had exposed a narrow, slippery margin that he thought would permit lining. A mistake. As the men were easing the first boat, the *Sweet Marie*, around a promontory of rocks, a crosscurrent tipped it sideways and drove it, full of water, between two boulders, where it stuck fast. Though they worked all day in the winter-cold water, they could not free it.

Camp that night was miserable — a small patch of fairly flat rock to sleep on, wet blankets, and very little wood for fire. A full moon soaked the gorge in eerie light. Wakened by it, one of the men sat stiffly up. Then he yelled at the others. The river had risen slightly, and the *Marie* had washed into a "hole" below the boulders, where it was being churned violently. They piled out to rescue it, failed, tried again by daylight, and at last managed to drag the stricken craft onto an uneven bank of rocks, bow pointed upward like the beak of an angry goose. The center of one side was smashed, but the keel was sound. Four of the crew led by McDonald set about cutting four feet out of the middle and then splicing the ends together. They worked in awkward positions on insecure footing, their nerves constantly assaulted by the bellow of the water at their heels. The rest of the men meanwhile cautiously lined down the rest of the boats, ran a survey along the granite cliffs, and roamed far afield to find firewood and lug it back to camp. After five days they had a new *Marie*, only eighteen feet long, that ran as well as the original.

Stanton was exhilarated. He customarily rode in the first boat, standing with his knees braced against the forward compartment while he held the bow line like a halter rope and shouted directions to the oarsmen, whose backs were to the rapids. Often, by his estimate, they reached speeds of thirty miles an hour. Now and then waves poured completely over him and occasionally knocked him sprawling. Yet he wrote, "To feel the boat under you go over and down a slope of ten or twenty feet on the incline of the rushing waters, and then dash into and

Even the cautious Powell had had to run the furious stretch.

split the huge waves at its foot, with their angry power slapping you first on one side and then on the other is an excitement grand in the extreme."

His imagination rioted. At one point he climbed to the Tonto Platform and wandered around looking at the vast cliffs and seeing "each cove with its picturesque Swiss chalet, and its happy mountain people with their herds of sheep and mountain goats, developing local business for our future railroad." And the mineral! "We found and sampled a very large vein of Quartz which seemed to be filled with fine ore."

Farther on, they passed into complex red granite broken by dikes of hornblende and stringers of quartz. One vein in particular stood out — "the Great Vein that Jack Sumner & Powell have said so much about . . . 3/4 of a mile above Bright Angel on the Rt. side. I did not stop and test it for various reasons, best known to myself, but located it for further use." What he probably meant was that he did not want the men, some as excited as he by the brief view, to file claims ahead of the railroad syndicate or perhaps even desert and go to mining before the trip was finished. To prevent this, he ran half a mile beyond the great vein, camped on the left bank, told the group to stay put, and then had Elmer Kane, a man he trusted, row him across the river so he could climb a promontory for another look.

Morale dropped after that, a sag to which the river contributed. They had so much trouble lining the *Bonnie Jean* through a ferocious rapid a little below Bright Angel Creek (probably Horn Creek Rapid) that they decided to let the shortened *Marie* run through unrestrained and then, after it had reached slow water below the rapid, row out and capture it with the *Bonnie Jean*. Another bad idea. The *Marie* banged into one rock, bounced off another, splintered, and swamped. After watching the destruction in horror, the men built a skidway of logs and portaged the *Water Lily* and its cargo around the murderous place.

For two days and eight rigorous miles McDonald sulked. His labor with the *Marie* had gone for nothing. He grumbled about Stanton's petty faultfinding and about working harder than anyone else. (He was also being paid more.) Glumly he predicted they would never get through the chasm the way they were going. But the truth, one of his companions recalled later, was that he wanted to desert, climb out of the canyon, gather supplies and return to exploit the mines ahead of all others.

The blow-up came at Crystal Creek. Stanton suggested that since the party would have to hurry through the rest of the canyon to escape starvation, everyone should help lighten the boats by discarding unnecessary possessions. McDonald snapped that he would not throw away anything of his for the sake of the company. If the boats needed lightening, he'd remove himself. Fine, said Stanton. The next morning he paid the rebel off with a check for $197, and McDonald started up Crystal Creek for the snow-covered North Rim with his possessions on his back.

The day after McDonald left, Stanton decided to go climbing himself, at least as far as the snow line. He may have been wondering whether McDonald really could get out. Or he may simply have wanted to obtain pictures of that stupendous section of the canyon known now as Hindu Amphitheater, and still seldom visited. John Hislop and Elmer Kane went with him to share the burden of the camera; the tripod was strapped to Kane's back. Because they expected to reach the snow and be back before dark, they carried along only a minimum of food and neither water nor blankets.

Like McDonald, they started up Crystal Creek, then veered east onto the Tonto Platform and aimed for an inside butte since named the Tower of Ra. (No one knows what route McDonald followed, but he certainly did not strike for an inner butte.) They teetered along a hair-thin ledge on the lower Redwall Cliffs and wormed past a projecting rock into a narrow chimney. They inched up that by bracing their knees against one wall and their backs against the other. A chockstone blocked them. Hislop got above it somehow, lay down, and extended a hand. Kane crouched while Stanton stood on his shoulders, then straightened until the engineer could catch Hislop's hand with his good arm.

They spent the night on top of this "island in the air" (Stanton's words) without water and only a fire for warmth. The dawn stunned the climbers. A rosy light spread across the vast cliffs opposite the point of sunrise. As the first rays streamed through, the great amphitheaters and majestic alcoves seemed to be born before their eyes. To the northwest, five or six miles beyond Crystal's narrow slot, Point Sublime stood sharply outlined against the sky. Powell, who thought the view from Sublime to be the most breathtaking in the canyon country, had persuaded the famed nineteenth century landscape artist Thomas Moran to paint it. Moran rendered it in his most grandiose style, and Congress paid him $10,000 for it. Stanton, sitting on the top of Ra, recalled the painting as static. The Grand Canyon never is. "It is a living, moving being, ever changing in form and color. . . . One stands enchanted, language fails, and description becomes impossible."

Searching for a better way than the chimney to descend, the climbers dropped into the saddle between Ra and Osiris Temple. That route, too, turned into a hair-raiser. At one point they had to use the camera strap for lowering Stanton into a dead tree that they shinnied down to the ground. On reaching a tributary of Crystal Creek, they found water in a pothole — their first drink in twenty-four hours — and were back in camp well before suppertime.

At Crystal Creek the surveyors were ninety-eight miles into the canyon. Their boats were overloaded; their provisions, inadequate. Their only escape route, as far as they knew, was Diamond Creek, one hundred and twenty-seven miles ahead. If they reached Diamond, they could follow easy tourist trails twenty-three miles up side gorges to the railroad stop of Peach Springs, where, if Stanton's orders had been carried out, additional film and food awaited them. So they hurried, insofar as the river let them hurry.

One boat flipped but was righted without damage. They prayed for high water to submerge the rock gardens through which they lined their boats — and then got more than they wanted. A sudden flood tossed them like chips, spun them in whirlpools. Then the weather turned so cold that in the mornings they had to thaw the camera and transit to make them usable. By the time they reached Diamond Creek they were out of tobacco and had only graham mush for food. But among the footprints on the sand bars was one of a woman's dainty boot. "One of the men, I shall not give his name, fell down and kissed it."

The three men who had proved least efficient were let go and replaced by one whose primary job would be cooking. To Stanton's delight he received a telegram from Denver stating that the film he had sent out by the prospector Felix Lantier was satisfactory. Now he felt better about the rest of the pictures he had been taking — all told about twenty-two hundred negatives to supplement sixteen hundred pages of field notes.

They resumed their river journey late in February 1890. So far Stanton had never been spilled into the water, but that record ended at Separation Rapid, where Powell's party had split. Like Powell, Stanton could see no way of lining the boats through it or portaging goods around. So they ran it. The engineer fully expected to be dashed against a cliff in the second section of the rapid, but his boat shot by. Looking back, he saw the second crew coming through in fine form and shouted his joy. Just then his boat bumped a rock. While he was off balance, a wave hit him from behind and swept him overboard. Choking, he came up fifty feet farther on, buoyed by his life jacket. Another wave rammed him back under. The next time he emerged the men in the second boat were able to catch him and jerk him out of the water as "mercilessly" — his word — as he had been thrown in.

Though Lava Cliff Rapid looked hopeless, they got through it, too, and a little farther on rowed out of the canyon at the Grand Wash Cliffs. Only five hundred more miles of relatively easy going separated them from the salt water of the Gulf. They reached it on April 26.

Stanton's backers were not impressed. They doubted his estimates and pointed out that new discoveries of oil in California had reduced the demand for coal. He campaigned for months, giving lectures and writing articles. Those labors, like McDonald's with the *Sweet Marie*, went for nothing.

Switching tactics, he obtained backing for taking a huge gold dredge into Glen Canyon and mining its gravel bars during the late 1890s. That venture also failed.

And McDonald? Though forced by the rugged terrain at the head of Crystal Creek to abandon his blankets and pack, he managed to struggle up the snowy cliffs to the top of the North Rim on the Kaibab Plateau. Chancing onto a summer camp of a cow outfit, he broke in for food and rest, and then made his way to Kanab. With the money Stanton had paid him, he purchased a prospecting outfit and some burros. As soon as the weather turned good, he made his way to the east side of the Walhalla Plateau, where the road to Cape Royal winds along today. He made no effort to reach the Bright Angel area but instead dragged his animals off the east rim of Walhalla through a break in the pale Coconino cliffs. From there he somehow — a stupendous feat — worked down into the drainage of Chuar Creek, near the point where he had talked to the prospector, Felix Lantier.

A little more than a mile up Chuar Creek from the river he found ore. He took samples to Denver in the fall of 1890 and persuaded a speculator named James Best to finance a mining company for exploiting the claims. Because of the difficulties of reaching the site with pack stock, the new partners decided to take their first party in by water, all the way from Green River, Utah.

McDonald supervised the building of two boats big enough to hold four men each. In the party that started out in 1891, with Best as captain, were four of Stanton's veterans — McDonald, John Hislop, Elmer Kane, and William H. Edwards. Before they were well inside Cataract Canyon, they smashed one of the boats beyond repair. "Hell to pay," someone scratched on the nearby cliff.

While he was off balance, a wave hit him from behind and swept him overboard.

31

Though they all managed to get out of the canyon, the disaster led to a breakup of the party at Lees Ferry.

Some kept trying on their own. Two resolute men took horses along the Kaibab Plateau and worked down into the head of Bright Angel Creek past "fountains of liquid diamonds . . . scenes from Arabian nights" (so reported the Salt Lake *Herald*, November 22, 1891) but found nothing of value. McDonald, traveling again by horseback, returned to Chuar Creek, staked another claim, recorded it in Flagstaff, but was unable to develop it. Discouraged he returned to Glen Canyon and eventually went to work for Stanton on the gold dredge. They'd had their difficulties, but they respected each other. Good men generally do.

Three

NEW TECHNIQUES

The first runs down the Green and Colorado rivers unmarked by deaths, desertions, or lost boats were made by men who had no grand designs in mind. Relatively uneducated, they wanted only to trap, prospect, and enjoy the adventures they experienced. As one of them, George Flavell put it, "We must expect some accidents and expect to hit some rocks. There is only one stone we must not hit . . . our Tomb Stone."

Flavell was the first to follow Stanton. Born in Philadelphia about 1863, he ran away from home when in his teens. Sometime before 1890 he adopted as his territory the lower Colorado River from the Grand Wash Cliffs to the Gulf. In that wide area he was known as Clark the Trapper. Coyotes, for whose hides the state of California then paid a bounty of $5 each, were his main prey. Much of his solitary travel was by rowboat. He was tall, sinewy, and enormously confident.

In the spring of 1893, he built a two-masted, flat-bottomed little ship that he sailed along the Mexican coast to Guaymas. Back in Yuma the next year, he and a friend were hired by two California journalists to remodel a thirty-two foot, ten-ton craft, the *Examiner*, and take them to Tiburon Island in the Gulf, where they hoped to pick up a story on the wild Seri Indians. Luckily the boatbuilders stayed behind after putting the news-seekers ashore and were able to escape in the dinghy when the Indians killed the others.

His thirst for adventure still unsated, Flavell next persuaded Ramón Montéz, a short, stocky young Mexican (some say Indian) from San Fernando, California, to join him on a run from Green River, Wyoming, through the Grand Canyon to Yuma. The two men created a sharp-prowed, square-sterned, flat-bottomed boat out of two-by-fours hewn from Oregon pine. They covered the frame with tongue-and-groove boards and planked the bottom double thick. As further protection from rocks they straightened out some light steel wagon tires and fastened them around the lower edges of the sides. The whole was fifteen and a half feet long and five of beam. It contained no compartments for storage or buoyancy. Flavell named the creation *Panthon*. He may have had "Phantom" in mind.

The pair left Green River on April 27, 1896. They had no intention of operating the way Powell's and Stanton's crewmen had. Those oarsmen, two to a boat, had rowed backwards into the rapids at full speed, counting on the heavy construction of their craft to withstand shocks. Flavell, by contrast, sat on a box near the center of the lightweight *Panthon*. In fast water he stood up, facing forward, and pushed on the oars when he needed to thrust through a wave. He tried to keep away from the rocks in the current — his predecessors seldom saw such rocks — by manipulating the oars as necessary. Montéz rode aft, sitting on the luggage, which was covered with waterproof sheets and lashed tight. He had a short sweep oar to help with the steering, but apparently he did not use it often. The few people who saw the wayfarers en route give differing accounts.

The rapids in Lodore Canyon spooked the adventurers enough that they lined down the four worst ones. Lining is difficult for only two men, however, so Flavell kept pushing ahead through more and more rough water until the feel of it was ingrained in his center of gravity. In Cataract they lined only once. Evidently, through, they had some close calls, for on reaching Lees Ferry on October 12, after pauses to prospect in Glen Canyon, they appropriated two of the life jackets that had been left there by the aborted Best expedition of 1891. They also increased the height of the boat's sides by ten inches. One tale, perhaps apocryphal, says that during the work Montéz announced he was quitting, to which Flavell replied, fingering his gun, "You can come along with me or you can float down dead." Montéz came.

"You can come along with me or you can float down dead."

On October 15 they took to the water again. In Badger Creek Rapid they hit a boulder with a thump that turned even Flavell cautious. They spent a wearisome day lining Soap Creek Rapid and might have lined Hance as well except for a party of tourists who had just ridden down from the rim on John Hance's new trail through Red Canyon. Showing off, Flavell thrust the boat down the "V" into water shredded by a maze of boulders. As he was yanking full strength on one of the oars, its blade caught on a rock, pulled out an oarlock and snapped in half. The *Panthon* ran up on a huge red boulder and hung there. After crawling out on the stone, replacing the oarlock, and untying a spare oar, the two men jumped back in. Before Flavell could get a good grip on the oars, one was torn from his grasp. They floundered the rest of the way like a bird with a broken wing. But they stayed upright, and that convinced Flavell he'd rather risk bad runs that do any more lining.

On they went, riding out even Lava Falls and Lava Cliff, according to his story, and after thirteen days in the canyon, they reached the Grand Wash Cliffs. Familiar ground now. They dawdled along, hunting as they went. At Needles, where the local newspaper gave their arrival a brief mention, Montéz dropped out. Flavell continued two hundred and fifty-seven miles downstream to Yuma, arriving January 9, 1897.

He didn't stay put, of course. A month later he was back in Needles. There he read in the paper that Nathaniel Galloway and William Richmond had just

completed a run down the Green and through the Grand Canyon. Promptly
Flavell located them and looked their boats over. The craft, one for each man,
were slightly longer than his, but a foot narrower and much more shallow, so that
they looked puny. He shook his head. They could not have made such a run —
not in those one-man boats.

But they had, they said, and proceeded to tell him how.

The more one learns about Nathaniel Galloway, commonly called Than, the
more certain it seems that he could have traveled as an equal with Jim Bridger,
Jedediah Smith, and the other fabled mountain men of the 1820s, much of
whose country Galloway trapped long after they had left it. He was a crack shot
and a superb tracker. He could tinker, repair, improvise, invent. One
acquaintance said all he needed for boating was a heavy dew. When George
Flavell met him in Needles in February 1897, Galloway was about forty-five and
growing bald, his sun-darkened face adorned with a heavy mustache. He was
nearly six feet tall and weighed one hundred and fifty pounds.

Like Flavell, Galloway had been using boats for years while making a living.
He needed light craft that he could haul in and out of the water alone — light
enough, too, to be maneuverable in rapids filled with boulders. The theory of
rowing backwards full tilt into danger, hoping to outspeed the current for the
sake of better control, made no sense to him. He entered rapids stern first, face
forward, judging his course by what he saw, not by shouts from a steersman in
the rear — an extra hand who would have to be paid. Whether Flavell or he used
the technique first can't be said positively. Circumstantial evidence favors
Galloway. He was older and had been on the river longer — rougher parts of the
river. And because Flavell stuck to the relatively smooth lower river except for
his big run with Montéz whereas Galloway regularly trapped the upper canyons,
it was Galloway's influence that spread among rough-water boatmen.

He built his boats at his home in Vernal, Utah. They averaged about sixteen
feet long, were narrow of beam and shallow, with square sterns and a
pronounced "rake" — that is, they were deepest in the midsection and then rose
toward bow and stern. To reach his favorite takeoff point on the Green, he
loaded the boat he had built for that year's work onto a wagon and hired a friend
to drive him north across the Uinta Mountains to the mouth of Henry's Fork,
where the West's first great fur-trade rendezvous had been held in 1825. There
he started downstream, following the path blazed by the originator of that
rendezvous, William H. Ashley. Since the 1960s, the lovely upper canyons that
entranced them both have been smothered under the waters of Flaming Gorge
Reservoir.

Normally Galloway worked alone, but in the fall of 1896 he took along his
thirteen-year-old son Parley for training. After bouncing through some exciting
rapids, they met, near Brown's Park at the head of Lodore Canyon, two
prospectors, Frank Leland and William Richmond, the latter twenty-three years
old. They, too, had started on the Green from Henry's Fork, towing behind
their clumsy boat a homemade sluice for washing gold dust. Hard going. When
Galloway suggested, at their joint campfire that night, a trapping trip through the
Grand Canyon, young Richmond agreed instantly. Not Leland. He had once
peered into the abyss near the mouth of the Little Colorado and in his opinion

only fools would try traversing it in cockleshell boats. When they just grinned, he turned their boat over to Richmond, took their dog, and walked back to the railroad in southern Wyoming.

In the howling waters of Lodore Canyon, Galloway decided that Richmond's boat would not do. Small matter. At the conclusion of an earlier trip he had hidden one of his own boats in the willows at the mouth of Minnie Maud Creek near the head of Desolation Canyon. Richmond could have it for $12.

After emerging from the Uinta Mountains, they landed and made their way to Galloway's home in Vernal, where young Parley dropped out and the others picked up fresh supplies. Returning to their boats, they drifted across the broad Uinta Valley into Desolation Canyon and retrieved Richmond's new boat. By this time it was late October 1896, but they were in no hurry. They trapped several beaver and lived high on migrating ducks and geese. After plucking the birds, Galloway stored their feathers in a canvas tick he carried. Pretty soon he was sleeping on the most comfortable mattress in the canyon.

To keep the cold, splashy water from wetting the furs and chilling themselves, they cut Richmond's canvas bed tarpaulin into pieces and decked the boats fore and aft. The furs still got wet, and so at Green River, Utah, they bought lumber and installed cargo compartments. The wooden decking proved to have another use; using it as a passenger seat, Richmond took Sadie Staker, the pretty schoolteacher at Lees Ferry — there were thirteen children there that year — for a New Year's Day ride down the easy Paria Riffle.

Later, while the two of them were lining Richmond's boat down the first of a pair of rapids deep in Marble Gorge, it broke loose from their holds on the rope and careened downstream. Panicked at the thought of riding the deck of Galloway's boat all the way to the first settlement below the Grand Canyon, Richmond floundered across the boulders onto a sandy beach and raced after the runaway. Ahead of him a red promontory thrust into the stream. Unable to circle the obstruction by land, he snatched up a five-foot piece of driftwood, took a wild leap into the water, and, holding the stick in front of him for support, kicked furiously after the boat. Overtaking it he climbed in and beached it just as it was nearing the head of the second rapid.

As the weather and water kept growing colder, Galloway set driftwood stakes in the corners of the decking and surrounded each rowing compartment with a strip of canvas, two feet high, broken by holes for the oars. They went the rest of the way through the canyon shielded by these contraptions, lining when they had to, running when they could. A sentence in Galloway's diary about the second section of Separation can suffice for all the big ones: "I am looking up at the heavens; now a seeming hell has opened to receive us." When their boats filled with water, they bailed out with their gold pans. That night, after drying out beside a big fire, they slept side by side on the feather bed.

One more bizarre experience remained. Where the Virgin River flowed into the Colorado River below the Grand Canyon was a ferry owned by Daniel Bonelli, a Mormon immigrant from Switzerland. Most of his customers were miners and stockmen. Most of his employees were Indians. When a Paiute called Mouse created a drunken ruckus one night, Bonelli fired him. Resentfully Mouse drifted over to a small mine being run by a Major Greenowat, eighty years old, and two young partners, Davis and Stern. Mouse prevailed on the young men to go with him to look at a vein of ore he said he had found. When the pair failed to return after several days, Greenowat went to Bonelli's to report. A search party was forming just as Galloway and Richmond appeared. They joined it. In time the bodies of the two men were found at the base of a steep bluff. Both had been shot and robbed of their guns and boots, but not of the money they carried.

The searchers lugged the corpses — dead for an estimated sixteen days — back to their camp, sealed them in coffins made out of their own rowboats, and prevailed on Galloway and Richmond to tow them, one bier behind each boat, to Needles. With the aged Major sitting on one of the decks, they covered the one hundred seventy-five miles of fast water, including Black and Boulder canyons, without stopping except to eat. They reached Needles on February 10, 1897. They sold their boats for $12 each; their furs went for about $600. Richmond was well satisfied. Galloway was not. It had been a long, tedious trip, he said, for so little profit. But it made for interesting talk with their predecessor, George Flavell. By telling him about the rock cairns he had built here and there along the way, they convinced him they had indeed traversed the Grand Canyon a few weeks behind him in their puny boats. They shook hands in mutual congratulation, but privately Galloway doubted that Flavell and Montéz had run every rapid in the gorge except Soap Creek. Others have felt that way, too, but Flavell's diary said they did.

And perhaps Galloway was not as bored with river as he thought. Back in Vernal, he grew restless and in the fall of 1897 went down the Green and Colorado to Lees Ferry. From there he turned back to the placer mines in Glen Canyon. He was working on one of the gravel bars in January 1898, when Robert Brewster Stanton rowed down the ice-clogged river, preparatory to starting his gold-dredging operations. He hired Galloway on the spot. This led to Julius Stone, a wealthy Ohio industrialist and sportsman who was backing Stanton, and to Galloway's second traverse of the entire canyon system. First, however, there occurred, in 1903, one of the least known and most puzzling of the many runs through the Grand Canyon — that of Hum Woolley and two totally unprepared companions.

. . . there occurred, in 1903, one of the least known and most puzzling of the many runs through the Grand Canyon . . .

Elias Benjamin (Hum) Woolley was an enterprising prospector who, it seems, devised a cheap way of looking over the Grand Canyon from end to end. His grubstaker was a widow who called herself Madame Schell, though her late husband had been named Jacques Traves. Madame Schell owned a large residence in Los Angeles, the bottom floor of which she rented to a family named Sanger. She also owned several gold claims near Quartzite, Arizona. She needed assessment work done on the claims — either actual mining or mining-related improvements to the property — to keep her provisional titles valid. She hired Hum Woolley, antecedents now unknown, to do the work.

Woolley could have reached Quartzite by traveling overland to the Colorado River and crossing it by public ferry. Instead he built an eighteen-foot boat in Madame Schell's backyard. Short and stocky, Hum wore a bristly mustache and was not particularly clean. But he knew what he was doing. The finished boat was raked neatly upward fore and aft, had a fifty-inch beam, and contained compartments five feet long at either end. In between was an eight-foot-long cockpit that evidently contained only a single seat whose location showed that

Woolley intended to face whatever rapids he entered, although in 1903 the Galloway technique was still not widely used.

He hired the cousins John King and Arthur Sanger as helpers. John, the older, educated as a physician, was to be cook; the only utensil he took along, other than those used for eating, was a dutch oven. Arthur was to be handyman. He was neat, soft, and though twenty-three years old, still lived unemployed at home. Presumably he agreed to go on the trip only because he had no idea of what it involved.

Satisfied at last with the boat he had built, Woolley took it apart and shipped the pieces by rail through Needles (about one hundred miles north of Quartzite) to Flagstaff, Arizona, take-off point for the Grand Canyon. The three men bought train tickets for the same destination. Financing, including the cost of the boat, came from Madame Schell. Either Woolley persuaded her he would bring back apronfuls of gold, or she was as ignorant as the Sangers about western geography.

In Flagstaff, Woolley hired a teamster to haul the disassembled boat to Lees Ferry, where the trio put it together in the fierce heat of late August. On September 1 they started out. That night Arthur wrote, "It was wonderful looking up at the towering cliffs and strater [sic] and colored Rocks, when suddenly we came to a number of terrible rapids."

As it often does, Badger Creek Rapid shook them up so that when they came to Soap they decided to portage the cargo around and line the boat through empty. King and Woolley handled the ropes while Arthur waded among the rocks, holding the craft away from their sharp edges. He did not like lining, but liked running less. September 4: "Thank God we are still alive, it is impossible to describe what we went through today. Only the wonderful river knowledge and oarsmanship of Hum — Woolley saved us from the vortex . . . I am scared."

So was John King. In Upper Granite Gorge, probably at Sockdolager, the cousins huddled down flat on the cockpit floor while Woolley headed in stern first. Wrote Arthur:

> I thought this was the end as we rushed up a great wave, then
> another until I was almost sick and dizzy with fear, Wolly would
> yank the boat this way and that, until one of the great waves or
> whirlpools suddenly swung us broad-side to a great wave coming
> up the river and towering at least 20 ft high, curling right over us
> . . . it came down and almost filled the boat again. the next one
> did fill it John and myself was clear under water Wolly shouted to
> lie still and paddled the boat over to the shore.

In the evenings Woolley tested the sand and gravel bars with a gold pan while King cooked and Arthur dried out beside the fire, nursing his "sprained anchols — hands — back — and cuts." It took them most of September to reach the end of the canyon at Grand Wash Cliffs. There the cousins camped several days with some miners while Woolley walked off, without water, into one of North America's bleakest deserts. Somewhere in the wastes he met, obviously by prearrangement, another prospector, Charles Bolster. Bolster crowded into the boat with them and they went on downriver two hundred and twenty-five miles to the landing at Ehrenberg. From there they hiked to Madame Schell's claims and did the assessment work.

That's all. Though the trip was only the fifth traverse of the canyon it received no notice. It would probably have remained unknown if P.T. Reilly, a river buff since the 1940s, had not chanced to meet Sanger at a lecture in Los Angeles and dug part of the story out of him. Part, because Sanger had never known quite where they were, had forgotten many details, and on several days had been too tired to enter its events in his diary. We still don't know who Hum Woolley was, how he prevailed on Madame Schell to finance the reckless trip, why he took along complete novices as helpers (many tough prospectors would have jumped at the chance), or how or for what purpose he met Charles Bolster in the middle of nowhere. Most of all, we would like to know where he learned to build and handle river boats with such skill. Sanger thought Hum had been through the Grand Canyon before, but there is no record of such a run. And so there we are, with only the shadows of what might have been a fascinating tale.

Indirectly, mining also put Nathaniel Galloway back on the river. Among his duties after Robert Brewster Stanton had hired him to work for the gold-dredging company in Glen Canyon — a company of which Stanton was vice-president, engineer, and general manager — was the construction of a scow big enough to hold a ten-ton drill for boring exploratory holes in the gravel and then floating the monster to likely spots here and there along the stream. On hand to watch much of the drilling was the company president, Julius Stone. Stone immediately struck up a lasting friendship with the pioneer boatman. They went hunting together in the lonesome Henry Mountains west of Glen Canyon — Stone later declared he had never met anyone else so conversant with the ways of wild animals — and after reading Galloway's account of his and William Richmond's trip down the Colorado, he corrected the journal's spelling and grammar and arranged to have it printed in a Cincinnati newspaper.

The mining venture failed dismally, and Stone returned to Ohio. He could not forget the river, however, and in 1907 he began corresponding with Galloway about a trip. Arrangements completed, Than took his four-year-old daughter with him to Detroit, where he designed and supervised, at Stone's expense, the building of four flat-bottomed boats of white oak and Michigan pine. Dry, they weighed only two hundred and forty-three pounds each, though they were sixteen and a half feet long, four feet wide at the gunwales, and eighteen inches deep, with a ten-inch rake fore and aft from the center. Each held two compartments in the bow and two more aft; one of each pair was more or less watertight for buoyancy as well as storage, and the others were decked with canvas. Uprights for holding splash shields could be set around the five-foot cockpit. At Stone's suggestion skags, which were a kind of detachable keel, were placed on the bottoms of the boats. Though dangerous in rapids — they caught on rocks — the addition made navigation easier in quiet water. Whenever the skags were removed, the holes that held them were filled with wooden plugs.

The trip was not to be solely for Stone's private pleasure. "Like a great soul in an unappreciative world," he wrote later, "the Colorado runs its deep, silent, lonely course, too little understood, too little appreciated, loved by few, feared by many, and only a name to the multitudes who have never seen it." Hoping to dispel the ignorance, he signed on an expert photographer whom he really did not like, his brother-in-law, Raymond Cogswell. A second guest was C.C. Sharp.

Galloway added as a helper Seymour Sylvester Dubendorff, twenty-seven years old, an all-around handyman on Vernal's weekly newspaper. The publication of Than's first journal had given him literary ambitions, and Dubie, as he was called, could help put a new book together. Dubie had other virtues as well. Though lacking in boating experience, he was amiable, skilled in other outdoor pursuits, strong as an ox, and, in Stone's words, "gritty as a flapjack rolled in sand."

Five men — four boats. The idea was that Cogswell, busy with the ponderous photographic equipment of the time, should be freed from the responsibilities of a boat. In Stone's mind Cogswell pressed the privilege too far and shirked not only camp chores but every other unpleasant task he could avoid. But he took two thousand pictures, each accompanied by copious notes concerning colors and conditions — data he planned to use if and when he tinted the prints.

They left Green River, Wyoming, on September 15, 1909, well provisioned and armed, and laden with Galloway's traps. They had no real trouble until Dubie capsized in Cataract Canyon. A little later, at Hite in Glen Canyon, Sharp dropped out, abandoning his expensive boat, which Cogswell had no interest in handling. The real shocker was reaching Lees Ferry and finding the supplies that should have been waiting there had not appeared. Though the new ferryman, Roy Rider (his name is commemorated in Rider Canyon, through which House Rock enters Marble Gorge) could give them only a few dried apples and raisins, they decided to run fast for Bright Angel rather than spend time going to Kanab for new stocks of food.

To increase their problems, the water was low, the rocks bad. They lined past part of Badger and almost all of Soap. When Stone doubled up with the pangs of pleurisy, Galloway came up with applications of a hot plaster whose ingredients are unidentified in the diaries each man was keeping at Stone's behest. The recipe was as far as Galloway's doctoring went. The patient himself had to keep a fire going all night so that each change of the plaster would be hot enough. He drooped with weariness, yet he wrote by moonlight at Badger Creek, "Here where the world is shut out, the spirit of the wilderness still abides and welcomes one into the full freedom and magic of the night and morning; uplifting and swaying the beholder with a sense of being that is delightful past compare."

Cogswell, too, felt the touch and tried to pin down with words the colors of the scenes he could photograph only in black and white. Tall cliffs took on "a fine rich pink in the evening light." Another place showed "True brown color in the shade, golden faun in the light." "Often waves in mild rapids and riffles have a decided lilac tint, intensified by the mud color of the water." "Our tent is in a fringe of willows which form a lovely tracery against the moonlit sky, the poetry of lines." Rapids held no appeal for him, though occasionally he had to ride through one sitting on the hatch of one of the compartments, generally in Dubendorff's boat. Even then he would try to jot down notes as the spray flew around him and at times try to use his camera, though it was not suited to action shots.

They were greenhorns no longer. Galloway praised the way they came through Marble Gorge without an upset. They solved some of their food problems by breaking into a prospector's cache, and Stone's pleurisy improved

The real shocker was reaching Lees Ferry and finding the supplies that should have been waiting there had not appeared.

41

enough so that on November 3, and in spite of noontime temperatures in excess of 100° Fahrenheit, he was able to walk up the Bright Angel Trail to the South Rim with Galloway and Cogswell (who lugged his camera along) to order a few muleloads of provisions sent down to the river. Dubie stayed with the boats.

They went through Horn Creek, Granite Falls, and Hermit Creek rapids unscathed. Then, on November 8, Dubie capsized again in the high waves of an unnamed rapid. Fortunately he was running last and Cogswell was not aboard. As he surfaced, he gashed his head on the gunwale of the boat, which was upside down and rearing wildly. Pushing clear, he rode the current about three hundred yards, mostly under water and catching his breath in the troughs. Climbing out at last, he looked back and saw that Galloway had managed to row over to the derelict, catch its painter, and tow it out of the fast water to refuge close to shore. There Stone and Galloway heaved it upright and made it fast. Blood streaming down his face, Dubie ran up to help bail. He was furious with embarassment. "I know I could run it," he kept chattering, "if I could just try it again." Yet by upsetting he achieved a kind of immortality. In 1923 a United States Geological Survey party named the rapid Dubendorff to commemorate the incident. At the same time, the canyons at either end of the rapid were named Galloway (the upper one) and Stone.

The last bad spot, Lava Cliff, taxed them. Although both Stone and Dubie were lame from bad falls, they helped portage every pound of cargo over the two-hundred-foot precipices and through dense stands of barrel cactus that Cogswell called nail kegs. Then one by one each got into his boat and eased it down the swift current to the head of the rapids, where the others, standing precariously on a narrow ledge and aided by a back wave, caught it and made it fast. Next they attached all the stern lines to a single boat. After Dubie had perched himself on a landing place halfway down the rapid, the others, sometimes working fifty feet above the raging water, eased the boat down to him. He caught it and pulled it in. Then another. And another. Night overtook them at the midway point, and they camped on the granite, listening to the boats rubbing against the rocks as they rose and fell with the waves.

The next day, November 14, they finished the lining. Pushed along by a strong wind they rowed into Needles at 10:00 A.M., November 19, "the most memorable and successful trip ever made down the Green and Colorado Rivers," Dubendorff proudly told his diary. "This trip goes to prove the efficacy of Mr. Galloway's method of running fast water, which has been much disputed."

There was more to crow about. Galloway was now the first man to have made the full run of the canyons twice. It was the first time a vacationer had hired a guide to take him down the river just for the fun of it. And although Stone had supposed he was in good condition on reaching Green River, Wyoming, in September, he found he had lost thirty-five pounds on the trip, which may also be a record of some sort.

Exultant, they decided to repeat the adventure in 1910, but Dubie's sudden death of Rocky Mountain spotted fever, the result of a tick bite, ended the plan. With him gone, Galloway's projected book never materialized, and he returned to his desultory running of the upper canyons. In 1913 he, too, died. Stone's *Canyon Country*, a quiet account of what had been to him a revelation rather than an accomplishment, did not appear until 1932. It was illustrated with Cogswell's photographs. Today the prints seem very static, and it is not until one reads the photographer's notes that one realizes what he was really seeing through the viewfinder those times when Stone was faulting him for his sluggishness.

Four

FREE-LANCING THE HARD WAY

B y 1907 Charles Silver Russell, a wandering promoter of mines, had come briefly to rest at Prescott, Arizona, as part-owner of the Perkins-Russell Print Company, which published both the town's weekly newspaper and a mining review designed to keep the brotherhood abreast of what was happening in the mineral regions of the West. He was of medium height, stocky, bossy, and physically powerful. Perhaps as a publicity stunt he decided to go prospecting by boat in the Grand Canyon, where, as he knew, several men were trying to develop "promising leads." His familiarity with publishing also suggested the possibility of coming out with a stack of salable pictures.

He prevailed on Edwin R. Monett, a miner of Goldfield, Nevada, to join him in the venture; together they put up $4,500. A third partner was Albert Loper, who had mined with Monett in Goldfield, Nevada, and with Russell in Telluride, Colorado. Loper, thirty-eight years old in 1907, had recently drifted over to the placer mines in Glen Canyon on the Colorado River and knew something about boats, an important point. He had no money, but Russell said he could repay his share of the expenses after the trip by giving illustrated lectures and selling pictures. Thus persuaded, Loper bought a camera, type uncertain but probably a 5″x7″ film-pack model. The other two invested in an older but more dependable glass-plate camera complete with black focusing cloth and developing tent. Russell was also able, as a newspaperman, to sell the story of their adventure to the Salt Lake City *Tribune*, the manuscript to be mailed in installments from stops along the way. In addition he contacted the Santa Fe Railroad and Fred Harvey's El Tovar Hotel on the South Rim, promising publicity tie-ins when the party arrived there.

Their fleet consisted of three sixteen-foot boats purchased from the

Michigan Steel Boat Company. The frames and the decking of the compartments at either end were of steel covered with wooden skins. Each rower sat in an open cockpit three and one half feet long. They left Green River, Utah, on September 20, 1907, Russell in the *Utah*, Monett in the *Nevada*, Bert Loper in the *Arizona*. The boats were heavily laden with food, camping equipment, a perforated gravel screen, gold pans, picks, shovels, retorts, and one hundred pounds of quicksilver, useful for picking up particles of free gold washing through sluice boxes.

Monett overturned twice in Cataract Canyon, but the most serious damage, time showed, was to Loper's camera, wetted enough by spray for the shutter to rust and jam. After they had reached the Hite Post Office on October 2, he sent it to the factory for repair. The three of them then prospected in Glen Canyon until November 6, when Loper returned to Hite for the camera. The other two drifted slowly on to Lees Ferry, where they settled down with the ferryman's family to wait for their companion. To save their own food, they freeloaded on their hosts until they wore out their welcome. On December 13 — a Friday — they started down Marble Canyon in bitter weather.

Loper reached the Ferry too late to overtake them. Loperphiles and Loperphobes have stirred his delay into a small tempest. Defenders say the repaired camera was unexpectedly long in arriving; he had split a seam in his boat and had to repair it; he waited for necessary supplies. Detractors sneer that he was afraid of the Grand Canyon and dragged his feet rather than run it. It seems more likely that he was a dawdler by nature and loitered along at his own pace, thinking the others would not dare go without him. They did; as a consequence Loper had to turn around and, alone, row and tow his boat one hundred and sixty-eight miles, a few miles a day, upstream against floating chunks of ice, a remarkable feat.

Monett could not catch the hang of river running. He went over again in Marble Canyon, and Russell barely saved the boat from escaping. A few days later, Monett hung up on a boulder in Hance near the head of Upper Granite Gorge, trapped in the cockpit, icy water cascading over him. Russell threw him a rope and they managed to get most of the cargo ashore, but could not budge the boat. Foolishly they did not tie it up when they went to bed. During the night it jiggled loose and drifted away. They had options. They could have climbed out of the canyon by either the new Hance Trail through Red Canyon or the Grandview Trail. But there would be no story in that, so on they went in the *Utah*, Monett riding through quiet water and easy rapids by sitting on the deck with his feet in the cockpit. The bad rapids he walked around, except Sockdolager, which he had to brave. The loose boat evidently sank along the way, for they never saw it again.

On January 3, 1908, they coasted one and seven-tenths miles past the mouth of Bright Angel Creek and landed at the point where Bright Angel Trail meets the river after its drop from the South Rim. There they cached the *Utah* and climbed the trail, ragged and unshaven, to keep their publicity appointments. The handful of tourists staying at El Tovar Hotel greeted them with raptures of excitement. They lived there luxuriously for four days, "confiscating," Monett wrote, "an awful lot of good eating matter," while Hayden Talbot, Fred Harvey's publicity man, interviewed them and photographer Karl Moon posed them for pictures. When they returned to the

. . . Loper had to turn around and, alone, row and tow his boat one hundred and sixty-eight miles, a few miles a day, upstream against floating chunks of ice, a remarkable feat.

45

river on January 7, a retinue of sightseers mounted on mules trooped along to watch the takeoff. Moon joined the procession, as did the brothers Ellsworth and Emery Kolb, who ran a photographic studio on the rim but were not part of the Fred Harvey stable.

More pictures. More cheers. On the adventurers swept. Somehow — sources fail here — they either ran through or worked a way around two major rapids, Horn Creek and Granite Falls. Then they came to a huge rapid since named Hermit, created by an outwash of boulders from Hermit Creek. Definitely it called for lining. After unloading their boat on the south side of the pool above the rapid, they decided they could work better on the north side. Rowing across, they rigged up. Unfortunately they let the boat slip too far into the current. It filled with water and, too heavy to hold, tore loose from their grasp. In dismay they watched it disappear through the tail waves.

The nearest shelter, as they had learned at El Tovar, was a small copper mine, farm plot, orchard, and tourist camp located in a wide place in Boucher Canyon, a few miles downstream. The melange was owned by gentle, white-bearded Louis Boucher, the "hermit" for whom the entire vast basin of Hermit Creek was later named. Buoyed by their cork life jackets, the marooned pair swam back to the south bank and, with what must have been considerable difficulty, wormed their way up the cliffs to the Tonto Platform. They followed its dim trails to Boucher Canyon. Though the hermit was not in residence when they arrived — his main camp and corrals were far up under the rim at Dripping Springs — he soon appeared, riding his favorite white mule.

He fed them, listened to their story, and told them things might not be so bad. A big eddy beside the rapid at the foot of Boucher Canyon trapped quantities of driftwood floating down the canyon. It might have trapped the *Utah* also.

They walked down to see — reluctantly, one suspects, for they were growing fed up with the canyon and, quite likely, with each other. Sure enough, there it was, battered and punctured, caught in a messy apron of driftwood fragments that bobbed sluggishly in the ripples of the eddy. Boucher had tools and a soldering iron and offered to lend them a light canvas boat they could tow and paddle upstream along the edge of the river, taking advantage of the eddies, to recover the possessions they had left on the riverbank just above Hermit Creek Rapid.

They looked at each other. There were dozens of rapids still ahead. How far could they stretch their luck? But even harder to face was the thought of going back to El Tovar, the only point of escape within reach, and letting the anticlimax be known right while Talbot's stories were being headlined across the country.

After agonizing vacillations, they retrieved the boat and went on.

Like Powell's men they were exhausted when they reached Separation Rapid. It terrified them. They saw no possibility of lining it or portaging around it. Run it? Climb out? They argued for two hours. Then Russell screwed up his nerve to try if Monett would work his way along the cliffs that had frustrated Powell, carrying the few remaining glass camera plates on his back for safekeeping. A fitting climax. "After the wildest ride of the trip," Russell wrote later, "I emerged through the rocks and waves at the lower end, entirely unharmed. . . . I would not have believed it possible." Monett made it, too, without cracking a single plate.

Not bad for men who had started as complete novices. As they neared Needles, California, Russell found someone to carry word of their arrival ahead. According to a story in the *New York Times*, dateline Needles, February 8, — Talbot had attracted national attention to them, all right — five hundred spectators cheered them up to the bank. The next night they were honored at a reception at the Railroad Hotel. In the flush of his excitement Russell declared in ringing speech that they were going to keep on down the river into the Gulf of California. They would follow the Mexican coast to some point that offered railroad transportation to the Atlantic and follow that coast to the Mississippi, turn up it to the Great Lakes, descend the St. Lawrence, and eventually reach New York City.

Not Monett. He vanishes from the records. Cooling down, Russell returned to Prescott. There he contemplated his rewards: a bit of fame, no gold, and only a few poor negatives. The pictures that Karl Moon had taken of the *Utah* and of Russell running a little rapid beside the Bright Angel Trail had not turned out much better. In search of something he could use for the stories he was contemplating, he wrote Emery Kolb on March 7, 1908, asking whether Emery had gotten anything printable.

Emery sent two samples and remarked in the accompanying letter that he and his brother Ellsworth were thinking of making a picture run from Wyoming to the Gulf. Marvelous, Russell replied, and suggested the brothers take along enough tourists to pay expenses, adding, "If it was arranged right I might be induced to go through again."

The proposal never came to a head, for not long after Russell's letter arrived the brothers heard, probably through Nathaniel Galloway's friends in Glen Canyon, that Than was preparing to escort an eastern dude, Julius Stone, down the river. Ellsworth fired off a letter asking for a job as trip photographer but was advised the place had been filled. When the Stone party walked up to the South Rim in November 1909, the brothers talked to them at length. Afterwards they kept in touch. When Dubendorff's death cancelled Stone's plans for a second trip, the Kolbs stepped into the gap and invited Stone to go with them. Business prevented, he said, but sent them complete specifications for the boats Galloway had designed, together with maps of the river and notes on "the method of passing down such various rapids as we could not run." What he said about possible competition from Cogswell's pictures is unknown, but it is not likely it would have mattered anyway, for by then the brothers had decided on a revolutionary new approach: the first motion pictures ever taken of the river.

At the time of making the decision the Kolbs were in the process of pulling themselves up by their own bootstraps. They had been born to an impoverished family in Smithfield, Pennsylvania, Ellsworth in 1876, Emery in 1881. Both went to work after finishing grade school. After being injured during his teens in a steel mill accident, Ellsworth quit in disgust and moved West, a roving roughneck. He fell in love with the Grand Canyon during the winter of 1901-02 when he worked briefly as a bellhop at the Bright Angel Hotel. Returning home on a flying visit, he sang such praises to his twenty-year-old brother Emery, who was running a drill press and studying photography in his spare time, that the younger Kolb followed him within weeks.

In 1903 they mired themselves in debt to buy, for $425, the shop of a bankrupt photographer in Williams. They hauled the building to the growing South Rim settlement, perched it on the edge of the canyon, and began taking photos of tourists lining up on their rented mules for a ride down the Bright Angel Trail. It must have been the most difficult souvenir picture-taking enterprise in the United States, for there is no natural water at the South Rim. Rather than pay the high cost of having it hauled in by the new railroad, the Kolbs built a shack for their developing tanks at Indian Gardens on the Tonto Platform. The trail there dropped three thousand two hundred feet in four and one-half miles. After snapping pictures, Emery dashed down the steep, twisting path, made the prints, and dashed back up in time to distribute them to the returning riders at seventy-five cents each.

Whenever time allowed, they hiked into Upper Granite Gorge to take scenic shots and do odd jobs at the tourist camp (now Phantom Ranch) that Dave Rust had put together near the mouth of Bright Angel Creek. They sometimes swam horses across the river for Rust and played around in the boat he kept near the creek mouth for short trips. By and large, though, they were no more at home on rough water when they shoved off from Green River, Wyoming, on September 8, 1911, than Russell and Monett had been. Yet the only help they hired was a young greenhorn who, by acting as swamper, could give them more time for their picture taking.

Riding through the rapids of Lodore Canyon sprawled out on the deck of a five hundred pound boat terrified the youth, and he quit as soon as opportunity allowed.

Riding through the rapids of Lodore Canyon sprawled out on the deck of a five hundred pound boat terrified the youth, and he quit as soon as opportunity allowed. After that the trip was entirely the Kolbs' — filming, cooking, lining, portaging, and running the boats as best they could on hints gleaned from Powell's and Dellenbaugh's books and the notes that Stone had sent.

They were a disparate pair. Emery, short, slim, and wiry, weighed about one hundred thirty pounds. He was tense and withdrawn, but quick tempered and always ready to fight. Married, he had a four-year-old daughter; he named his boat *Edith* after her. Ellsworth, often called Ed, was about forty pounds heavier, easy going and friendly but reckless to a fault. A bachelor, he named his boat *Defiance*. In the studio they quarreled constantly. Their inability to get along would lead, in the early 1920s, to a breaking up of their partnership. But no animosities revealed themselves on this trip, either in their writings or in the recollections of those they encountered along the way. Indeed, they spent many anxious hours selflessly fishing each other out of uncomfortable situations.

They proved themselves, if proof was needed, in Cataract Canyon. They raced after and retrieved the *Edith* after it had washed loose from the bank and was plunging off through one of the major rapids "like a thing possessed." They crashed into boulders, were smothered under collapsing billows, and sometimes were left next to helpless with broken oarlocks. They never lined once, partly because Emery was sick part of the time — they had to lay over one day to let him recuperate. Yet they traversed Cataract in four days' running time, a record as far as they could determine.

Later Ellsworth summarized the experience in one generalized account:

I saw the mad, wild water hurled at the curving wall. Jagged rocks,

like the bared fangs of some dream-monster, appeared now and then
in the leaping, tumbling waves. Then down toward the turmoil —
dwarfed to nothingness by the magnitude of the walls — sped the
tiny shell-like boat. . . . The oar-blades were tipped high to
avoid loss in the first comber; then the boat was buried in the
foam, and staggered through on the other side. It was buffeted
here and there, now covered with a ton of water, now topping
a ten-foot wave. Like a skilled boxer . . . the oarsman shot
in his oars for two quick strokes, to straighten the boat with
the current or dodge a threatening boulder. . . . One would think
the chances about one to a hundred that he would get through. But
by some sort of system, undoubtedly aided, many times, by good
luck, the man and his boat won to land.

Alternating between their big 8"x10" plate camera and the heavy, awkward,
hand-cranked picture machine, they occasionally took pictures of each other in
their boats. More often, however, Emery did the filming while Ellsworth
recklessly sought out whatever spots seemed likely to make the best pictures. Of
his risky stunts, the most dangerous came at Soap Creek Rapid in Marble
Canyon, twelve miles below Lees Ferry.

Late in the afternoon Emery set up the motion picture camera where he had
a good view of a twisting channel between a monstrous hole and a massive
boulder a few feet farther downstream. Tatters of water leaped everywhere.
Down through it came Ellsworth in the *Defiance*. He skirted the hole but grazed
the lower rock. The *Defiance* reeled onto its side, throwing Ellsworth overboard.
He kept hold of the gunwales, however, and as the boat pivoted around the
boulder and righted itself, he climbed back aboard, retrieved the dangling oars,
and landed on a beach below the rapid. He had been in the water only half a
dozen seconds, but the brief bath has kept him from being recognized as the first
person to run Soap Creek Rapid.

He was unaware of the lost record, but he did know that portaging the
heavy, waterlogged *Edith* down the big drop would be an ordeal. To avoid it, he
helped Emery bail out and unload the *Defiance* and then trudged back upstream
through the deepening twilight. Uneasily Emery set fire to a pile of driftwood on
the bank and then climbed into the *Defiance*, ready to row to his brother's help if
needed.

This time Ellsworth's boat turned completely over, trapping him under the
cockpit. Scrambling free, he clung to the upside down boat and let it drag him
along. All he could see through repeated dousings was the fire. Then the *Defiance*
loomed through the dusk and one hundred thirty pound Emery somehow
dragged his bigger brother aboard, numb with cold. They overtook the *Edith* at
the head of the next rapid but could not get a good hold on the runaway and
were hauled, struggling and swearing, a mile down the river before they could
land. The next morning, taking advantage of every little eddy, they towed the
Defiance back to the bottom of Soap Creek for reloading.

The experience led them to vow to portage more often, but one laborious
trial was enough to put them back to running everything they saw, with a partial
exception at Hance. They lugged the *Defiance* and its duffle halfway down past
that rapid's spray-filled rock jungle, and then lost patience. Ellsworth climbed
into the reloaded *Defiance* and took off down the bottom half. Emery ran the

whole way in the *Edith*. A rock bounced him out once but he climbed back in as fast as Ellsworth had in Soap Creek. Luck. They knew it — but kept counting on it.

Twelve more hard, cold miles and a steep climb up the Bright Angel Trail brought them home. There they learned news that had been kept from them at every mail stop upstream: Emery's wife Blanche was ill. He rushed her to Los Angeles for treatment. A month later, assured she would be all right, he returned to the canyon, bringing the film that had been developed. Good shots, some of it, and it encouraged them to resume the trip.

Nearly a foot of snow covered the ground when they started down the trail on December 19, 1911. They took their younger brother Ernest with them, promising that he could ride and walk as far as Bass Camp eighteen miles downstream; from there he could climb the Bass Trail to the rim. Also with them was Bert Lauzon, an affable, daring, twenty-four-year-old prospector. The low water bared more rocks, and Ernest soon learned what an upset in winter-cold water was like. Even so he left Bass Camp reluctantly.

Four miles farther along, on the day before Christmas, Emery and Ellsworth, running separately, cracked up at almost the same instant in what has become known as Waltenberg Rapid. Emery managed to reach shore in the badly stove *Edith*, but Ellsworth, adrift in the river, was buffeted so long by the icy water that he could not stand after crawling free. Meantime Lauzon, who had walked around the maelstrom, leaped into the stream and caught the *Defiance* before it was carried over the next rapid. They spent the next day, Christmas, replacing the *Edith's* broken ribs with mesquite cut out of the niches where it grew on the cliff walls. They patched the gaping hole near the bow with loose boards they had carried along and covered the spot with canvas and galvanized iron.

So it went. Emery upset again. Freezing weather greeted them at Lava Falls, but the hot springs nearby offered one recompense; when the three men, in the water as much as out, were chilled from wrestling the boats over the streamside boulders, they ran to the springs and thawed out for a moment. Later, where Diamond Creek breaks through the walls, they left the river to buy fresh provisions at Peach Springs. And in one way the portages grew easier: a sheathing of ice on the boulders lining Separation and Lava Cliff rapids lubricated the labors of shoving the boats along.

They reached Needles on January 18, 1912. Altogether they had spent one hundred and one days on or beside the Green and Colorado rivers in seventy-six different camps. They had overturned five times in the Grand Canyon; waves or collisions with rocks had dumped one or another of them into the water eight times. But from the run — the eighth one through the canyon — came a movie that was shown nearly every day for almost three-quarters of a century in the studio on the rim — the longest run ever of any motion picture anywhere. Emery gave upwards of thirty thousand talks in connection with the studio showings and during lecture tours throughout the country. For the sake of the book he was writing, Ellsworth completed the traverse of the river by riding the spring flood of 1913 from Needles to the Gulf. Together the film and the book helped make the canyons of the Colorado one of the best known natural wonders on earth.

Charles Russell saw the Kolb film sometime after it began its run in 1912. He thought it poor — jerky, ill-lighted, badly organized. On returning to the mine he was then managing in Mexico, he brooded about it. Why not make a better film and take some of the plaudits and money away from the Kolbs? Not with Monett, however, who had proved to be an inept boatman, but with Bert Loper. (Clearly Russell had gotten over any resentment he may have felt over Bert's failure to appear at Lees Ferry in 1907.) They exchanged letters, and on the strength of Russell's promise of $550 as an advance against expenses, Loper agreed. Grandiosely then Russell paid out $5,000 for cameras and four miles of film, though all he knew about making movies was derived from a conversation with Karl Moon at the Grand Canyon. The Santa Fe and Denver & Rio Grande railroads agreed to buy some still shots from him, and a Salt Lake City newspaper noticed the trip with a gratifying headline:

WILL FACE DEATH
TO SECURE FILMS

Equipped again with steel boats — they were lighter and shallower than Loper liked — they pushed off from Green River, Utah, on July 19, 1914. The river was high for that time of year, and Loper proposed they slow the rush of their boats through Cataract Canyon by dragging metal chains from the sterns.

Rapid 14 looked dramatic — almost catastrophic, in fact — and they prepared for a spectacular shot, Russell in his boat, Loper on the bank with the camera. Russell surged through the head of the rapid in fine fashion, but hit a boulder among the towering tail waves. The blow punctured one of the boat's airtight compartments. It flipped, throwing Russell out. He clung to the overturned craft as it drifted toward quiet water. As it began to sink, he floundered ashore and looked back. No boat. Evidently the dragging chain had caught between two rocks and had pulled it, full of water, to the bottom. They looked for two days without finding it.

Loper's boat was still whole. They stored their heavy cameras in it, hid it, and made their way back over arduous rockfalls to a trail that zigzagged up into a region of weird turrets, colored sands, and startling fissures known now as the Doll House, part of Canyonlands National Park. A five-day hike with little water and only some candy and raisins for food brought them to Hite. There they rented horses and rode back to Salt Lake City and then Green River to begin again.

A quarrel broke out when Loper started building a boat more to his liking than the one Russell had lost. He wanted Russell to pay for the materials; Russell insisted that Loper use the $550 advance (which, one suspects, Bert had already spent). He named the craft the *Ross Wheeler* after a friend who had recently been murdered, entrusted it to an acquaintance — don't let Russell have it! — and then got a job with a Bureau of Reclamation crew that was exploring, with drills, for a dam site at the head of Cataract Canyon.

Furious, Russell hired two men to replace him: Bill Reeder, whose rowing experience was limited to the quiet water above and below the town of Green River, and August Tadje, who claimed to be a cameraman though his only experience had been working as a property man for a movie company that had been taking background shots in Salt Lake City. He took the *Ross Wheeler* away from its guardian at Green River, perhaps by means of a writ of attachment, and all three crowded into it to float down the mirrorlike waters of Stillwater and

Labyrinth canyons. Near Cataract they encountered Loper. Amid a storm of bad language Russell and he flew at each other, fists flailing.

Afterwards each claimed to have bested the other, though Tadje says they were pulled apart by onlookers. In any event Russell kept the *Ross Wheeler* and plunged on down Cataract Canyon to the point where Loper's boat had been hidden after the first disaster. Russell appropriated it, too, along with its cache of cameras, film, and such food as remained unspoiled. Launching it, he promptly sank almost at the spot where he had gone down before. Fortunately they had stowed the cameras and film in the larger *Ross Wheeler*.

No more walking out for Charles Russell. They managed to get the *Ross* through the rest of the rapids and in due time reached Hite. There Reeder quit. Russell and Tadje returned to Salt Lake City, hired Tadje's brother-in-law, Goddard Quist, as swamper, then loaded a new boat on a wagon and drove back to Hite to continue the journey. It was December 6 and cold. With grisly humor they named the new boat *Titanic II* after the ocean liner that had been sunk by an iceberg in the Atlantic a little more than two years before.

Ice plagued them, too, as they floated out of Glen Canyon into Marble Gorge. Each morning they had to chop the boats loose and during the day dodge the jagged white cakes tumbling down the main current. At Badger Creek they decided to leave until warmer weather arrived. After caching the boats and with great effort leaning the trunk of a dead tree against an otherwise impassable cliff, they reached the top and stumbled back to Lees Ferry, drinking "only a little green water along the way." A stagecoach took them on to Salt Lake City.

On January 15, 1915, as the time neared for the resumption of the trip, Tadje let his terror overflow into an almost incoherent letter to the Kolbs. Was it possible to buy waterproof clothing? How much extra pay should he, hired as a cameraman, demand for being required to labor with the boats at the portages? And then the cry for help. "If anything should happen if you care to look for one or more of us on foot trying to save our lives. We may build watch fires or signal fires as you call them."

The letter reached the Kolbs on March 9. By then the trio were back on the river. Russell's boat turned over in one rapid; Quist hung up on a rock in another. Tadje busily filmed all this but found the scenes too tame. Though he would not ride through heavy water himself, he wanted one of the others to provide him with a truly spectacular spill. Quist, sensing that he was being exploited, said resentfully some years later, "I was sure each morning that I would be dead before night."

"I was sure each morning that I would be dead before night."

On reaching the foot of Bright Angel Trail, the trio pulled the boats onto the bank and climbed to the South Rim for rest and relaxation. There Quist told Russell he'd had enough and demanded his pay. Russell wrote him a check for $100 — on brown wrapping paper with a burned match, one story says, though surely there were pens and good paper somewhere on the rim. The recipient cashed it at El Tovar and when it bounced he faded quietly away.

Meanwhile Russell had hired a local hanger-on, Jake Jeffs, to take Quist's place at the oars of *Titanic II*. At that point their troubles truly began. Jeffs jiggled down a riffle, wallowed into an eddy from which he could not break free, and went into hysterics. Russell and Tadje managed to pull him to the bank, and he fled. So, in effect, did the *Titanic II,* which broke loose and vanished as the two men were trying to line it out of the eddy and around a point of rocks.

In grumbling resignation they pulled the durable, Loper-built *Ross Wheeler* out of reach of high water and hoofed up Bright Angel Trail to the rim. By telephone they ordered another steel boat from St. Louis. It was to be sixteen feet long and four of beam, and they seem never to have named it. Meantime they ran across a job-seeker with whom Tadje had worked on the same Salt Lake City film. His name was Clement, and though he knew nothing of white water, Russell hired him as an all-around handyman.

During the three-week wait for the boat, they built an awkward wooden dolly supported on eighteen-inch wheels attached to axles of iron pipe. When the boat arrived, they loaded it on the dolly and started down the steep trail, across rubble and around tight curves. Whenever a mule train of tourists appeared — it happened at least twice and occasionally four times a day — they had to ease the contraption off to one side, sometimes at the edge of sheer precipices, and cover it with canvas so that the animals would not spook. During the first stretch of the journey they walked back to the top to spend each night. As they neared Indian Gardens, they used a cabin there for shelter. A good samaritan with a horse helped pull the improvised truck across the relatively flat Tonto Platform, but when they reached the corkscrew trail down through the lower granite cliffs they were on their own again. Altogether the journey took a week. They then discovered that a rock rolling down the hill had punched a hole through the side of the *Ross Wheeler.* Tadje walked all the way to the rim and back for patching material.

Finally they were moving again. Hellish work. Lining Horn Creek, lining Granite Falls, portaging Hermit. But they were grinding out pictures and regaining confidence. At Crystal, a much less formidable rapid than it has been since the great boulder outwash of 1966, Russell decided to run the new boat through for the camera. Near the lower end, close to the left bank, he rammed it immovably between two huge boulders.

Back to the rim — and no trail this time. They climbed Slate Canyon, a generally dry tributary that debouches into the Colorado River from the south, until the cliffs boxed them in. Swinging left on dangerous ledges, they found a crack in the Tapeats sandstone and at last stood on the Tonto Platform. Tadje and Clement started across it, intending to reenter Slate Canyon above the barrier they had circled. Russell balked. He knew from his 1908 experiences that Boucher Trail lay somewhere to the east and he suggested following the Tonto Platform until they reached it. The others declined to go with him. One can only surmise why. Russell had been acting oddly of late, sitting apart in camp and holding earnest discourses with himself. Perhaps his talk of a trail was more vaporing. Tadje and Clement were friends and fellow Mormons. In this crisis they decided to count on themselves.

It proved to be a hair-raising choice. When the Grand Canyon's premier hiker, Harvey Butchart, tried to reconstruct their route up Slate Canyon and through the Coconino sandstone, he had to use ropes. They used a pole they found for worming up one perpendicular niche. They went piggyback up another chimney — one of them jammed himself into the crack while the other climbed his back, stood on his shoulders and head, found lodgement, and then let the other use him as a ladder. Over and over, until Clement topped out and collapsed, half fainting, into a scuff of snow. Tadje, stuck in the chimney behind him, bellowed over and over for help. Rousing at last, Clement returned through the gathering dusk and tugged him free. By then both were suffering torments of thirst. Unsatisfied by the mix of snow, twigs, and dirt he managed to scrape off the ground, Tadje found a piece of pitch clinging to the limb of a piñon pine and began chewing it to start the saliva flowing. Clement asked, with his eyes, what it was. "I opened my mouth to show him," Tadje recalled later, "and he reached in and grabbed it and put it in his own mouth. We then just looked at each other."

They stumbled south through the trees until they chanced onto a road that took them to a ranger station. The ranger refused to believe their story but fed them and let them rest. The next morning they went on west to Bass's hotel, hoping to find word of Russell there. Russell, of course, had gone east. Bass excoriated them for having abandoned their companion — and just then he wandered in, declaimed dramatically, "I have been lost," and keeled over.

Recovered, they rented a windlass, ropes, grappling hooks, and other equipment from Bass, packed the tools on burros, and returned to the river by way of Boucher Trail, the closest access to Crystal. How they reached Crystal itself remains a small mystery. Anyway, after they had unpacked, Clement took the donkeys back to their owner while Russell and Tadje worked on the stranded boat. Finally they pulled it free and maneuvered it into a back eddy. Russell climbed in to run it through the bottom of the rapid to a quiet beach. Instead he rammed it right back into the rocks. Wearily, they hooked up the windlass and began heaving again. This time the boat rolled onto its side and split open. Cameras, film, everything fell out and sank to the bottom. Why the precious baggage hadn't been unloaded first is another mystery. Perhaps there was no trail to carry it over.

When Clement returned, they started downstream with the *Ross Wheeler* for Bass's riverside camp ten miles away, thinking to have replacements sent them down the Bass Trail. There are several spooky rapids in that stretch — Sapphire, Ruby, Serpentine — and on top of the soaking from the rapids a cold rain began to fall. It kept falling as they made camp a short distance above Bass's place. Sitting there sodden and defeated, they decided to hell with it and the next morning walked out Bass Trail, leaving the *Ross Wheeler* rocking gently at the margin of the river.

The story needs three postscripts.

First. Deciding that the *Ross Wheeler* might come in handy some day, John Waltenberg, William Bass's occasional employee and partner, winched it up the bank out of reach of floods. It is still visible there if one knows where to look.

Second. Four years after leaving the river, Charles Russell went insane and had to be institutionalized.

Third. Shortly before Christmas 1916, a year and a half after his fight with Russell, Albert Loper married. He was forty-seven; his bride Rachel was eighteen. Because she refused to live in the stone cabin he had built beside his placer mine and garden patch in Glen Canyon, he found work in Carbon County as a coal miner. Between jobs he returned to the canyon to mine a little gold, talk to old friends, and just sit looking off across the river. In 1921 and 1922 he acted as a boatman for survey parties scouting the San Juan and upper Green rivers for dam sites. He was eager to join the climactic expedition through the Grand Canyon in 1923 but was rejected as being too old.

Old? At fifty-four? Bert brooded about that even after a heart attack a few years later made him switch from coal mining to acting as caretaker of the Masonic Temple in Salt Lake City. He still visited Glen Canyon occasionally, and although his river adventures had not been particularly extensive, he became known as the sage of the Colorado. In the winter of 1938-39, while recovering in the hospital from a gall bladder operation, he was visited by young Don Harris of the United States Geological Survey. Harris and two twenty-five-year-old friends wanted to make a movie of the Grand Canyon — that perennial itch. Could Loper offer suggestions? He could, the main one being that by summer he'd be able to go along if the others paid his expenses.

They went in two boats, Don and Bert rowing and the others riding as passengers. It was a good trip and ended just days before Bert's seventieth birthday. In high spirits the group vowed to repeat the excursion in 1949 in celebration of Loper's eightieth.

Bert probably took the impulsive promise more seriously than the others did. He built a new boat of plywood, named it the *Grand Canyon*, and after World War II had ended took at least fourteen parties of Boy Scouts through Glen Canyon on rafts. Early in July 1949, a month shy of Bert's eightieth, Don Harris brought four men to Lees Ferry for the promised run. Except for Harris, none had been on the 1939 trip. Harry Aleson, perhaps the first of the Grand Canyon's true river rats, and Louise Fetzner, riding together in a war-surplus neoprene raft, attached themselves to the group, so that altogether seven people started downstream. The heat was fierce and Bert was clearly not feeling well; at one point he said that if anything happened to him he wanted to be buried beside the river. He refused to let anyone spell him at the oars.

He entered the big rapid at mile 24.5, Marble Canyon, without pausing to look it over.

After lunch on July 8 he started out first with Wayne Nichol as passenger. He entered the big rapid at mile 24.5, Marble Canyon, without pausing to look it over. Suddenly he turned rigid. Nichol yelled but there was no response and the boat flipped. Nichol caught the lifeline that circled it and let it drag him ahead. Looking back, he saw Loper floating along, buoyed by his life jacket, his eyes open, the victim, almost surely, of another heart attack.

A mile farther down, where the current slowed before plunging into another rapid, Nichol managed to crawl onto the bottom of the overturned boat. Extricating one oar, he worked his way into an eddy just as Loper floated by into the rapid. Unable to do anything constructive, Nichol leaped from the circling boat onto the shore. The next boat in line picked him up. Meanwhile Loper's boat broke out of the eddy and followed its owner into the rough water below. The party paid it no heed but spent the rest of daylight searching for Loper.

At dusk they found his boat lodged on a rock bar sixteen miles downstream. The next morning they dragged it above the flood line and painted on its bow, "Bert Loper, Grand Old Man of the Colorado, Born: July 31, 1869. Died: July 8, 1949."

And still there is a postscript. On April 2, 1975, a hiker found a human skeleton hidden by brush near the mouth of Cardenas Creek, forty-seven miles from the rapid in which Bert had overturned. Park rangers took the bones by

55

helicopter to Northern Arizona University at Flagstaff for examination. A close study by anthropologists and artist Barton Wright's drawing of the features that the skull might have supported (Barton had never seen a picture of Loper) convinced those involved that the remains were indeed Bert's. They were then sent to Sandy, Utah, for interment beside Rachel, who had died February 8, 1975, less than two months before the hiker had made his discovery.

Five

DAM SITES

Before the economic potentials of the Colorado River could be realized, the erratic stream flow — it varied from less than two thousand cubic feet per second (cfs) during dry periods to two hundred thousand cfs or more during floods — would have to be, in engineering jargon, "smoothed out." This meant building dams and reservoirs. Big dams for checking the torrents that every now and then rampaged through the towns along the lower river. Big reservoirs to settle silt and store water needed for ambitious irrigation systems and metropolitan developments. Plus power and recreation, all embraced in what one Secretary of the Interior called "a comprehensive plan of development by which this great river, now a natural menace, may be converted into a national resource."

Private power companies — the Southern California Edison Company and Utah Power & Light — joined the United States Geological Survey in launching the topographic surveys fundamental to the work. They began in 1921. (That same year the seven states of the river basin agreed to form a commission, chaired by Secretary of Commerce Herbert Hoover, to determine how the waters of the Colorado were to be divided among them.) Bert Loper was head boatman of the little fleet that surveyed the canyons of the San Juan. The next year he shifted north to Lodore and Desolation canyons on the Green. Meanwhile the Kolb brothers handled the assignment for Cataract Canyon: in 1921 Ellsworth ran each of the expedition's boats through every rapid — not without difficulty — while Emery, still using his faithful *Edith*, cranked away with his movie camera.

The Colorado River Commission's final meeting was scheduled for November 1922 in Santa Fe. Hoping to attract publicity and provide the delegates with background for their deliberations, the public and private surveyors decided to take the boats that had been used on the Cataract survey out of their storage sheds at Lees Ferry, equip them with outboard motors, and putt-putt up through Glen Canyon to Hall's Crossing. There they would pick up a gaggle of dignitaries and float them back through Glen Canyon, showing them the sights and instructing them on past accomplishments and future plans. Included in the gathering were Arthur Powell Davis, director of the Bureau of Reclamation; Colonel Claude H. Birdseye, Chief Engineer of the Topographic Branch of the United States Geological Survey; officials of various railroads and power companies; a representative of Herbert Hoover's; and John A. Widstoe, former president of the University of Utah and Utah's delegate on the Colorado River Commission.

The man in charge of the flotilla was Eugene Clyde LaRue, chief hydrologist of the USGS. He was tall and thin, wore a small black mustache, sometimes experienced vertigo on high places, and, during the pangs of intermittent stomach aches, seemed unduly brusque to those around him. He was forty-three years old in 1922. He had been working on Colorado River plans for nearly a decade and had a special ax to grind. Many engineers believed that the river could be controlled best by a high dam located below the Grand Canyon in either Black or Boulder canyons. LaRue disagreed. He believed the high dam should be located at a site he had discovered four miles above Lees Ferry. This would smooth out the river in the Grand Canyon, and engineers could then construct several hydroelectric projects at sites to be chosen during a survey the following year, 1923.

In the crew hired to take the boats upstream to Hall's Crossing was another man with an ax to grind — Lewis R. Freeman. He was almost the same age as LaRue. He had won letters in football, baseball, and track at Stanford University during 1896, 1897, and 1898, but afterwards had let himself become fat — two hundred and fifty-seven pounds according to a river acquaintance, Frank Dodge. In spite of his weight Freeman made his living as an outdoorsman — as one example, he had traveled alone in a rowboat down the entire length of the Columbia River — and then writing about his experiences. When the canyons of the Colorado began making news, he hurried there. LaRue, desirous of publicity about the river, put him on as a boatman.

Except for troubles with silt in the motors, the upriver trip was uneventful. On the way down, the dignitaries took time out to walk up to Rainbow Bridge and to inspect LaRue's dam site. How much influence, if any, the junket had on the commission's deliberations is problematical, but during their acrimonious discussions in Santa Fe the conferees finally hammered out the historic Colorado River Compact. Unable to decide on allotments for each state, they agreed instead to divide the river's waters between its upper and lower basins. Lees Ferry was selected as the boundary point. An all-important gauging station for measuring stream flow was placed there, just below the mouth of the Paria, at what was called Mile Zero. Henceforth all mileages, both upstream and down, would be calculated from that point. Of still greater significance, the ratification of the compact by the legislatures of the states concerned would guarantee the eventual construction, either above or below the Grand Canyon, of what would then be the biggest dam in the world.

This was news. To capitalize on it, Freeman hurried home to Pasadena and in four months turned out several articles and a book entitled *The Colorado River Yesterday, Today, and Tomorrow*. To learn still more about the "tomorrows" he sped back to Flagstaff, Arizona, and joined the crew Colonel Birdseye and LaRue were assembling for the 1923 survey of the Grand Canyon. With him he brought what was probably the first typewriter ever to travel through the canyon.

One geologist, a cook, and five surveyors, including Birdseye, made up the core of the party. The surveyors, their food, and equipment were to be transported in five boats. Three of the craft were those stored at Lees Ferry; a fourth eighteen-footer, named *Grand*, was ordered built in Long Beach, California, and shipped by rail to Flagstaff. Because these big, heavy boats lacked maneuverability, the Colonel added, at Freeman's suggestion, the *Mojave*, a fourteen-foot, steel-framed canvas affair buoyed by oil cans and protected from rocks by a girdle of inner tubes. This contraption, designed to land the surveyors on difficult perches beside rapids, was to be the responsibility of one of the party's rodmen, Frank Dodge, who in time would develop into one of the finest river runners on the Colorado. He was thirty-one, short, stocky, powerful, and already growing bald. Born and raised on the island of Oahu in Hawaii, he was an excellent swimmer and surfer. He knew horses — he had worked on the island's cattle ranches — and on coming to the mainland had turned into a wanderer, supporting himself with odd jobs until joining the USGS as an all-around handyman. His employers found him overly fond of the bottle; his companions delighted in his antics.

The four principal boatmen — Freeman, Leigh Lint, H.E. Blake, and Emery Kolb — were veterans of earlier USGS surveys. To Kolb, whom Birdseye asked to serve as head of the rivermen, the trip looked like a marvelous opportunity for taking additional pictures of the canyon with better equipment than he and Ellsworth had used in 1911-12, and thus cash in on the public's rising interest in the project. Birdseye brought him up short. Picture making, he wrote Emery on February 10, 1923, would interfere with the work Kolb had been hired to do and "unless you consider the success of the government expedition to the entire exclusion of your private interests, we will secure another boatman." The USGS, he added, and he meant LaRue, would take its own movies for its own publicity purposes. In addition, Emery must be prepared to help newsreel photographers who came down the different trails to film the expedition.

Emery exploded. "I feel," he fumed at Birdseye, "it would be self-extermination to take part in a trip where others obtain motion pictures, as it is in such pictures, more than anything else, we make our living."

The wrangling continued almost until departure time, when at last Birdseye said Kolb could take along one small camera if he promised to use it only when it did not interfere with his duties. The government would provide the film and expect a positive print in return. Emery's salary as head boatman was raised to $500 a month (the others received $200) and with some ill grace he yielded.

The party left Flagstaff for the canyon on the afternoon of July 17 — three trucks and three passenger cars traveling a next to impassable road in crushing heat. Emery's wife Blanche was along, as was his pretty daughter Edith, her dark hair cut in a Dutch bob, and Edith's friend, Catherine Pahl of Los Angeles. The new boat was so heavy and protruded so far from the rear of the truck carrying it that when the vehicle was ascending a hill the heaviest men in the party had to stand on the running boards and lie across the hood — Freeman, who was to navigate the *Grand,* came in handy here — to keep the front wheels on the ground.

They spent twelve days at Lees Ferry patching, caulking, and painting the old boats, which they renamed *Glen* (it carried the cook outfit), *Boulder,* and *Marble. Marble,* somewhat shorter than the others, was to be Kolb's boat and would carry no passengers. When the surveyors needed river transportation, they would divide up among the other boats and sprawl out flat, one on each stern and one on the bow.

Daytime temperatures at the Ferry hit 115° Fahrenheit, and there was a lot of jumping into the muddy river to cool off. According to the new gauging station it was running about 35,600 cubic feet per second and was more dangerous than the men realized. Once Dodge had to rush out in the *Mojave* to pull Lint from a whirlpool. And when Kolb was told he could not film a "departure" scene being staged on July 31 for LaRue's cameras, he created a whirlpool of his own by resigning on the spot, but eventually was soothed by the harried Birdseye. As for Dodge, he appeared in none of the official pictures of the "start"; he was somewhere in the shade, sleeping off a load of prohibition-era brew distilled from figs by the gauging station attendant.

In spite of the contretemps, no early Grand Canyon trip was more meticulously planned. Waterproof containers for equipment had been specially designed and repeatedly tested. Roger Birdseye, a nephew of the Colonel's, had been employed to assemble either pack trains or Indian bearers, depending on the trails to be used, for bringing fresh supplies from the rim to the slowly moving party. A radio powered by a dry battery was brought along to pick up warnings of any flooding caused by cloudbursts. The party's geologist, Raymond C. Moore, contrived a speaker for it out of a baking powder tin and a funnel, good enough, when rapids weren't too noisy, to be heard for forty feet. It did need a one-hundred-sixty-foot antenna, however, one end attached to a driftwood pole set in the sand and the other to a bush or boulder high on a nearby cliff.

On August 1 they plunged into Marble Canyon and that night camped at Badger Creek Rapid in a drenching rain that sent cascades of red water spouting spectacularly over the rims. The next day most of them voted to run Soap Creek Rapid, but Kolb said no; they shouldn't risk a wreck so early in the trip. Exhausted that night after skidding the boats on logs around the worst part of the thundering water, they turned on the radio and learned that President Harding had died. Shaken, Birdseye said that on the tenth, the day scheduled for the funeral, they would do no running.

Instrument work between those glorious red walls slowed them, during the next week, to a forward progress of only thirty-two miles. They were not dull days. Plummets of sunlight struck arrowheads of gold from the water (Freeman's words) and reflections rippled across the walls. While waiting for the surveyors the boatmen sang and played in protected coves. Rowing was a challenge. The laden boats rolled heavily in the thick waves and sometimes were spun completely around. Blake, at the oars of the *Glen,* hit a rock and jarred Birdseye overboard, and then a few days later went in himself when an oarlock snapped. Dodge's canvas *Mojave* buckled under him at mile 24.5, where Loper would die years later. One of the wooden boats picked him up off a clot of driftwood and then retrieved the *Mojave* — to no avail. While Dodge was lining it along the

61

edge of a rapid a little farther along, it slipped sideways into a hole, ripped apart, and wrapped itself around a boulder. From then on Dodge, too, was a passenger.

The rides terrified the passengers at first. Donning life jackets, they lay flat on the planking and clung to the lifelines that were stretched across the decks. Seen from that angle, the waves looked mountainous; laden with silt, they crashed thunderously on the riders. But after surviving a few runs, the men caught "rapids fever" and wanted to float when they could have walked. They invented a game: who could go through with a lighted pipe or cigarette in his mouth? When that palled, Dodge hitched up ropes like bridle reins so that he could stand on the bow where he wouldn't block the oarsman's view (they were running stern first). Then, rearing back, he rode out the rough water like a Roman on horseback — a risk increased by the way his upright position lifted the boat's center of gravity and added to its instability. Yet the stunt was so exciting to watch that, as far as the records show, not even Birdseye objected.

On the evening before President Harding's funeral, they reached Boulder Rapid, named for a massive block of stone in its center. The elements contributed a fitting backdrop to the pause Birdseye had ordered — a sandstorm followed by cannonades of thunder and deluges of rain. Their fire expired. As if to meet the weather on its own terms, LaRue and some of the others stripped off their wet clothes and raced back and forth along the beach. The next morning, after a miserable night in soaked beds, they looked for the grave of Peter Hansbrough of the Brown-Stanton expedition, located near the reddish, seven-hundred-foot cliffs of Point Hansbrough. They did not find it, but the search itself added solemnity to the account of the President's funeral they heard over their radio. Later, when Birdseye compiled the party's topographic map of the region, he changed the name of Boulder Rapid to President Harding Rapid.

Because surveyors descending old prospector trails had already run some level lines in the vicinity of the Little Colorado River, the Birdseye party reached their supply point at Hance Rapid ahead of schedule. To hurry Roger Birdseye's packtrain of supplies along the way and also to have heavier oarlocks forged, Kolb, Lint, and Blake climbed the Hance Trail to the old Grand View Hotel, closed by then, and hitched a ride to Grand Canyon Village.

On August 18 they returned with the pack mules — and with Edith Kolb, chaperoned by a Mrs. Gilliland. Hance is a long, dangerous rapid, and by then the river had fallen enough to expose its sawblades of rock. So that the boats could run it empty — lightness made them easier to manage — the pack mules, groaning over the the boulders, were forced to take the new supplies to the foot of the rapid. After watching her father make a dazzling run through its churning water, Edith decided to try. Leigh Lint put her on the stern deck of his boat so she would be facing forward, took off, and quite unintentionally dived over a boulder into a yawning hole. By ramming forward as hard as he could on the handles of the oars in their strong new oarlocks, he drove the boat through the standing wave below the hole like a surfacing ouzel. Edith disembarked soaking wet and grinning widely, the first woman, as far as is known, to run a major rapid in the Grand Canyon. She swore that when the boat was knifing down into the hole she saw the very bedrock of the stream. A triumph — but watching it had made Birdseye break out in a sweat. No more women in the party's boats, he ordered.

The restrictions did not apply to photographers. Farther downstream, where

She swore that when the boat was knifing down into the hole she saw the very bedrock of the stream.

the Bright Angel Trail parallels the river for a mile or so, Freeman put a Fox Movietone cameraman in an open hatch of the boat and ran through Pipe Spring Rapid so that the man could film the bucking of the boat in the waves. Tourists watching from the trail yelled, cheered, and took more pictures. At Hermit Creek, Blanche and Edith Kolb and thirty-two additional tourists appeared with the pack train. Because several Park and Santa Fe Railroad officials were in the group, the boatmen put on a good show for them, which LaRue filmed for the USGS. Unable to withstand the excitement, Kolb unlimbered his own small camera. Birdseye told him to put it away and get on with his performance. Kolb resigned in a temper. Fine, said Birdseye, and turned his boat over to Dodge. Then Blanche Kolb intervened; the genial Dodge told Birdseye they would need all the experienced manpower they could get farther downstream, and why didn't everyone calm down and start again? Agreed — and then they had to placate Ward, the cook, who started to stalk off because he was being asked to feed too many dignitaries. Birdseye soft-talked him back: the delay of sending outside for a new cook would seriously disrupt schedules, but Roger Birdseye would bring a replacement down Havasu Creek, and Ward could leave there.

On they went, through squalls of rain. Roger brought another packload of supplies down the Bass Trail on August 29. Kolb, hired to be careful, was just that and on September 8 had the grumbling crew portage all the supplies and equipment around Waltenberg's tumultuous fifteen-foot drop so the boats could be run through empty. But on September 12, six weeks and one hundred fifty miles from Lees Ferry, the cautious head boatman suffered the indignity of being the first one to overturn a boat.

A sharp, unnamed cataract dropped down to a sandbar that had been designated as the night's campground. Dodge and some of the surveyors were already there, and, as he often did, Dodge stood beside the smooth, swift water at the foot of the rapid, watching the boats come through. He saw Kolb's *Marble* miss its course by a fraction of a yard, nose-dive into a hole, roll over, and emerge bottomside up. When Kolb finally appeared a hundred feet farther down, he looked dazed and was barely able to cling to the bobbing craft. Later he said he had been trapped in the cockpit.

By then Dodge was in the water, angling to intercept the boat seventy feet out from shore. In spite of eddies and the speed of the current, he timed the converging vectors perfectly, climbed onto the craft's bottom and helped Kolb, who seemed muddled by shock, climb aboard. Leigh Lint, who had pursued the derelict through the rapid, then took the boat's painter and headed for shore. After they had landed, the others came down, righted the boat and laboriously towed it back upstream to camp. Birdseye, who had been uneasy about Dodge's sudden promotion/demotion at Hermit, gave the rescuer a raise in pay and then broke out a dram. In the hilarity of relief they named the rapid Upset, a designation it has borne ever since.

Seven miles farther on, at the mouth of Havasu Creek, they met the ever-faithful Roger Birdseye shepherding a red-bearded cook, Felix Kominsky, who was almost as fat as Freeman, and nineteen Indian bearers carrying hundreds of pounds of supplies. The former cook left, and because the radio had failed they sent it out for repairs, with the request that it be returned at the mouth of Diamond Creek, the next supply point.

Surveying for dam sites in the narrow gorge kept them tied up for a few days. The water was very low as they moved slowly on toward Lava Falls. The sky was bright. Lacking a radio to pick up the alerts that were being broadcast to them, they had no reason to suspect that a monstrous flood, caused by a cloudburst over the basin of the Little Colorado River, was pouring into the canyon behind them.

Just before reaching Lava Falls they landed on the left bank, unloaded the boats, and then, unable to hear each other yell above the unremitting roar of the rapids, partly portaged and partly lined the craft past the upper cauldron. By evening the worst was behind them, and they eased the boats into a tight, rocky niche and then brought down the cargo and reloaded, planning to run the rest of the rough water in the morning. Because the haven was not a good camping place, they left the cook outfit and their bedrolls at the head of the rapid.

They were trooping back through the dusk toward the camp when a swift rise in the river warned of trouble. Forgetting supper, they scrambled back to the cove. Already lateral waves created by the surges in midstream were banging the boats against the rocks and each other. They pulled the wooden craft up the narrow beach to the foot of a low cliff of travertine and then, as the water continued to rise, realized that what they had supposed would be an overnight haven for the boats was in fact a trap.

Kolb had lined this same stretch of the river twelve years before, and now he remembered — or thought he remembered — that there was a more commodious beach farther downstream. They eased the *Boulder* into the current for a scouting mission. Kolb took the oars; Lint rode on the deck with an acetylene torch. Cautiously they crept down such slack water as there was, working close to the black rocks on the bank in an effort to keep away from the main current. The cove was not as far off as it seemed in the dim, noisy darkness — only a hundred feet or so — and its floor was not sand, but hard, sloping limestone. They landed and pulled the heavy boat as high as they could and then returned to the others through sharp travertine and slashing sawgrass. Moonlight glowing on the opposite wall made the elephantine waves in midstream look like canvas billowing in a wind. The stink of the turgid water was sickening.

Because the *Marble* had not yet been loaded, they decided to leave it where it was, hauling it up the travertine cliff as far as necessary with block and tackle. The *Grand* and *Glen*, two men in each, moved on down to the limestone landing. They worked at their different stations until about 3:00 A.M., manhandling the boats even higher. Then, in spite of the noise, they slept fitfully, awakening at dawn to an awesome sight. By Birdseye's estimate the river had risen twenty-one feet and was flowing 125,000 cubic feet per second. (Actually, the top recording at the Bright Angel gauging station was 98,500 feet.) The volume of water smoothed out the former rough areas at the head of the rapid and then, opposite their coves, broke into a maelstrom of explosive mud. Driftwood trees and logs were sucked into gigantic whirlpools and then belched out like rockets.

During the day the rise slowed and stopped, but the battered boats remained a constant chore. Lower levels the next day made the bored prisoners fret to leave. Kolb held them one more day.

Roger Birdseye was waiting anxiously at Diamond Creek with the last load of supplies — and the repaired radio. They stayed there four days, the boatmen repairing the craft while the surveyors ran their level lines far up the nearby side canyons. Then on again to Separation Rapid. Like Powell half a century before, they could not find solid enough footing for portaging or lining the boats (though others had) and so all of them rode. Freeman had LaRue and Moore as passengers in the *Grand*. While dodging a boulder, he was rolled by a transverse wave. All three, even fat Freeman, had to struggle to stay afloat in the violent water. Moore, who was closest to the boat, finally crawled onto its bottom, held tight with one hand to a lifeline and with the other caught Freeman just in time to keep him from being crushed between the heavy boat and a cliff. Together, they pulled LaRue out of a whirlpool, badly dazed. Then Blake and Dodge came up in the *Glen*, caught the painter of the overturned boat — they were almost through Separation's third section by then — and towed it into a cove where they righted it. A little farther on they made an arduous portage around Lava Cliff Rapid, and the rest was easy. They reached Needles October 16 and disbanded four days later.

Scientifically, this was the most significant trip since Powell's. Thanks to Roger Birdseye's efficient supply system, they had been able to stay in the Grand Canyon for a longer period than earlier parties had. As a result, Raymond Moore had found time to broaden the geologic knowledge of the canyon. The surveyors would produce from their figures the first topographic map of much of the canyon bottom. In addition they had examined twenty-one potential dam sites, an essential step toward what they called "the conquest of the Colorado."

In addition they had examined twenty-one potential dam sites, an essential step toward what they called "the conquest of the Colorado."

Voluminous publicity greeted the triumph. Birdseye, Moore, and Freeman wrote articles for large-circulation newspapers and magazines. Freeman added a popular book, *Down the Colorado*. Birdseye, LaRue, and Kolb worked out illustrated lectures in such a way that they did not interfere with each other. Controversy over where the river's — and the world's — biggest dam would be built kept interest alive. Inevitably, publicity-hungry watchers began trying, in strange and startling ways, to capitalize on that interest for their own ends.

Six

THE OPPORTUNISTS

Eugene LaRue lost his job with the USGS because he could not hold his tongue. Even after the Bureau of Reclamation had decided to control the Colorado River by means of a high dam in either Boulder or Black canyons, he kept insisting, publicly and stridently, that a better site was the one he had located in Glen Canyon, four miles above Lees Ferry. His superiors told him to shut up or get out. Stubbornly turning his back on fifteen years of hydrological work along the river, he left government service and became a private consultant.

Almost his first work was with the Pathé-Bray Company of Hollywood, which had been put together late in 1926 by J.R. Bray, the inventor of animated cartoons, and the Pathé people for the specific purpose of making a film on river running. Maybe the picture would be a documentary harking back to Powell and entitled "The Pride of the Colorado." Or perhaps it would be a romantic adventure called "The Bride of the Colorado." The main thing was to put *something* on the screen while interest in the dam, and the river, was high. LaRue's job was to assemble a flotilla of boats and lead it down the canyons below Green River, Utah. His pay was to be the then astonishing figure of $150 a day.

Now it so happened that a serious, middle-aged war veteran back in New York City had the same idea at the same time. His name was Clyde Eddy. Born in Texas on March 30, 1889, he grew up mostly in Colorado and Utah. Though he served a hitch in the Navy beginning in 1906, he entered World War I as an infantryman, experiencing an uncomfortable amount of rugged action. Mustered out, he took a cross-country trip with his wife Kathleen. During it they rode mules with several other tourists down the Hermit Trail from the South Rim to the river. The sight of the water heaving in the rapids brought Eddy to his own obsession. "This is my river," he told Kathleen and seldom quit thinking about it after that, even though he soon had a son named Richard and a good position with the drug firm of E.R. Squibb & Sons. He was short, husky through the chest, had a pronounced widow's peak and a wide mouth that seldom smiled.

After reading everything about the river he could find, he decided on three Powell-type boats built of mahogany fortified by closely spaced ribs of oak. Two were twenty-two feet long, five of beam, and weighed half a ton each; he named them *Coronado* and *Powell*. The third, the *Dellenbaugh,* was sixteen feet. Each had two seats for four oarsman, and tightly built compartments fore, aft, and between the seats. Some of the cost was paid by the manufacturers of Mercurochrome, who saw advertising value in pictures of river runners doctoring their cuts with their antiseptic. The International Newsreel Company agreed to send along a cameraman and a liberal supply of film, and Metro-Goldwyn-Mayer evinced interest in making a documentary out of the raw product. But most of the money came from Eddy's savings.

About the time he was thoroughly committed, he learned of Pathé-Bray. He had a time jump on them, however, and decided to go ahead with an unpaid crew of, as he called them, "pink-wristed" collegians. He had fought beside such men in trenches and admired their coolness and daring in tough situations. So he advertised in university newspapers and on fraternity bulletin boards: "Volunteers are wanted for important geological-geographical expedition scheduled to leave New York City about June 10 to be gone about six or eight weeks." Nothing about movies. Nothing about destination. An instinctively secretive man, Clyde Eddy did not want any hint of his purpose to reach Pathé-Bray and jar them into speeding up their own film making.

As a guide he hired, by mail, Parley Galloway, Nathaniel's forty-year-old son. Parley had not seen the river below the junction of the Green and Colorado, but had thoroughly absorbed his father's teachings, and he turned out to be the glue that held the group together. As a final touch, Eddy purchased a black bear cub from the New York zoo and had it shipped to Green River, Utah, to serve as trip mascot. Later he added Rags, "mostly Airedale," from the Salt Lake City pound. Let Pathé-Bray top that for human interest.

More than a hundred college students answered his ad. He corresponded with forty and eventually picked three from Harvard, two from Coe, two from Notre Dame, one from Northwestern, and a ninth, Gordon Adger, a non-collegian recommended by the American Museum of Natural History. They assembled in Green River, along with Frank Blackwell, the International Newsreel cameraman, on June 22.[1] They dawdled around for five days, loading the boats and waiting for the river, swollen with late-melting snow from the Rockies, to drop. During the delay a hobo slid out of a passing boxcar and wandered over, thumbs hooked in the bib straps of his overalls. He clearly knew boats. McGregory, he said his name was and indicated a willingness to go along. The idea of an experienced man among his tyros disarmed Eddy, and he hired McGregory on the spot. The cameraman, Blackwell, was less enthusiastic. As the rigors of what lay ahead dawned on him, he wired his employer, asking to be withdrawn. No answer arrived and when the party shoved off, he went along sitting morosely on one of the decks.

Cataract Canyon was wild, and frequent rains kept adding to its thunder.

. . . decided to go ahead with an unpaid crew of, as he called them, "pink-wristed" collegians.

1. In Eddy's book, *Down the World's Most Dangerous River*, the cameraman is named Bradley. In Eddy's own diary and those of other crewmen he is Blackwell. I cannot explain this.

67

The first big rapid snatched one of the laden boats from the grasp of the men who were trying to line it down close to the shore, swept it into a hole, and turned it over like a chip. They managed to retrieve it, but after that Eddy insisted that every pound of cargo be portaged to the bottom of each bad rapid so that the boats could be let down empty.

Dragging the loads out of the compartments and then stumbling and grunting through the rain-soaked brush and over the slippery rocks was an ordeal. The pink-wristed collegians, who had purchased their own gear and had paid their own fares to Green River and who were receiving only rations for their work, objected to the excessive caution. Though they respected Galloway, they soon realized that Eddy knew no more about river running than they and was drawing his sonorous instructions from his reading. "Never before," wrote Robert Bartl in his diary, "have I been on such a slipshod camping trip *[sic!]*. . . . I don't understand how one man could assume such responsibility with so little knowledge of what he was doing."

Eddy sensed the scorn and brooded about it. The men did not understand the weight of the decisions that rested on him. He dared not risk either lives or boats, for how could they survive without the latter? He fretted constantly about welding "this wild loose aggregation into a functioning human machine." But he kept on acting like a martinet. Each morning he woke the young men with a piercing blast on a metal whistle, and he tried to set examples: "I decided that, in view of the circumstances, I could do nothing better for the morale of the expedition than to shave."

The bear cub, who had been named Cataract, and the dog, Rags, furnished better distraction. They played together every day, rolling and growling. The cub's ambitions were bigger than its body. It worked valiantly to win the mock battles; Rags stood just so much and then showed who was boss by bowling the cub over and walking disdainfully away. Cataract played with the men, too, hiding behind a bush like a cat and then leaping out to grapple an ankle between its paws. As mealtime neared it was leashed to keep it away from the food, but occasionally it broke loose, a flying little ball of hyperactive fur, upsetting pots and pans and dragging away whatever had caught its attention. After being fed, it lay down and sucked on a paw, crooning softly. It took the same stance in the bottom of a boat's cockpit until water boiled in; then it climbed to a drier seat on one of the decks, clinging tenaciously with its long claws. Rags, traveling in a different boat, reversed procedures, standing on the deck until a rapid neared and then jumping into the cockpit.

They reached Lees Ferry at noon on July 9. There the cameraman received word from his home office that he could leave. Two of the collegians quit with him. Eddy was distraught. The climax of the trip lay ahead and he had neither camera nor photographer for recording it! He had picked up a notion, moreover, that the Pathé-Bray expedition planned to be on the river by August. Feeling his rival's breath on his neck, he rented a battered old truck and, boiling and bouncing in the heat, chugged off to Kanab to buy supplies and telegraph for a replacement to meet him at the Grand Canyon's South Rim.

On returning, he learned that two of the college students, Bob Bartl and Ed Holt, had walked away from their job of repairing the boats and had hitched a ride to Kanab to cool off. Somehow he had missed them along the way. In a passion he turned the truck around and started back.

He found them hiking under the punishing sun with a thirty-nine-year-old native of Dubuque, Iowa, Oscar Jaeger. On returning from Kanab they had caught a ride with a rancher and, falling asleep in the car, had waked up at the VT Ranch on top of the Kaibab Plateau, far out of their way. Jaeger had appeared at about the same time, a drifter wandering through the Southwest, looking at the sights through the lens of a small, hand-held motion picture camera. Bartl and Holt promptly signed him on. No pay, of course, unless Eddy loosened up, which he didn't.

The camera wasn't much compared to the model Blackwell had been using, but it calmed Eddy. Nine days of rest had revived the crew and they were exuberant when they headed into Marble Canyon on a sweeping forty thousand cubic feet per second of thick water — all, that is, except McGregory. Suddenly he dropped his oar, yelling, "I quit! I quit!" and demanded to be put ashore. Not even pausing to collect his duffel, he clambered away over the low cliffs. At that Oscar Jaeger, who had been sitting on one of the decks, became an instant oarsman.

They bobbed through a riffle or two and came to a roaring rapid Eddy and Galloway decided was Soap Creek. (Actually it was Badger.) Remembering that his predecessors had portaged around Soap, Eddy ordered a similar procedure. After they had taken off again, a thunderstorm blasted rain and sand into their faces. Up in the lead boat Galloway heard the booming of another rapid, saw no place to land, and signaled frantically for standard rough-water procedure — life jackets on, boots off and tied to the cleats in the cockpits.

This was the real Soap, though fortunately for his nerves Eddy didn't know it. They shot down the "V" stern first — the Galloway technique. A wave slapped Jaeger off his seat. "Sky and earth and water were arrayed against us," Eddy wrote months later, "and I found joy in the unequal conflict. I swore each time I threw my body to one side or the other of the boat and the river became a living thing, a monster clutching with dripping fingers to snatch away our lives. . . . There I was, cursing the dragon in his lair, defying him to do his worst." Later on, far downstream at Separation Rapid, he would again heave and curse and, for good measure, snap his teeth. Here were the basics. For this he had risked not just his young men but also Kathleen's and Richard's happiness — for "an exhilarating voyage into a storyland where dreams are real and the constant pressure of danger gives richness to life."

And drama to books.

They risked running Hance, Sockdolager, and Grapevine. In each the neophytes lost control and the boats spun wildly. In Sockdolager the bear was washed overboard but clung to the gunwales. Jaeger paused in his frenzied bailing long enough to drag the animal back and was bitten in the leg for his pains. But the only ones who capsized were Eddy and Galloway, at the bottom of Sockdolager when they thought they were home free.

On reaching the foot of Bright Angel Trail, Eddy left two men to watch the boats and walked with the rest to the rim. The only thing there was a letter from his father asking when he was going to grow up.

High water had put them ahead of schedule so they waited two more days for mail, stuffing themselves meanwhile with peach pie and talking to Emery Kolb about what lay ahead. Some supplies and film arrived, along with a wire from International News saying they could not spare either a cameraman or

Jaeger paused in his frenzied bailing long enough to drag the animal back and was bitten in the leg for his pains.

69

camera. His last hope of obtaining professional quality pictures gone, he mailed the wire to his wife and told her to find a lawyer. "We'll sue!"

On they went, portaging around the rough rapids in heat that drained the color from the walls and left the rocks too hot to touch. After lunch he could hardly push the men out of their patches of shade to continue. If they could find just one cold drink! But except for occasional side streams the only water they had came from the warm, heavily silted river. They sliced cactus or put a little evaporated milk into buckets of the stuff and let it settle overnight — but then discovered that the milk now and then soured in their hot canteens.

After a stop to repair oarlocks, they went on, forgetting Rags, who was asleep in the shade of a small overhang. Waking, the dog pursued them with frantic yelps until a promontory stopped him. The boats put in as soon as they could and Eddy, Adger, and Bartl went back, climbing one hundred fifty feet to a narrow ledge, worming along it, and then descending to the trapped animal. Boosting him up, one man to another, was precarious, but after the rescue was finished they all felt better — for awhile.

In Waltenberg Rapid they knocked a hole in the *Powell* and had to repair it in the heat. Eighteen miles farther on, at Dubendorff Rapid, they lined the *Dellenbaugh*, the sixteen-footer, down to a jutting thrust of boulders and lifted it safely over. Unable to heave the big *Powell* up in its turn, they tried to line it around. The stern swung too far out, the current seized it, and jammed the boat against an outer boulder. Even with a block and tackle they could not budge it.

They spent the next day huddled in what shade they could find, hoping the river would drop a little and relieve some of the pressure. No luck. On the third day Adger swung out along the bow line with an ax and chopped a way into the forward and middle compartments but couldn't reach the back one. Together Carey and he unloaded the supplies, but the reduced weight was no solution. The river turned redder and rose, perhaps from a flood down the Little Colorado. Giving up on the fourth day, the eleven men, the bear, and the dog crowded with part of the salvaged material into the two remaining boats — one of them the little *Dellenbaugh* — and went on.

Lava Falls, Separation, Lava Cliff — a litany of exhaustion and fear. Even Galloway admitted that because of the constant strain he grew scared each time he heard a new roar ahead. But they made it, though food ran uncomfortably short. They swept out of the Grand Canyon, ran Boulder and Black canyons in heat they thought would fry their brains, and on the night of August 6 were cooled off more than they liked by a shrieking mix of blowing sand and rain. The next morning Cataract was so bedraggled that he allowed Eddy to hold him, an unusual condescension, while he licked at some crackers and canned milk. "I realized I had grown fond of him," the adventurer wrote later.

Fond enough to take Cataract back to the New York zoo? Well, no. In Needles Eddy sold the bear for $40. The party disintegrated quickly, no great fondness among them though Bartl did take Rags home to Wisconsin with him.

Back in New York, Eddy contemplated the fruits of his toil. Blackwell had taken some fair pictures in Cataract Canyon, but Jaeger had produced little. For one thing he had been too stingy with film, taking only short flashes of events and not changing as long as any film at all remained in the camera. What he produced came out jerky and bobtailed, or not at all if he happened to be caught short just as the action had been growing good.

As Eddy was moping around, trying to stir himself to write some articles, a call came from Pathé-Bray on November 14. Their expedition was lost in Glen Canyon. Would he come west and join the search?

Would he!

On November 24 he started north from Flagstaff with a truckload of the movie company's equipment. His arrival at Gable's Camp, a radio broadcasting station that Gilbert Gable, vice-president of the Bray Company, had set up on the desert thirty miles south of Lees Ferry, was an excuse for a special bulletin to the *New York Times*. By then Eddy realized he was being used as part of a publicity stunt, but never mind, he had made an impact, *he* was the one who had been summoned.

The next day he drove down the steep dugway to Lees Ferry (the new Navajo Bridge across Marble Canyon six miles downstream from the ferry was not yet open) and sat around until 1:00 P.M. on November 30, when the six boats of the lost expedition arrived in a smart line. He found out then what had happened.

The movie party left Green River, Utah, on November 10, two months later than LaRue had recommended. Frank Dodge was head boatmen of a crew that contained, among others, two Russian lifeguards from Southern California; both were excellent swimmers and had had some experience with surf boats though none on rivers. No actors yet. They would meet the group at the Grand Canyon. This part of the trip was for documentary and background shots, to be filmed by a pair of topflight cameramen, Glen Kerschner and Pat Gannon, working under Leigh Smith, a well-known director. A publicist was along, of course, Devergne Barber, a six-foot-four-inch reporter for the *New York Times* and staff writer for *Liberty* magazine. Barber's technical right hand was army sergeant Vernon T. Herrick, operator of the flotilla's battery-powered radio. The idea was for Barber to write daily reports on the expedition's progress that Herrick would send to Gable's Camp. From there the material would be relayed to a station in Salt Lake City and become part of the nation's news.

Finally there was a cook, and at the last minute a dog named Pansy. By then the group knew the details of Eddy's runs, and Pansy's presence may have been inspired by Rags, though no one said so. Anyway, Rags and Pansy were the pioneer river running dogs of the Colorado River canyons.

The six boats LaRue had ordered built in California were painted white for visibility. Smaller than Eddy's, each was handled by a single oarsman. The seven passengers and Pansy had to perch on the decks. LaRue and Leigh Smith rode with Dodge. The cook and camerman Pat Gannon rode with Owen Clark, formerly a boat operator at Lees Ferry. Pansy had a deck to herself. As events developed, the passengers walked almost as much as they rode. In quiet stretches the boats kept hanging up on sandbars. In Cataract, the rocks were exposed like the bristles of a steel currycomb, necessitating frequent portages. Leigh Smith was constantly calling for stops so that the photographers could climb precariously up the walls for spectacular shots — or else the picture takers sat still waiting for the right light. "All of us," Barber growled in his diary, "are beginning to wonder why cameramen are allowed to live."

Cataract Canyon ran north and south, its walls half a mile high. Days were short and so there was little sunlight. Air and water were frigid, torturing the boatmen, who, with occasional boosts from the passengers, were continually soaked from lining the craft. By the time they were in the middle of the gorge, they were ten days behind schedule. Though at one point Herrick climbed a talus slope to a tree and hung an antenna sixty feet above ground, he could not contact anyone with the radio. Now and then, however, they were able to receive messages from Gable's, one of which ordered, "Keep boats clean so they will photograph against dark water."

They lined the last of Cataract's rapids on a cloudy Thanksgiving Day, warming themselves now and then over fires kept burning on the bank. LaRue rewarded them with a surprise. He built a table out of driftwood, and had the cook prepare, from a hidden store of food, a feast of baked ham, canned corn and peas, fruit, and lemon pie. They gave thanks for having successfully passed through forty-six bad rapids and fell with vim to their last good meal, for food was running low. Soon they had only red beans and mush.

On November 26 (by then Eddy was at Lees Ferry), Herrick picked up another message. "Your continued silence causing alarm. Show immediately red flare if in danger, white flare if okay. Help on the way."

Sour laughter. They had no flares. And just how was help coming? By boats struggling slowly down the river after them? By a pack train from the rim that didn't even know where they were? They labored on across Glen Canyon's clutching sandbars, their clothing frozen and their empty stomachs growling. On the twenty-eighth they encountered an Indian camp and bought a haunch of venison. Meanwhile J.R. Bray had persuaded the Army to send out a search plane from California. It landed on an improvised strip near Gable's and was nearly blown upside down by the wind while waiting for a fresh supply of fuel to arrive from Flagstaff. Functional at last, it took off and passed over Lees Ferry just as the expedition's boats were landing there.

Everyone signaled frantically but the pilot (he had a navigator and radio operator with him) decided that the people down below, excited at seeing a rare airplane, were just waving and that the boats were part of the ferry station's equipment. On they flew, low, buffeted by headwinds at Navajo Mountain, to the junction of the Green and Colorado, more than two hundred miles from Lees Ferry. No boats. Then back to Gable's, where they blew a tire as they landed. Gilbert Gable turned the fruitless errand into an epic. Never before, he exclaimed over the air, had a plane flown up the river at so low an altitude — "one of the most perilous flights in aviation history." (By then Lindberg's crossing of the Atlantic was three years old.) And Leigh Smith, who was on the point of dropping out rather than run the Grand Canyon, announced, "When we see the film on the screen it will repay us all."

If they saw it. The pay checks Bray sent to the boatmen had not been countersigned by a second official and were worthless. The boatmen vowed to walk out then and there. Eddy jumped to the rescue. He had been appointed director of photography in Smith's place, and he wanted something to direct. He smooth talked the men into continuing to Phantom Ranch and then sitting tight until paid. That would put real pressure on the company, for the big scenes were to be filmed at Hermit Rapids, seven miles below Phantom. The principals

They labored on across Glen Canyon's clutching sandbars, their clothing frozen and their empty stomachs growling.

72

would have gathered by the time the flotilla arrived, and there would be no time to bring in strikebreakers. In short, they'd win there but might not here.

On they went. During the bone-numbing lining of both Badger and Soap, Eddy discovered that he had been mixed up about their identities during his earlier trip and that his party, after portaging around Badger, had actually run notorious Soap Creek Rapid. He exulted. The first time! Someone corrected him. Ellsworth Kolb had gone through in 1911. Ah, but Ellsworth had upset. Eddy could still claim the first successful trip.

Lugging the heavy radio and its batteries around the rapids was an ordeal, but it was also a relief to be able to hunker around it on long evenings and listen to distant stations. One night the principals of the coming romance went to Gable's to boost the canyon party's morale by praising their efforts over the air. The male lead was John Boles, a six-foot Texan, star of stage and screen. Opposite him was Rose Blossom, a five-foot, ninety-seven-pound blonde, who so far had had only one small part in a Pathé offering. The encouragement they offered the boaters remained unheard. Static was bad that night.

The cold intensified. Spray in the rapids froze on the passengers' clothing. The boatmen, except for Dodge, who seemed impervious, could not finish a lining without pausing at the fires the cook kept burning for them on the banks. At night they crawled into their sleeping bags fully clothed and were still too cold to sleep. At the Little Colorado a vicious sandstorm made fire lighting impossible and drove them to bed supperless.

There were accidents. At Sheer Wall the cook was washed overboard but retrieved. (Barber, reporting over the radio by Gable's, waxed facetious: "John is a good cook and we would hate to lose him.") The radio boat turned over at mile 21.5, but watertight compartments saved the apparatus. At Cave Springs just below the point where Richards and Hansbrough of the Stanton expedition had drowned, boatman Dean Daily hit a rock and was thrown into the icy water, but swam after the craft, caught it and climbed in. At Hance they heaved the boats onto their shoulders and walked them around on the icy boulders. During one passage Nick Samoff slipped and crushed his foot. Eddy got the Russian's boot off and treated the injury. Samoff lay as still as death; he had fainted.

They got through Sockdolager at about 1:00 P.M. on December 13, a drizzly, cheerless day. After warming up beside a fire, they started on through Upper Granite Gorge, eager to reach Bright Angel Creek, nine miles away, before dark. Grapevine gave them a shaking but they made it without mishap and were shouting triumphantly back and forth when Daily, his vision obscured by the gathering twilight, again ran head-on into a boulder. His passenger, Devergne Barber, careened overboard. He came up under the boat and was held there by his life jacket, his head banging against the rock. Sensing his plight, Herrick whipped off his boots, jumped in, and with Daily's help got him back into the boat, half dead.

There was no place to land right there and so, perforce, Barber mumbled he was willing to go on. In gathering darkness they ran Mile 83 by depending on luck and their ears, but Dodge wasn't willing to take a similar chance at Zoroaster, a murderous rapid in low water. While the passengers, Pansy and Barber included, groped among the boulders in the dark, Dodge led the white boats through the heavy water, each oarsman guided by the faint glimmer of the one ahead. At the foot of the rapid, the passengers returned to the cold, wet decks. A narrow canyon enclosed by sheer walls of dark granite, an inky sky — spooky. To keep contact, they yelled, lit matches, played their flashlight beams across the water. When they landed close to the mouth of Bright Angel Creek, Barber's clothes were frozen solid. He had to be helped out of the boat and up the trail to Phantom Ranch.

While the rest were warming themselves with coffee and steaks, Eddy telephoned Bray at the South Rim to report their arrival and ask that the boatmen's wages be sent down — God knew the money had been earned. But again the checks arrived without countersignatures. No way would they go to Hermit Rapid, the outraged boatmen declared. Eddy telephoned the ultimatum to Bray and the next morning hiked up the trail, in snow the last thousand feet, to collect. The following noon he was back on horseback with $3,000, only to turn right around and leave for home. It is not possible to be sure why. With Leigh Smith ready to resume work at Hermit Creek, he may have been dismissed as superfluous. He may have sensed what some reminiscences hint at: his officiousness grated on the men's nerves in spite of his help, and he may have gone off in a pout. In his mimeographed autobiography, Dodge suggested Pathé-Bray was keeping him tied up long enough so that he couldn't write about his own earlier trip in time to take the edge off their publicity. But the easiest explanation is perhaps the most likely: he had been away from his family and his job at Squibb & Sons so long that year that their patience was wearing thin.

Barber, Samoff, and Pansy also dropped out at Bright Angel — plus enough others so that only three boats continued downstream to Hermit Creek. At various times during the next week as many as a hundred spectators clustered at trail's end to watch the antics. Possibly Rose Blossom and John Boles, who had been doing routine scenes on the rim with the canyon as a backdrop, were curious enough to join the onlookers for a time, but there is no mention of them in any reminiscence. The boatmen, performing now as stuntmen, took their places during the action shots.

Day after cold day, says Frank Dodge (a free and cheery soul who is not be read too literally) they ran through Hermit Rapid, dragged the boats back, and repeated. One assignment was to pull manikins off the wing of a supposedly wrecked airplane, props that had been packed down the trail on mules. They sawed a boat almost in two so that it would break apart against a rock dramatically smothered in surging foam. They had to ram it into the barrier again and again before the wounded craft obliged. The climax was the rescue. Dodge, short and square, put on the lanky Boles's outdoor clothes. Owen Clark donned a skirt, long stockings, and a golden wig. The boat swooped "her" away from whatever danger threatened on shore and she lay down on the after deck, her curves, says the narrator, all in the wrong places.

Dodge, who was at the oars, meant to skim past a raging hole but miscalculated and plunged into it. The boat flipped. Somehow they got it and themselves out of the vortex, righted the craft, climbed in and reached a quiet eddy. Clark was bleeding profusely from a cut in his cheek, his stockings were loose, the wig askew and stained with blood. But Dodge decided that at the distance they were from the cameras, the scheduled love scene would still look convincing.

He grappled with Clark. "It's the money I love," he declared passionately, "not your ugly mug."

Clark struggled. "You can't even steer a boat, you clumsy —"
They thrashed about. The boat tipped and in they went again.
Cut.

Ever publicity conscious, the Pathé-Bray people hauled one of the boats up the Hermit Trail and shipped it to Los Angeles for use in a parade celebrating the return of the explorers. All the party (except Eddy) were guests at a sumptuous banquet. They filmed some camp scenes in a studio and were the main attractions at the opening of a new theater in Long Beach. But the "Bride/Pride of the Colorado" was never released. Twenty-two years later one official told interviewer Dock Marston that the lead actress was incredibly bad and that he finally persuaded Pathé-Bray to halt the filming. Another explanation is that the two companies fell into a legal squabble over rights that checked the release. Perhaps the best way to end the story is to forget the failures and the quarrels and remember the experience as the photographer Glen Kerschner always recalled it, "I have made pictures in the far corners of the world, but the Colorado is the most spectacular, most beautiful, most stupendous subject any man ever photographed."

Not a word about actors. Evidently, in his opinion, they did not — perhaps could not — measure up to the setting.

In 1934 Clyde Eddy returned to the river, this time in response to an invitation from a river-running Utah doctor. Eighteen years before, admirers of John Wesley Powell had commemorated his epic journey of 1869 by placing a granite-and-bronze marker on a South Rim promontory between Maricopa and Hopi points. The names of Oramel and Seneca Howland and William Dunn, who had left the party at Separation Canyon and later had been killed by Indians, were omitted from the marker because, it was argued, they had deserted the Major. Robert Brewster Stanton held a different opinion: Powell's ineptitude and ill treatment had driven the trio away. The manuscript in which Stanton's findings were embedded was so bulky, however, that no publisher would issue it. After his death this was remedied by Julius Stone, who had traversed the canyons in 1909 with Nathaniel Galloway and Seymour Dubendorff. He hired an editor, James Chalfant, to polish those parts of Stanton's material dealing with both James White and Powell. In 1932 he financed the publication of the results as *Colorado River Controversies*.

A group of Utah river runners, inspired by Russell G. Frazier, a heavyset medical doctor of the copper mining town of Bingham Canyon, used the data in *Controversies* as an excuse for a traverse of the Grand Canyon. At Separation they would bolt to the walls a bronze plaque bearing the names of the Howlands and Bill Dunn. Dr. Frazier invited Eddy to join the group both for the sake of his experience and for the attention his name would bring to this act of historical justice. Eddy, seeing a movie and another illustrated book in the trip, jumped at the chance.

The sinew for the party was provided by the brothers Bus and Alton Hatch, Frank Swain, and Royce Mowrey, all related and all of Vernal, Utah, home of the legendary Nathaniel Galloway and his son Parley. The quartet had caught river fever after Swain, a part-time deputy sheriff, had jailed Parley Galloway for the non-support of his divorced wife and children. Thereafter the quartet spent almost as much time behind the bars as Parley, talking about the river.

Following Parley's directions, Bus Hatch built an open skiff that he could run through rapids either bow or stern first — a skiff he wrecked during a trip through Lodore Canyon on the Green River with his brother, Frank Swain, and Royce Mowrey. In spite of that they kept on trying and achieved enough local fame to attract Russell Frazier who made some trips with them. When Frazier put the 1934 expedition together, Swain was chosen as head boatman. Eddy's cameraman, Fred Jayne, and another guest, Bill Fahrni, brought the total to eight.

They launched their four Hatch-built boats at Lees Ferry on July 19. Those were the drought years that created the dust bowl farther east, and the Colorado was flowing a meager sixteen hundred cfs, almost the lowest on record. Rock gardens blossomed in every rapid. Running them was an invitation to an upset, but lining was such an ordeal that they tackled every one they dared — and more. Fahrni broke his hand in Soap Creek but continued. They flipped again and again. Eventually Swain's boat was so battered it had to be abandoned. Even before then the cameraman had quit and walked out the Bright Angel Trail, leaving the picture taking to Eddy.

The trip was historic, nevertheless. While poking around the cave where Stanton had cached his gear after Brown, Richards, and Hansbrough had died, Bus Hatch found what he took to be "toy horses or sheep" skillfully fashioned out of split willow twigs. Radiocarbon studies have dated them at three to four thousand years before the present, the oldest known traces of humans in the Grand Canyon.[2]

Bus Hatch found what he took to be "toy horses or sheep" skillfully fashioned out of split willow twigs.

With great effort the travelers bolted their plaque to the granite at Separation. They miscalculated elevations, however, and a few years later water backed up by Hoover Dam inundated the memento. In 1939, Frazier made another run, this one by motorboat up Lake Mead, to set another. Julius Stone, then aged eighty-five, went along. But they erred, too. The enormous amounts of silt the river deposited in the upper stretches of Lake Mead raised the level of the old streambed, and in 1943 the plaque had to be moved to yet another location.

A baffling river. In 1934 Eddy again failed to get the pictures he wanted and knew he would never produce a movie or write a second book. Toward the end of the trip, while sitting on a rock watching the moon and writing by flashlight, he scribbled moodily, "The Colorado defeats everybody." It wasn't even a consolation to reflect that except for Than Galloway no one else had yet logged as many miles on the stream, under as extreme conditions of heat and cold, high water and low, as he had.

2. Civilian Conservation Corps workers found three split-twig figurines in a canyon cave in 1933, but Hatch gave his to Clark Wissler of the American Museum of Natural History and they were the ones that caught attention. Since then about three hundred similar figurines have been found at scattered sites in Arizona, Nevada, Utah, and California.

1. *Despite losing an arm during the Civil War, John Wesley Powell led the first boat trips through the canyons of the Colorado River.*

2. *Green River Station, Union Pacific Railway, Wyoming, 1871, starting point of the two Powell expeditions.*

4. *Frederick Dellenbaugh as he looked during Powell's second expedition, 1871–72.*

3. *John Sumner the year before Powell's first expedition through Grand Canyon.*

5. *Billy Hawkins, a Colorado mountain man who accompanied Powell's first expedition. He and Hall were the only ones to continue to the river's mouth.*

6. *Young Andrew Hall was hired just before the first Powell expedition left Green River, Wyoming, May 24, 1869.*

7. *Powell's second expedition poses before leaving Green River, Wyoming, in May 1870.*

8. *Powell's* Emma Dean, *second boat of that name. He added the chair, which made the boat top heavy, in order to have a better view of the river and the other boats.*

9. *Hot-tempered Harry McDonald, shown here in a cork life vest, was a skilled frontiersman of unknown antecedents. He was more interested in prospecting than surveying.*

10. *Sturdy John Hislop rendered yeoman service on both of Stanton's hard-luck expeditions.*

11. *Frank Mason Brown's dream of constructing a railroad through the canyon cost him his life.*

12. *Elmer Kane, photographed by Nims on December 25, 1889 before the Stanton survey party left Lees Ferry.*

13. *George Washington Gibson, Stanton's servant, accompanied the first survey attempt as cook.*

14. *William Richmond and Nathaniel Galloway after their 1897 trip. Galloway popularized the stern-first technique of running rapids and was the first man to make two traverses of the Grand Canyon.*

15. *Galloway (standing) and Julius Stone. Stone was the first person to run the river solely for pleasure.*

16. *Arthur Sanger, scared stiff most of the way, made the fifth traverse of Grand Canyon in 1906 with the mysterious Hum Woolley.*

17. Raymond Cogswell, Julius Stone's brother-in-law, took two thousand scenic photos of the canyons of the Colorado during the fall of 1909.

18. Dubendorff Rapid, mile 131.6, was named in 1923 for Seymour Dubendorff, who upset there in 1909 during the Stone party's memorable trip.

19. Julius Stone's tribute to "Dubie" after the latter's death in 1910 at the age of twenty-eight from the bite of a Rocky Mountain tick.

My Companionship with Mr S. S. Dubendorff brought me a new realization of what a man could do and be under many extremely difficult as well as dangerous conditions, and in his death there has gone out of my life an association that detracted nothing and added much that was rich and fine

Julius F. Stone

20. Charles Russell (left) and Edwin Monett at Needles, California, February 10, 1908, at the end of Russell's first hair-brained adventure in the canyon.

21. Ellsworth Kolb and his brother Emery made the first motion pictures of the Colorado canyons during a reckless, trouble-filled trip in 1911.

23. *Bert Loper as he looked after his first run through the Grand Canyon in 1939, just short of his seventieth birthday. When he tried to repeat the trip ten years later, he died in Marble Canyon.*

22. *Goddard Quist, who floated with Russell and August Tadje through Glen Canyon to the Bright Angel Trail where he quit in disgust, during the winter of 1914–15.*

24. *August Tadje, would-be photographer, standing in the boat* Titanic II *while filming the exploits of his companions.*

25. *Charles Russell in the* Ross Wheeler, *built by Bert Loper, who named it for a murdered friend.*

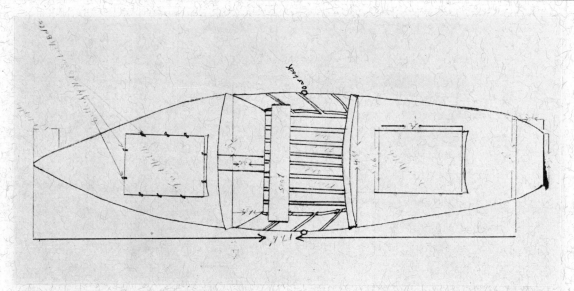

26. *The Kolb brothers and the USGS surveyors on the Green and Colorado rivers, 1921–23, built their boats according to blueprints provided by Julius Stone.*

27. *Eugene Blake, boatman for USGS party of 1923, works on a Galloway-Stone type boat, the* Glen, *Lees Ferry.*

28. *Hydrologist Eugene C. LaRue, proponent of a high dam above Lees Ferry.*

29. *Born in Hawaii, an expert swimmer and horseman, Frank Dodge became "the best oarsman who ever shot a rapid" on the Colorado.*

30. *Edith Kolb, the first woman known to have run a major rapid in Grand Canyon.*

31. *Lewis Freeman bailing his boat at the foot of Waltenberg Rapid, September 5, 1923.*

32. *Claude Birdseye, left, led the USGS 1923 survey for dam sites in the Grand Canyon. His cousin, Roger Birdseye, packed supplies down various trails to the party.*

34. Raymond C. Moore before the start of the 1923 survey.

33. Frank Dodge in the canvas boat Mojave *as the USGS 1923 party left Lees Ferry.*

35. Felix Kominsky, cook for the Birdseye party on the 1923 survey trip.

36. Leigh Lint loaded for portage in Cataract Canyon.

Seager   Adger   Weatherhead & Bear   Bartl   Eddy   Holt   Rags   Carey   Galloway   Callaway

37. The Eddy Party of 1927. Eddy is in the center, looking glum as usual. Note bear cub in Weatherhead's arms and Rags in front row.

38. The boat Dellenbaugh *is muscled ashore for repairs after flipping at the boot of Sockdolager with Eddy and guide Parley Galloway. Eddy is at right bow.*

39. *Though Parley Galloway, Nathaniel's son, had never seen the Grand Canyon before 1927, he got Clyde Eddy's green-horns through.*

40. *Oscar Jaeger photographing the* Powell *on the rocks at Dubendorff Rapid, July, 1927.*

41. Bill Adger of the 1927 Eddy party comes ashore after salvaging cargo from the Powell, *trapped against a rock in Dubendorff Rapid.*

43. *Despite many hardships, Hollywood cameraman Glen Kershner, declared the Colorado canyons to be the "most stupendous subject any man ever photographed."*

42. *Leigh Smith, director of "The Bride (or Pride?) of the Colorado," had enough river running on reaching Lees Ferry and went overland to Hermit Rapid, scene of the picture's muddled climax.*

44. *Pansy, mascot of the Pathé-Bray film makers. Raggs, mascot of the Eddy party, preceded her by a few months as the first dog to run the Colordao River canyons.*

45. *Devergne "Bob" Barber of the* New York Times *nearly perished of exposure in Upper Granite Gorge during the Pathé-Bray moviemaking expedition of 1927.*

46. *Owen Clark, another of the roughneck boatmen of the 1920s, doubled for the heroine of "The Bride of the Colorado" during rescue scenes in icy Hermit Rapid. The film was never released.*

47. *Bus Hatch accompanied Clyde Eddy on his return trip through the canyon in 1934.*

48. *Glen and Bessie Hyde disappeared in lower Granite Gorge in the Fall of 1928 and were never seen again.*

49. *Buzz Holmstrom (he was working at Pierce Ferry) chats with Emery Kolb and Norm Nevills at the end of the first Nevills expedition in 1938.*

50. *Norman Nevills of Mexican Hat, Utah, pioneered commercial river trips on the Colorado.*

51. *Amos Burg, Buzz Holmstrom, and Willis Johnson in 1938 at Lake Mead. Burg's boat* Charlie *was the first inflatable boat to travel through Grand Canyon.*

52. *Boatmen who chose not to run rapids had to "line" around them, a laborious chore. Here Norman Nevills and crewman Joe Desloge work past a boulder at the edge of Lava Falls.*

53. The first women to traverse the Colorado River through Grand Canyon were Dr. Elzada Clover (left) and Lois Jotter, with the first Nevills expedition in 1938.

54. Don Harris, who went through Cataract Canyon with Clover and Jotter in 1938, later accompanied Bert Loper on his final run.

55. *Barry Goldwater, who went through Cataract and Grand canyons with Nevills in 1940, stands beside the plaque that commemorates Norm's and Doris' deaths in a plane accident on September 19, 1949.*

56. *Alexander "Zee" Grant took the first kayak through the Grand Canyon in 1941 while accompanying a Nevills trip.*

57. *Mildred Baker and Doris Nevills in 1940 became the first women to traverse all the canyons from Green River, Wyoming, to Hoover Dam. Paying guests helped with camp chores.*

58. *Margaret and Otis "Dock" Marston began traveling with Nevills in 1942. Later, after serving as a paid boatman, Marston became an indefatigable collector of Colorado River history and pictures.*

59. *Aleson and Georgie White show off the six-foot inflatable raft they rode, sometimes, downriver from Parashant Wash, mile 198.5, in 1946. The previous year they had tried swimming the stream.*

60. *Harry Aleson with motor of a boat he wrecked at Granite Spring Rapids, mile 220.4, in 1944 during one of his attempts to power up the canyon.*

61. Aleson with Moore and Swenson, part of the crew of the UP LAKE which attempted to go up the Grand Canyon from Diamond Creek in February 1944.

62. Ed Hudson and the Esmeralda II, Tapeats Creek, 1949. The Esmeralda II was the first motoboat to go down the canyon. Wrecked the next year, its salvage created bitter arguments.

63. The Hudson-Marston expedition before shoving off from Lees Ferry. Left to right: Joe Desloge, Guy Forcier, Dock Marston, Jordan Rust, Ed Hudson, Jr., Ed Hudson, Willie Taylor and Bill Belknap. June 12, 1950.

64. Esmeralda II *arrives at Lake Mead. Ed Hudson and Dock Marston drove her from Lees Ferry to Lake Mead in four and one-half days, June 1949. Left to right: Dock Marston, Ed Hudson, Willie Taylor, Ed Hudson, Jr., and Bestor Robinson.*

65. *Rod Sanderson of Page, Arizona, and Jim Jordan drove the first outboard motors through the Grand Canyon in June 1951.*

66. *Dock Marston powers up Unkar Rapid in June, 1950. Passengers are Taylor, Desloge and Forcier.*

68. *John Daggett (left) and Bill Beer float-ed through Grand Canyon without boats, using neoprene packs as water wings, May, 1955.*

67. *Initiation rites in lower Grand Canyon. Jim Rigg delivers the splash, Tad Nichols the swat. Frank Wright supervises at left.*

69. *After taking over Nevills' company with Frank Wright, Jim Rigg (right) added inboard motors to the fleet, tried to salvage the* Esmeralda II, *and in 1951, with his brother Bob (left) rowed a wooden cataract boat through the canyon in two and one-half days.*

70. *Georgie White and her husband J.R. in August, 1955.*

71. *Hitching three big rafts together into a G-rig (named for Georgie White) was "The Woman of the River's" contribution to mass transit in the canyon. Photograph was taken June 3, 1958, at Lees Ferry.*

72. *P.T. Reilly in 1949 as a Nevills boat-man. In 1964, after notable runs on high water, he joined Martin Litton in putting wooden dories on the river and battling high dams in the canyon.*

73. *New Zealander Jon Hamilton drives jet boat up Lava Falls Rapid, July 1960, during the only successful up-river run of Grand Canyon.*

74. *Buzz Belknap runs Granite Park Rapid in a sportyak, August 1963.*

75. *River historian Dock Marston runs Mile 217 Rapid in a seven-foot plastic sportyak, smallest boat to traverse Grand Canyon. August 1963.*

Seven

FOR THE SAKE OF FAME

B essie Hyde, the first woman to run all of Cataract Canyon and most of the Grand Canyon, was born Bessie Haley in Washington, DC, on December 29, 1905. Later the family moved to Parkersburg, West Virginia. There Bessie, aged nineteen, five feet tall and ninety pounds in weight, graduated second in her high school class of seventy-eight. Toward the end of her sophomore year at Marshall College in nearby Huntington, West Virginia, she secretly married Earl Hemlick of Parkersburg. After finishing the school year, she abruptly left, alone, for San Francisco.

A pregnancy may have been involved. Earl later said he sent her money for an "operation" whose nature he did not identify. There is no mention of a child in surviving records, but she did include this poem among fifty she wrote in California and gathered into an unpublished collection, "Wandering Leaves":

> *This soft bundle*
> *so close to me,*
> *Is yours and mine*
> *Come, love, and see.*
> *I'm glad the stork,*
> *In hurried flight,*
> *Took time to stop*
> *In here tonight.*

The lightweight bundle isn't necessarily autobiographical, of course. Neither is "Mermaid Doll," in the same collection, but, in hindsight, its prescience is uncanny:

78

Oh! Mama, dear, please come.
My dolly must be drowned.
When I put her on the creek,
She sank without a sound.
Wee Betty's [Bessie's?] eyes filled with tears.
Where could poor dolly Be?
Perhaps she's turned into a mermaid
And drifted out to sea.

Bessie studied art in San Francisco from August 16, 1926, to February 25, 1927. During that period she became friendly with an aspiring movie actress, Greta Grandstedt, and at an unknown date went with her by overnight ship to Los Angeles. On this boat they encountered Glen Hyde, twenty-nine, son of a substantial farmer (a widower) who lived outside Twin Falls, Idaho, close to the Snake River. Though Glen was more than six feet tall, he was attracted to wee Bessie. Soon he persuaded her to move to Elko, Nevada, within driving range of Twin Falls, and apply for a divorce under Nevada's lenient laws. Her divorce from Earl Hemlick became final on April 11, 1928. The next day Glen and Bessie were married in Twin Falls.

Rivers were important to young Hyde. He had done a little floating on the Peace as a teen-ager when his family had been living in British Columbia. Later, in Idaho, he had met Captain Harry Guleke, already legendary for freighting mining machinery and supplies to men working in the howling canyons of the Salmon River and its Middle Fork, the famed River of No Return. The boat Guleke used was a scow thirty-seven feet long, eight wide, and five deep. Guidance came from two twenty-five foot sweeps protruding from bow and stern, their last ten feet consisting of wide, thin blades. With Guleke's help, Glen built a sixteen-foot scow with five-foot sweeps. In this boat he and his sister, Jeanne, spent ten days in the fall of 1926 traveling entirely across Idaho from the town of Salmon down the Salmon River to the Snake and on to Lewiston — a pretty good test for any amateur boatman, or woman.

It is likely that the Eddy and Pathé-Bray expeditions of 1927 turned Glen's attention to the Colorado. Eddy had used a bear as an attention-grabber, but Hyde thought he had a better attraction — a wife. The first husband-and-wife team on the river. The first woman to traverse the best known of all canyons, the Grand. On top of that, Bessie was fluent and artistic. She could write and illustrate a book; they could tour the country lecturing.

According to Glen's sister, Bessie was enthusiastic about the idea. Early in October, after most of the fall chores were finished on the farm, they traveled to Green River, Utah. There Glen set about building a flat-bottomed scow twenty feet long, five wide, and three deep. Bill Reeder, who had been with Charles Russell in Cataract in 1914, shook his head over it. Looked like a coffin to him. Glen shrugged off the doomsaying. Together Bessie and he loaded in, besides food, tools, and utensils, a set of bed springs, a mattress, and a small stove so that they need not leave the boat to camp unless they wished to. They did not take life jackets; they were strong swimmers, they told Emery Kolb later, and didn't need artificial aids.

They shoved off on October 20, 1928, planning to reach Needles,

Eddy had used a bear as an attention-grabber, but Hyde thought he had a better attraction — a wife.

California, where Glen's father would be waiting anxiously, on December 9. Little is known of the trip. In quiet water, Glen turned the scow sideways and used the sweeps like oars. They lined bad rapids; the thought of the two of them, one a ninety-pound woman, struggling to let the heavy craft down through mazes of water-washed boulders staggers the imagination. Once when Bessie was manipulating a sweep in tousled currents, the blade caught on a rock and knocked her overboard. Glen, reacting fast, hauled her back uninjured.

At Lees Ferry (out of business by then because the Navajo Bridge had been completed in June) the few boatmen still hanging around inspected the contraption minutely. They admired its construction, said the sweeps were beautifully balanced, and agreed that Glen handled them like a wizard. Nevertheless, Jeremiah Johnson, the former ferryman, urged them to give up their crazy notion. Owen Clark, who had been with the Pathé-Bray expedition and who in 1928 was keeping flow records at the river-gauging station, said they should have a second boat along for safety. Glen answered that they had handled the worst Cataract could throw at them and they'd make the rest as easily. Bessie, according to Clark, admitted having been scared at times, but remained enthusiastic. To an interviewer who she thought might relay her remarks to newspapers, she declared, "I've been thoroughly drenched a dozen times, but I am enjoying every moment of it."

Marble Canyon and Upper Granite Gorge took the cheeriness out of her. They were riding a medium-low nine thousand cubic feet per second. The weather was cold, rocks were a problem, and in Sockdolager she learned in one terrifying second that her husband was not indestructible. The handle of his sweep bucked up, hit him under the chin, and knocked him overboard. She threw out a rope, its end already fixed to the scow, then caught both sweeps, and struggled to keep the craft going straight ahead. Glen was groggy, but he was also an excellent swimmer. With a desperate reach he caught the trailing rope, held on until the water quieted, and with Bessie's frantic help wallowed back aboard.

On November 15, twenty-six days out of Green River, they landed at the foot of Bright Angel Trail and hiked the seven miles to the South Rim. There Bessie luxuriated in a hot bath and good food, but her zest was gone. Seeing a pair of Edith Kolb's new shoes, she wondered wistfully whether she would ever wear pretty shoes again. Again people tried to dissuade them, and again Glen refused to heed. He would not even take the life jackets Emery Kolb offered him, and he stubbornly ordered that two mule loads of supplies meet them at the foot of Hermit Trail.

When they reached Hermit at noon on November 18 (a photographer went there from Bright Angel with them) the handful of people who met them noticed that Bessie was very subdued. One observer said Glen had to force her back onto the boat after lunch, but that may be one of those memories that form out of thin air when accidents are talked about after they have happened. Anyway on they went.

For a person who planned to write a book about her experiences, Bessie kept a notably sparse diary. Her map of each day's run consisted of sequences of circles, dashes, and vertical hash marks — the dashes for still water, circles for easy rapids, uprights for difficult ones, like this: 0 — /// — / 0 ///// — /0/0 — . Her written entries shed no light on her emotional reactions to the river, the majestic scenery, or the simple problems of staying alive. She was sick on the twentieth. On the twenty-third, at Bedrock, they cracked a plank in the scow and had to lay over while Glen repaired it. On the twenty-seventh she did a laundry in a hot spring, probably the one beside Lava Falls. Wind blew hard on the twenty-eighth; on Thanksgiving Day, the twenty-ninth, they saw a deer.

They should have reached Needles, where the elder Hyde was waiting, on December 9. They did not. As more days dragged by without word, he let his imagination turn the scow into the villain of the piece. Somehow, he told himself, the ungainly craft had escaped from them, leaving them stranded. The picture that occurred to him most often was of an island surrounded by such terrible water that they could not cross to either bank. Or perhaps they were in a cove surrounded by unscalable cliffs, waiting for help, existing, perhaps, on a few provisions they had miraculously retrieved, or on game; for Glen had taken a rifle along. Yet even if they were dead, he had to know it beyond doubt. Glen was his only son, the mother long since dead in British Columbia.

Day after slow day went by, until nearly a month had passed since the November noon when Bessie and Glen had left Hermit Creek. If a search was to be launched it would have to be soon. Terribly agitated, the elder Hyde telephoned the governor of Idaho, urging him to call army headquarters in Washington, asking that search planes be dispatched from the nearest base in California or Arizona. He got in touch with Bessie's parents as well, pleading that they make a similar appeal through the governor of West Virginia. Then, boarding a train, he rode to the Grand Canyon so that he could respond on the scene to whatever news the air search yielded.

Six planes straggled into the Red Butte airport on December 18. When the first one was gassed up and ready to take off down the canyon, P.P. Patraw, assistant superintendent of Grand Canyon National Park, and Bob Francy, an all-around handyman who knew the area well, went along as observers. During the previous summer Francy and some friends, fortified by a block and tackle, had dragged one of the boats the Pathé-Bray people had left at Hermit Creek back upstream to Bright Angel, where he used it to collect driftwood from the river for the fireplaces at Phantom Ranch. No other boat was available nearer than Lees Ferry, and so his could be a real prize if the young Hydes were spotted somewhere in the gorge.

The flight was wild, between the canyon walls scarcely seventy-five feet above water level, and in a way it worked. The fliers saw the scow at rest in a quiet pool twelve miles below the mouth of Diamond Creek – one hundred thirty-eight heart-chilling miles from Francy's boat at Bright Angel. There was no sign of life anywhere.

To the canyon people the situation looked hopeless, but Glen's father refused to give up. Diamond Creek offered one of the few points by which the river could be reached without excessive toil; in fact, a drilling crew testing the rock foundations for a possible dam had established a temporary camp there a few years before. Why couldn't the abandoned camp be used as a base for a ground search?

Emery Kolb supported the idea. At Hyde's request, he had been contacted in Phoenix, where he was undergoing a physical check-up, and he returned without waiting to hear the results. (One tale says the doctors recommended an appendectomy — which he never got around to having.) To acquaint himself fully with the circumstances, he too arranged to be flown down the canyon to look over the scene. He returned to suggest that a small party take oars and camping equipment to the old drill site. They could build a boat out of the remnants of the old shacks and use it for floating down to the scow and then go down the stream to another take-out point at Spencer Canyon.

Fine — if the lost pair were stranded below the mouth of Diamond Creek. But, said Hyde, what if they were somewhere above?

So the ball went back to Francy and his boat, sweetened by Hyde's promise of $1,000 for firm information about the fate of his son and daughter-in-law. Francy enlisted a friend, Jack Harbin, as helper. Assistant Superintendent Patraw went along to lend an official hand.

Each wore red flannel long johns, two pairs of jeans, and a heavy sheepskin coat, and still it was a miserable experience. The river was dropping and frequently they had to lift the boat past the exposed rocks. Water buckets froze each night in their cheerless camps. Once while Harbin was in the boat, fending it off bankside rocks, Patraw mishandled a line and dumped him in the river. Afterwards Harbin kept snarling at him until, on reaching the Bass Trail, Patraw quit and hiked out, losing his way in the snow near the top and wandering for nearly two days before reaching habitation.

Meanwhile Emery Kolb, Hyde, Chief Ranger Jim Brooks, and John Nelson, deputy sheriff at Peach Springs, made their way by car and horse to the mouth of Diamond Creek (mile 225.7). Ellsworth Kolb, who was then living in Los Angeles, met them there in response to a wire from Emery. While the Kolbs and Brooks tore down a shack and built a boat, Hyde and Nelson hiked as far upstream as they could, hoping to find some trace of the missing pair. Nothing.

The finished boat had room in it for only three. They ruled Hyde out — even he saw he would be a burden — and on Christmas Day the Kolbs and Brooks headed downstream. The rapid at Mile 232 can be wicked during low water — and it was low then. The main current beats full tilt against a low cliff of beautifully fluted granite a hundred feet below a tight, fast tongue. A boatman has to skirt a big hole and pull hard left through heavy waves in order to miss a series of fang-rocks partly submerged in the racing current. Because of the complex difficulties, the Kolbs and Brooks decided to line down along the shore opposite the cliff, and that was difficult, too, because of the strength of the current. The thought occurred: the young Hydes, clinging desperately to a lining rope, could have been jerked into water too fast for even Glen to manage. Or, if they had been running the rapid, the scow might have smacked against the cliff hard enough to throw them overboard.

The scow, floating peacefully at Mile 237, seemed to confirm the conjecture. There was some water in it, probably from splashings, but the mattress, the stove, the camping gear, and the pair's personal possessions were neatly in place. So there had been no upset: boat and boaters had simply parted company.

The searchers retrieved Bessie's diary, box camera, and such other items as they thought relatives would like. The scow rocked gently under their feet, its rope caught firmly on the stream bottom. Unable to work it free, they cut it — and afterwards were criticized because there might have been a body down

The rapid at Mile 232 can be wicked during low water — and it was low then.

there, clinging with a death grip to the rope's knotted end. Freed, the scow floated off a little ways and ran immovably between the cliff-girt shore and a boulder. They abandoned it there.

With Emery at the oars of their campmade boat and all of them shivering in the icy weather, they pushed on two and one-half miles to Separation Rapid and boomed straight ahead without a pause to scout it. Halfway through they hit a boulder with a shuddering crash. Ranger Brooks, perched precariously on the icy foredeck, was catapulted into the stream. His pants caught on some loose projection of the boat, and he was dragged under water to the foot of the rapid before he could be extricated. A bad camp followed, on beds that had been soaked and then frozen in the leaky hatches.

The elder Hyde and Nelson met them with riding horses at the mouth of Spencer Canyon, just above Lava Cliff Rapid, mile 246. As soon as he could, Hyde thumbed through Bessie's diary and found a last glimmer of hope there. On November 27, the two had been at Lava Falls. On the twenty-eighth high winds had vexed them. The last entry, dated November 30, spoke of bad rapids without specifying a place. Tossing and turning in bed that night, the father convinced himself that they could not have traveled in their clumsy scow, on low water, against headwinds, the forty-six miles from Lava Falls to Diamond Creek during that short interval. Therefore the accident must have occurred above Diamond Creek, not at Mile 232, as the Kolbs and Brooks surmised. The two, injured probably, were waiting for help in the canyon bottom, he reasoned, or somewhere on the walls, unable to climb higher.

Grimly he continued the search. He told Bob Francy and Jack Harbin, who had walked twenty miles up Havasu Creek to the Indian village of Supai to contact him by telephone at the South Rim, to press on down to Diamond Creek, searching every sandbar for tracks. At his behest Hualapai Indian trackers scoured the reservation south of the stretch of canyon between Lava Falls and Diamond Creek for any sign that might be there. He hired cowboys to search the desolate benches and mountains on the north side of the canyon. Accompanied by Jack Nelson, he himself backpacked laboriously into the gorge below Lava Falls, but found nothing.

The Kolbs did not charge him for their work, but when Francy and Harbin asked for the $1000 he had promised, he refused on the grounds they had unearthed no facts. Yet they had paid for their own supplies, including replenishments bought at Supai, and of necessity they had abandoned Francy's hard-earned boat at the mouth of Diamond. Not until they threatened suit did he settle for $700.

Ironically, much of this was unnecessary. In 1931, people prowling through the drill camp found Glen and Bessie's names written in pencil with the date November 31 [sic], 1928, written on a board inside the old blacksmith shop. So they had reached Diamond Creek, and in all likelihood, the accident took place the next day at Mile 232. But because no bodies were ever found speculation continued for years that one or the other or both survived the river and went into hiding for reasons of their own. One favorite surmise has Bessie shooting her heartless husband and then somehow escaping across miles of cliff and desert without leaving a trace. Even P.T. Reilly, a serious river historian who compiled a list of deaths in the Colorado Canyons *(Utah Historical Quarterly*, Spring 1969, pages 250-51) accepts Glen's drowning but puts a question mark beside wee Bessie's name.

Be all that as it may, she did come, in her search for fame, within forty-seven miles of being the first woman to traverse the Colorado's canyons. There are some who feel she deserved a plaque fully as much as the Howland brothers and William Dunn, who got only eight miles farther than she before they left the river and perished.

Eight

BUZZ

Buzz Holmstrom — only his widowed mother called him by his given name, Haldane — went alone down the Green and Colorado rivers in 1937 not because he wanted fame or money but because he could find no one to go with him. The year before he had written Emery Kolb, offering his services as boatman for any group contemplating a trip anywhere on the river. Emery had referred him to Frank Dodge, who had just contracted to take two scientists from Carnegie Tech in Pittsburgh and two from Cal Tech in Pasadena through the Grand Canyon to study the ancient crystalline rocks of the inner gorges. Dodge planned to use three big, expensive, mahogany-planked boats, each weighing a thousand pounds empty, and had already signed up a crew — himself, Owen Clark, M.F. Spencer, and, as back-up, Frank Moore. Sorry.

Buzz, who was twenty-eight, with close-cropped hair atop a round, stubborn-looking countenance, declined to be put off. He'd build his own boat and make the eleven-hundred-mile run from Green River, Wyoming, to Boulder Dam with a friend.

Whenever he could break away from his job as a filling-station attendant in his home town of Coquille, Oregon, he scoured the nearby forest for suitable wood. Finally he found a down log of thoroughly cured Port Orford cedar, a wood often used in those days for venetian blinds because of its tensile strength and resistance to warping. After cutting out a piece of the log's midsection, he levered it by hand half a mile to a road, hauled it to town, and had it milled to his specifications. Then he began his carpentry.

The end result was a four-hundred-and-fifty-pound boat fifteen feet long, five wide and almost flat bottomed — he put in an inch-and-a-half arc for strength. It had a ten-inch rake fore and aft; this raised both ends out of the water, making the boat easy to pivot. Also if he ran into a submerged rock the boat would tend to slide up it, softening the impact. Buoyancy and storage space were provided by water-tight compartments in front of and behind a small center cockpit. The bow was pointed, the stern square. As all boatmen were doing by then, he planned to go down swift water facing forward.

He sent pictures of the craft, which he seems not to have named, to Emery Kolb for comment. Emery said it looked fine, but Buzz's companion, who would have had to ride most of the eleven hundred miles sprawled on one of the decks, didn't agree. He backed out.

So there it was. Either Buzz postponed the adventure or went alone.

He might well have paused. Up to that time his experience had been limited to three trips, two of them in the tumultuous canyons of Oregon's Rogue River. The first time he had smashed up on a rock in midstream. A mediocre swimmer, he had stripped off his heavy outer garments before flailing ashore and then had walked to the nearest fishing resort clad only in his longjohn underwear. As soon as he could, he tried the run again and succeeded. That victory under his belt, he had taken on, in October 1936, the famed Salmon, "River of No Return," in Idaho. His success convinced him he could also go down the Colorado — alone, if necessary. And now it was.

Certain corollaries followed. No one had yet run every stretch of white water from the head of Lodore Canyon on the Green to the Grand Wash Cliffs at the bottom of the Grand Canyon. The worst rapids they had avoided by lining boats through them or portaging around them. Either procedure would be an ordeal for a lone man: hence the temptation to skip the labor by running through risky places would be almost overwhelming. Yet if he smashed up, as he had in the Rogue, could he get out?

Well, he'd take those worries one at a time. He knew he had a remarkably substantial, comparatively light-weight boat. He knew his compact body was in good shape. He was methodical. He pored over every government map and every book on the river he could find. He took Ellsworth Kolb's *Through the Grand Canyon from Wyoming to Mexico* with him, calling it his good friend. He could be content with dry rice, flour, beans, raisins, prunes, bacon, coffee, and a few canned goods for food; a frying pan with a lid, a pot, a cup, a tent, a sleeping bag, a bucket, several pieces of rope, nails, block and tackle, and a camera and film for equipment. He had a beat-up car and trailer to get himself and the boat to his put-in at Green River, Wyoming. In his pocket he carried $100 for replenishing his needs along the way. A few things — new oars, for instance — he ordered sent to him at a bus stop called Marble Canyon, where the Navajo Bridge crossed the river four miles below Lees Ferry.

He also had a very private goal. He knew from letters he had exchanged with Frank Dodge that the Cal Tech-Carnegie Tech scientific party planned to take off from Lees Ferry, Arizona, on October 10 and travel slowly.[1] Buzz planned to leave Green River, roughly eight hundred miles farther upstream, on October 4. Suppose he overtook them. Just for kicks. Just to see their faces. Solo. Something no one else had ever done.

He did not let the idea push him unduly. On the way to Green River he detoured through Salt Lake City to talk to Bert Loper, legendary already though he had not yet run the Grand Canyon. Bert offered good information about the

A mediocre swimmer, he had stripped off his heavy outer garments before flailing ashore and then had walked to the nearest fishing resort clad only in his longjohn underwear.

1. The scientists actually started on October 11.

87

upper river, and, better yet, encouragement, for Bert, too, had been a loner in his day. Mostly, though, Buzz had to learn by doing.

October 9. 2:30 P.M. Red Creek Rapid, still well above Lodore. "It is," Holmstrom wrote in his journal,

> a dirty son-of-a-gun to put it mild — steep, long, and rocky. . . . I might have tried to run it if close to home and everything favorable, but there is too much to lose, so I portaged the boat [alone, four hundred and fifty pounds] over a beaver dam down a little side channel. . . . Then the trouble began. It was over a quarter of a mile from the duffel at the head [of the rapid] to the boat at the foot. I made it all in three loads, but I am sure a donkey's ear would have burned with shame watching me. . . . If there are many more long portages about half my stuff is going overboard.

And then, just before turning into bed beside the fire that had provided light for his writing, he added, "Well, tomorrow is the day that Dodge's outfit is supposed to start from Lees Ferry." He had already cut their lead to little less than seven hundred miles.

The low water of autumn exposed mazes of deadly rocks in Lodore and Whirlpool canyons. Four times he lugged duffel around rages of water. Twice he lined the lightened boat ahead, at Disaster Falls and part way through Triplet. He ran the other two bad stretches. The boat danced gaily without its load, swinging readily to his tugs on the oars until, in the middle of Hell's Half Mile, an oarlock jerked out of its socket and he hit a rock with a bang that jarred his heart into his mouth. No damage, fortunately. Meanwhile he was learning to bake fluffy biscuits in his frying pan, with coals underneath it and on the lid. The dough-gods became the staple of his diet, warm ones in camp, cold ones, along with cold bacon, for lunch.

He broke out of Split Mountain on October 17, treated himself to a hotel room in the tiny riverside town of Jensen, Utah, and hitched a ride to Vernal, to talk to Bus Hatch, Swain, and Mowrey. Then back to the river — to rain, wind, and slack water where the Green winds across the broad Uinta Valley, and on into the sharp rapids and past the occasional neat farms in Desolation and Gray canyons. The stores in Green River City, Utah, carried neither new tennis shoes nor oars, both of which he wanted badly, but he did manage to exchange his heavy block and tackle and its ponderous ropes for a lighter set. On October 25 he pushed on again toward forbidding Cataract Canyon. He had four oars, one cracked, one so badly warped that using it twisted the skin off his palms, and two good spares for use in heavy going. His spirits stayed buoyant. "Dodge's outfit," he wrote that night, "should be out fifteen days now. I sure would like to have good luck so I could catch them."

At 11:30 A.M., October 28, he reached the point where the Colorado sweeps into the Green from the left. Cataract ahead. He spent the next few hours discarding excess food and cleaning accumulated mud from the cockpit — ounces counted — rigging lifelines around the boat, setting up splashboards to keep at least some waves out of the cockpit, and preparing a bag of raisins, prunes, and chocolate in case he got separated from the boat. By dark he had run the first five rapids without incident.

The next two and a half days were a different story. At rapid number sixteen, by his count, he had to haul the boat out of the water and skid it over the streamside rocks on a sort of causeway of driftwood logs and poles he wrenched into place with difficulty. "An awful job. My hands are very sore from the handles on the boat." A hundred yards of that convinced him he wanted no more portages. He discarded still more food, cans, even flashlight batteries. Then, after a long study of each bad place, he ran straight ahead into the long quiet of Glen Canyon.

For a time he drifted slowly, talking to miners, looking at old placer mines, investigating Anasazi ruins, feasting on fish. Then, late on November 3, he learned that two days earlier Dodge's group had been interviewed on the South Rim radio station above Bright Angel Creek, scarcely two hundred miles ahead. The adrenalin surged then. During the next day and a half he skimmed across more than a hundred of those miles, eager to pick up the supplies he had ordered sent to the hamlet of Marble Canyon. He did not pause at Lees Ferry; the Navajo Bridge had ended its business, and the two residents of the remaining shacks, Frank Dodge and Owen Clark, were with the scientists. He'd see them soon, he told himself — and then came the shocks. Navajo Bridge was not near the river, as he had supposed, but four hundred and sixty-seven feet above it. Desperately he swung into a break in the left cliff a short distance upstream from one of its abutments, tied his boat securely, and tackled the precipice, "an awful climb. I don't know how I can carry anything down there." And after he had walked across the bridge to Marble Canyon, he discovered it had no post office and nothing was there to carry. He'd have to go to Flagstaff.

He arrived late at night by bus, wandered disconsolately around town for a while, and then slept fitfully on the floor of the terminal among a group of CCC boys. The next morning was cold and rainy. He picked up his new oars and wandered some more, shopping and talking, for he had an easy way with people. The storekeeper he dealt with was willing to trust him for what he bought — Buzz's $100 had melted away — but Buzz refused and made out a check on the Coquille bank on piece of brown paper. Dead tired, he caught the bus back to Marble Canyon and managed to get himself and his replenishments to the boat. Shoving off, he floated to the head of Badger Creek Rapid, three miles below the bridge, and made camp in a sandstorm. For the first time, Dodge's group seemed a long, long way ahead.

He was still depressed and the wind was still blowing when he scouted Badger at sunrise the next morning, November 8. Bad, he thought, but tried to be upbeat about it. "I can get some good practice lining here." Tracks on the bank suggested that was what his predecessors had done. (As, in fact, they had, putting four men on the stern rope and two on the painter of each. The water had been low, about fifty-five hundred cubic feet a second, and rocks bristled everywhere. Dodge was in and out of the craft, running things. Cal Tech's Ian Campbell watched agog. "To see Dodge using hand signals and facial expressions to guide the linesmen above the roar of the rapids is as inspiring as seeing a great orchestra leader in the middle of a difficult passage.") Six or seven men to a boat. But Buzz Holmstrom was alone. He lugged about two-thirds of his duffel to the foot of the rapid, came back studying the currents, and thought, To hell with it. Climbing into the lightened boat, he dropped over the top on the right side, headed straight for a monstrous boulder, and then, as he had planned, caught a current veering around the obstruction, and let it suck him past.

The same thing happened at Soap Creek Rapid. He carried two loads of cargo to a quiet place in the middle, went back intending to line — then jumped into the boat and zipped down the very channel, so he figured from his reading, that had twice upset Ellsworth Kolb. After reloading he treated himself to coffee. "I feel better if I have something warm at noon."

Success made him feel too good. He gave only a cursory look at North Canyon Rapid, nine miles below Soap, and was caught by the big waves in the center of the constricted channel.

> The boat was flooded down on a rock in the trough and stuck there. All I could see was water on all sides. . . . The oars looked awfully small and useless in those circumstances, so I let go of them and grabbed the gunwales and expected to go over, under, or end over end, but she came loose, shot out of the wave and headed for the ledge on the left of the big waves. Then I grabbed the oars and ran the rest OK. I am going back up there, a half mile, in the morning and try to analyze it to see for sure just what my mistake was. Mostly carelessness, I am sure.

He did go back, but it was really a ritual — an apology to the river for not heeding what its waves and currents could have told him. He already knew what he had done wrong, and he also knew, after the experience was over, what he and the boat were capable of when he set his mind to it. The lessons of eight hundred miles of water came to a focus that day; processes had established their own efficiencies. He was down to the bone of things. He cleaned the mud out of the cockpit again and discarded more weight — his tent, even one of his two bars of soap.

Routines became fixed. The November days were short, and he wanted to be moving as soon as there was light enough to read the water. This meant getting up in the dark, cooking and packing by firelight. Because his watch had grown erratic, he tried to learn to tell time by the stars so he wouldn't have to crawl out of bed before he had to. The narrow view of the sky between the high, winding walls reduced the effectiveness of the experiment, but he reveled in the desert sky anyway — stars more numerous and brilliant than in the misty air of coastal Oregon. And the canyon, he thought, was more beautiful by moonlight than by day — too wonderful, almost, to bear. "It really hurts to go thro [sic] here in a way, there are so many things and on such a grand scale I cannot describe them."

As soon as he put one rapid with a bad reputation behind him, he began worrying about the next. Paradoxically, however, he did not fret much about how he could escape if he were wrecked, an insouciance he scolded himself for in his diary. He checked every rapid carefully, sometimes, as at Hance, from both banks. If the water looked really risky, he lightened the boat by packing some of his duffel around. To calm his nerves he bit off a chew of tobacco just before starting, spit on his hands for a better grip on the oars, and slid down the tongue singing "Barnacle Bill the Sailor" at the top of his lungs.

At 3:30 P.M., November 11, he went into camp just above the Kaibab suspension bridge near Bright Angel Creek — a few hours less than four days

He cleaned the mud out of the cockpit again and discarded more weight — his tent, even one of his two bars of soap.

from Badger Creek. He had run every rapid along the way, something never done before. Give some of the credit to his aloneness. If a companion had been along, he probably would have lined or portaged the scariest ones.

Toward dark he bathed and washed his underwear during a sandstorm. Without bothering to cook breakfast the next morning, he climbed the trail to Grand Canyon Village, bought what he needed for the rest of the trip, and in the evening visited the radio station, which was maintaining contact with the scientists, who were carrying a two-way set with them. They were camped at the mouth of Kanab Creek that evening, fifty-six miles below Bright Angel Creek, and the operator at the village told them Buzz Holmstrom was on his way, though whether the message went through they could not learn.

The next day Emery Kolb and his grandson, Edith's child, Sonny Lehnert, helped Buzz pack his supplies down the trail. In return for the bed the Kolbs had given him the night before, he let the two use his sleeping bag while he burrowed into the sand with only a poncho for cover. It was cold; he scarcely slept but was agreeable enough in the morning to let Emery run the boat beside the trail for a ways so the child could have his first ride on the Colorado.

He wanted to hurry then but couldn't. Horn Creek, spray flying fifteen feet above the towering waves, spun him so he grabbed the gunwales to keep from being thrown overboard. Granite Falls snatched an oar from his right hand — he recovered it quickly — and then Hermit cracked it. Serpentine, twisting like a snake, was "nasty, nasty," and when he went through Waltenberg with the sun in his eyes, "the boat struck a rock under a hump, and hung, stern tipped down, until water from above lifted the boat and shot it thro [sic] at fifty per, and a second later the same thing was repeated, pretty hard this time." But he found a quiet camping place, no rapids roaring, and "I sit here like a king in front of my fire, governed by no man-made laws." But hardly free. "The boat takes on more personality all the time. My fate and its are pretty well sealed together. If it is broken or sinks, so do I."

The thought was with him the next day, November 16, when he reached Dubendorff Rapid, where Seymour Dubendorff had overturned in 1909 and Clyde Eddy had lost a boat in 1927. "I don't like the looks of it," he wrote but decided to run it nevertheless. He piled his duffel on one bank and a bag of prunes and raisins on the other so he'd have something to eat no matter which side he might be washed up on. The trick was to hold close beside a rocky island in midstream, out of the big waves, and then, just short of a rat's nest of boulders that splintered the current into bedlam, to cut strongly to the right past the tip of the island into a deep, rockless channel.

Biting into a chew, spitting on his hands — down, past the thunder of the waves, around the island, bellowing "Barnacle Bill." He was at the bottom before he realized he was singing two lines he had been unable to remember since leaving home:

> *My whiskers grew so bloomin' fast*
> *The seahorses ate 'em instead of grass.*

And so the miles went, past lovely, fern-bordered Deer Creek Falls, past Kanab (had Dodge's party heard the message?), past Matkatamiba and Havasu. Then, after a tentless night in the rain, Lava Falls. The snarl, the violence amid the black boulders — he portaged this time, along the left side on skids he brought over from the right. By dark the boat was down. He walked back in a roaring wind to where he had left his gear and tried to cook in a shower of sand and glowing coals. Failing, he crawled into bed. As usual he arose in the pre-dawn dark and took a deep drink of water that had been settling in his bucket. At daylight he discovered two rats had drowned in it — out of remorse, he decided, for having eaten most of his butter.

His sharp eyes noticed, beside Lava Falls, a splinter of mahogany that had been knocked from one of the scientists' boats. A little farther on, he found where they had set a pile of driftwood afire. The big lift came at Granite Park, thirty miles below Lava. A board elevated above the sandy beach on a tripod of sticks carried the letters "Hello, Buzz!" Beside the embers of a campfire was a can of cocoa. He mixed a drink eagerly. They knew he was coming! — though, as he learned later, they had not received the message at Kanab, but a repeat of it at their Havasu camp.

He caught them the next noon at Diamond Creek. They had been moving slowly — six weeks in the canyon, including a climb to the South Rim, as compared to Buzz's fourteen days.

Words poured out — greetings, questions, interruptions, kidding, stories. After lunch Buzz drifted with them three miles to Travertine Canyon, stopping now and then to let the five geologists do their work. (Edwin McKee of the National Park Service had joined the party at the foot of Bass Trail.) At the campfire that night he told the rapt audience how he had built the boat and the way it had performed on its thousand-mile journey.

He could have continued with them through the last big rapids — Mile 232, Separation, Lava Cliff — but after what he had done already, he had to finish alone. He refused the money and food they offered him, except for a little salt, and the next morning went on, kite high from one of the happiest times of his life. He had pursued them just for this — to see people who would understand what he had done and what he felt deep down beyond his own powers to articulate.

As he rowed along he did a little soul searching. He had won no victory, he decided, for there had been no combat. The river was not treacherous, as some said. Its current, waves, boils, and whirlpools spoke plainly to those who heeded. As for himself, "I have already had my reward, in the doing of the things, the stars, cliffs and canyons, the roar of the rapids, the moon, the uncertainty and worry, the relief when thro each one — the campfires at night — the real respect and friendship of the rivermen I met."

Separation Rapid caused only minor trouble, but Lava Cliff was a heart stopper. He dodged submerged rocks, grazed one huge boulder, and in avoiding a yawning trough was shot toward a lethal cliff, escaping a collision only when water billowing back from the granite spun him away. After landing at the rapid's foot, he described his procedures on paper, scrambled back along the difficult cliffs, and left the message in a can taped to a rock for the party behind him.

It took him three days to row across Lake Mead to Boulder Dam. On November 25, Thanksgiving Day, he patted its smooth cement, said "I'm Pop-Eye, the Sailor Man," went ashore, and wired his mother he was safe. Knots of people surrounded him and in the confusion he just possibly recalled one of the last canyon entries in his journal: "I think my greatest danger is ahead — that I might get swell-headed over this thing. I am going to try to keep my mouth shut about it, go back to work in the old way and have it only for a memory for myself.''

There was no way he could stay silent. Flat broke, he succumbed to an offer of $100 from a Los Angeles radio station to participate in an adventure program. On his way back to Wyoming to pick up his car and trailer, he visited Dr. Russell Frazier in Bingham, Utah, and worked in the copper mines to earn money for the last leg of this trip. Frazier brought in a Salt Lake City reporter to interview him. A clipping of the story reached the *Saturday Evening Post;* its editors wired contributor Robert Ormond Case of Portland to get an article. It was published, purportedly in Holmstrom's own words, on February 26, 1938.

Exploitive offers poured in. One Californian, after leading off with a statement that a traveling exhibit of the mummy of John Wilkes Booth had grossed $10,000, suggested using the boat as a touring attraction and selling postcards and pamphlets on the side. A more interesting proposal came from Amos Burg, a genuine riverman and member of the famous Explorers Club in New York City. Burg had canoed or boated at least a part of every major river in North America except the Colorado. Now he suggested that Holmstrom and he duplicate Buzz's trip in the fall of 1938, taking short newsreel movies to sell to major film companies and a longer feature to be shown at the San Francisco's World's Fair, with Buzz as narrator. They could also take still pictures to illustrate a book. A major problem would be finances. Like Holmstrom, Burg lacked adequate funds for such a trip, but thought he could obtain sponsors one way or another.

About that time an unexpected angel appeared — Julius F. Stone, who had gone down the river in 1909 with Nathaniel Galloway and Seymour Dubendorff. Stone was in touch with Dr. Russell Frazier about another trip part way down the Colorado. The doctor had rediscovered the steps the Spanish explorer, Silvestre Velez de Escalante, had hewn into the sandstone walls of lower Glen Canyon in 1776 in order to cross the river, and he felt the place merited a memorial tablet, to be bolted to the pink rock by a proper expedition. He planned to launch the trip from Green River, Utah, late in the summer of 1938. Though Stone was eighty-three years old, Frazier invited him to come along. In the course of their correspondence, he mentioned Holmstrom's solo run and evidently remarked on how short of cash Buzz was. Promptly Stone sent the young man $500 — pure generosity, for it seems he had no idea then that Holmstrom might be planning another trip.

That tipped the scales for Buzz. He was still bashful, still did not strut or brag, but he found it impossible to settle down to pumping gas, and he was ready to start on the instant. Burg slowed him down. He was talking with the Goodyear Rubber Company about making him a special rubber raft to use on the Colorado River. In addition there were movie cameras and film to buy, more backers to search for. The trip could not possibly start until September. Meanwhile Buzz should travel, drumming up interest.

Promotion was not Holmstrom's forte. After a radio talk in San Francisco, he gave up and drifted down to Lake Mead to pick up his boat, which was stored there. To earn more money he took a job as spieler on a sightseeing cruiser. He learned, too, that competition for attention was going to be severe that year. In addition to Frazier's trip (featured after its completion in the *Saturday Evening Post*, which then had the biggest circulation of any magazine in the world), there

A more interesting proposal came from Amos Burg, a genuine riverman and member of the famous Explorers Club in New York City.

93

was Norman Nevills. He planned to launch a new tourist business by taking along, that summer, the first women ever to traverse the Grand Canyon — more of that in the next chapter. Buzz disapproved, saying publicly, "Women have their place in the world, but they do not belong in the Canyons of the Colorado." Nevertheless, when word reached Lake Mead that the Nevills expedition was lost somewhere above Lees Ferry, he jumped into a car and rushed to the abandoned station to join a rescue mission. If his idea was to draw attention, however indirectly, to the Holmstrom-Burg project, it failed, for when he reached the ferry on a blistering July day, the party was already out of Glen Canyon and eating watermelons before continuing into the Grand Canyon. No one interviewed him.

Burg, meanwhile, had found no sponsors except Goodyear, which furnished a rubber boat, *Charlie,* eighteen feet long, five wide, and painted bright yellow for visibility. He had spent all his money on cameras and film, both black-and-white and color, and Buzz had to pay the freight costs of getting *Charlie* to Green River, Wyoming. Buzz stuck to his wooden boat, which he painted red and named *Julius F.* for his patron.

Hoping to give scope to their trip, they set out on August 26, 1938, from the gorgeous Green River Lakes, near the Green's source in the spectacular Wind River Mountains of Wyoming. A foolish move. The late-summer water was so low and the river's meanders so time consuming that they fell behind schedule and after fifty miles hired a car and trailer to haul the boats back to the town of Green River, Wyoming. There a friend of Burg's from Portland joined them for the run through Lodore. They handled the "rollicking rapids" (Burg's words) of Desolation and Gray on their own. In Green River, Utah, they found a new roustabout, Willis (Bill) Johnson, a stocky, amiable, yarn-spinning Mormon who was, Burg said, a Rock of Gibraltar throughout.

It was a good run. They liked each other, worked well together, accepted each other's personality quirks. After they reached the junction with the Colorado, water levels picked up, creating more turbulence than there had been the year before but covering many troublesome rocks. Delighting in what he called "perfect conditions," Buzz ran all the rapids in Cataract, often without removing any duffel and sometimes with Bill Johnson clinging to the deck. The rubber boat, *Charlie,* the first on the Colorado, weighed only eighty pounds and bounced and bent so much that they often lined it. That and the cameras slowed progress, and Amos was not as inclined as Buzz to rise early. Each night he slept on an air mattress in a tent, both of which Bill prepared daily for him, and he wore a necktie all the way down the river.

Though they could have arranged to have supplies left at Lees Ferry, as the other parties that year did, this was supposed to be a reenactment of Buzz's first trip. So he climbed the cliffs near the bridge, went to Flagstaff to mail out film for development, returned loaded with material and lowered it to the boats with ropes.

The whirlpools in Badger, Soap Creek, and Hance spun *Charlie* dizzily, but Buzz, exulting in the roller-coaster water, ran the *Julius F.* straight through without unloading an ounce. In form and color the silt-laden waves, said Burg, resembled "molten lava." After a pause to climb to the South Rim, they rushed on — Burg had appointments to keep. Buzz's boat nearly swamped in Serpentine Rapid and was holed by a rock in Waltenberg, a shock that led them to portage the rubber raft around that rapid. More cautious now, Buzz lightened his load before running Dubendorff (they lined *Charlie)* and when they came to Lava Falls, Willis wrote soberly in his journal, "We believe Buzz is the best boatman in the world, but I don't suppose he will attempt to run this death trap."

He did, though, and stayed upright while the cameras cranked. Never having heard of George Flavell's exploits in 1896, they assumed Buzz was the first to ride out Lava's maelstrom. "We were so overjoyed and happy," Bill wrote, "that later we climbed back along the right shore of the falls and Buzz explained to us how he run it. It was exciting for awhile." It was almost the last excitement, for Lake Mead, filling rapidly had covered Lava Cliff and half of Separation. The owner of a power boat helped them buck the strong wind blowing across the reservoir, and on November 6 the trip ended, with Buzz Holmstrom the first man known to have run every rapid on the Colorado.

Burg hurried east to keep lecture appointments. Feeling let down and drained, Buzz and Bill knocked around the West, working for a time at the copper mines in Bingham Canyon. Amos sold a ten-minute film to Paramount and that was all; the market that year was saturated with Colorado River material. Buzz ended poorer than he had started — until, out of the blue, he was given the most unusual job a boatman ever had. A Mrs. Clegg, a widow living in Vancouver, British Columbia, wanted to go across the continent to New York City by boat.

He got her there, with help along the early stretches from Willis Johnson and a few others, and with one automobile passage across the Continental Divide from Idaho Falls, Idaho, to Gardiner, Montana. Though war had been declared in Europe by the time of their arrival in New York City, Mrs. Clegg sailed for England. Buzz, uncomfortable in the metropolis, went to Washington and hit Colonel Birdseye, head of the USGS, for a job. Nothing came of it until the fall of 1940, when he was hired to take two engineers on a month's trip through Desolation and Gray canyons, platting dam sites.

Shortly after Pearl Harbor he enlisted in the Navy, became a carpenter's mate, served in both the Atlantic and South Pacific, where he had a bout with malaria, and was mustered out in October 1945. He stayed in Coquille until the following spring, when he was employed to boat supplies for a surveying party working the Grande Ronde River in eastern Oregon. On May 18, 1946, he walked into the cook shack and borrowed a rifle, saying, "I am going to shoot a chicken," supposedly a sage hen. He walked off about half a mile across a sagebrush plain, past a scattering of yellow pines, and, either accidentally or deliberately, shot himself through the temple.

He had given no hint of suicidal intentions beforehand. He left no notes. There was no investigation. One can only speculate about that last moment.

Nine

BOATS FOR HIRE

One summer night in 1937, Elzada U. Clover, a forty-year-old professor of botany at the University of Michigan stopped at Mexican Hat, Utah, a remote trading post, tourist lodge, and a house or two located within sight of a strange, sombrero-shaped pinnacle near the San Juan River. She was collecting *Cactaceae* — her specialty — and it was natural for her to ask Norman Nevills, twenty-nine, the son of the lodge's owner, if he had any suggestions.

Norm jumped at the question with the intense enthusiasm characteristic of him. He was brown-haired, of medium height, lean, handsome, and agile as a cat. Later, as his fame increased, estimates of his character would grow controversial, but few denied his charm. He turned it full force on Elzada Clover.

Could she find sponsors for a truly notable expedition — one to study not only cactus but other forms of plant and animal life throughout the botanically unknown canyons of the Colorado River? An historically important expedition, for she and other women, too, if possible, would be the first of their sex to traverse the last American wilderness. From it could come a best-selling book, coauthored by Elzada Clover and Norman Nevills.

Elzie, as he was probably calling her by then, glowed in return. She was bespectacled, plump, cheerful, and naive. She could be determined. And now it looked as if her life might yet hold one great adventure. Other members of Michigan's science department might join them, she responded. The University and a Colorado Springs collector for whom she sometimes worked might help with money . . .

They separated and Norm went eagerly to work. For the first time in his life he had a big project of his own. He had been born in Chico, California, on April

An historically important expedition, for she and other women, too, if possible, would be the first of their sex to traverse the last American wilderness.

96

9, 1908, an only child. His father W.E. Nevills, a roaming prospector, had spent considerable time on the upper Yukon and in 1920 had followed a brief oil excitement into southeastern Utah. Liking the country, he stayed. Except for occasional visits, young Norm remained in California, attended the College of the Pacific at Stockton for a little over two years, and then joined the family in Mexican Hat. Because not enough tourists went through the town on the rough dirt road leading to Monument Valley to make the lodge pay, they supplemented their income with whatever work they could find. An occasional chore that Norm liked was helping prospectors and geologists assemble gear and boats for trips into the San Juan's twisting, highly scenic lower canyon.

In 1933, when he was twenty-five, he was bowled over by a blue-eyed, nineteen-year-old tourist from Oregon. He pursued her, saw her three times, and persuaded her to marry him that October. Legend avers (and his daughter Joan Staveley agrees) that for his honeymoon he built a boat out of boards taken from an old horse trough and an outdoor privy, used his mother's curtain rods for ribs, and the rods of abandoned oil well pumps as handles for oars. In this contraption he and his bride floated, early in 1934, sixty miles along the San Juan to Copper Canyon, where an automobile rattling down a mine road into the gorge picked them up and returned them to Mexican Hat. Neither the hasty courtship nor the unorthodox wedding trip gave Doris Nevills second thoughts about her marriage. Throughout the few years of life they had together, she remained devoted to her husband and was an essential element in his success.

After the honeymoon, Norm acquired more boats and floated at least two parties of vacationers down the San Juan to Glen Canyon and on to Lees Ferry. If Elzada Clover's expedition succeeded, he might extend that nascent tourist trade into the Grand Canyon. But the first thing he would need would be better boats than the ones he had, and so he set about creating them. Design came from his own fertile imagination and from his father, who had once developed a boat for running the fast water of the Yukon. With promises of national publicity he persuaded a manufacturer of extra-strong marine plywood to give him materials. His helper, whenever spare time allowed, was a young employee of the United States Geological Survey, Laphene Harris, known to his friends as Don.

Nevills named their three creations "cataract boats." Detractors called them "sadirons" because they were shaped like the old-fashioned irons women heated on stoves for ironing clothes. Each weighed six hundred pounds, was sixteen feet long and unusually broad of beam and stern. The cockpit was forward of the middle, leaving an ample afterdeck on which a single passenger could lie flat while riding through rapids. The interiors contained the usual watertight compartments, arranged according to Nevills' taste. Their names were *Mexican Hat*, *Botany*, and *WEN*, the elder Nevills' initials.

Elzada, meanwhile, had lined up two passengers, her lab assistant, Lois Jotter, twenty-four, tallish, rawboned, freckled, and mischievous; and Eugene Atkinson of the Zoology Department. The University and the Colorado Springs collector put up the $250 fare each paid. On his part Nevills rounded up William Gibson, a young San Francisco artist. If Norm's and Doris' time was considered (Doris arranged menus and packed supplies while caring for a year-old daughter) the $1,000 total did not cover expenses, but the fledgling capitalist was willing to give up present returns for future prospects.

Nevills was one boatman; Harris, who traveled free, was another. Because

Atkinson had had some experience canoeing with Boy Scouts in the Michigan woods, he became the third. They left Green River, Utah, on June 20, intending to run Cataract Canyon, explore Indian ruins in Glen Canyon, hike to Rainbow Bridge, and still reach Lees Ferry on July 4.

It was not a good trip. Nevills had never been in charge of a group before, and he barked orders instead of giving suggestions. Atkinson, who took offense readily, responded in kind. He was something of a braggart anyway, bustling around with a gun on his hip and making a show of setting mousetraps and shooting animals to gather specimens. Lois Jotter liked sleeping late and, as a paying guest, resented the abruptness with which either Nevills or Clover wakened her to help prepare breakfast. Alternating rains and stifling heat did nothing to calm tempers. Food was skimpy and lacked variety. Unlike some of the men, the two women did not sleep in their clothes, but undressed each night and in the morning found dressing under a blanket something of a problem. They captured rain water in one of the boats for washing their hair.

Before entering Cataract, Nevills delivered a pep talk that the listeners felt betrayed the state of his nerves more than it quieted theirs. The river was high that year, and Cataract's big drops were wilder than anything the neophytes had imagined. At the outset there was a misadventure. While Norm was studying, at great length, the first explosion of rough water, the *Mexican Hat* drifted off into the turbulence. Don Harris and Lois Jotter sprinted to the *WEN* and took off after the escapee. After shooting four medium-tough rapids, they caught the runaway in an eddy. They pulled both boats onto a narrow strip of beach, and Harris, leaving Lois to watch the craft, started afoot upstream to report. Difficult cliffs stopped him for the night. Before the party was reunited the next morning, both Lois and Don had spent lonely, hungry, miserable hours in a downpour.

The successful pursuit of the *Mexican Hat* made Nevills' elaborate scouting of each turbulent spot look more unnecessary than ever. Feeling degraded, he snapped recriminations at Atkinson for not having secured the boat before leaving it, watered down his thanks to Harris and Jotter by telling them they had been damn lucky, and went right on examining each flurry of rough water at length, as most careful boatmen do. The *Botany* nevertheless flipped in one bad rapid, and afterwards he insisted on lining the boats through places the others considered merely exciting.

By the time the party reached Glen Canyon, it was split into cliques — the younger ones, Jotter, Harris, and Atkinson forming one group; Nevills and Clover the other; with the artist Gibson balancing uneasily in the middle. Lois constantly annoyed Nevills, he wrote his wife, by whispering behind his back, and there was open talk of defections at Lees Ferry. Nevills harangued them earnestly and then, ignoring the fact that they were running four days late, stuck to the program he had outlined — exploring Indian ruins in the side canyons and hiking five miles up the erosion-scarred flanks of Navajo Mountain to see spectacular Rainbow Bridge. But the women gathered few cacti; there just wasn't enough storage space in the boats.

At Rainbow Bridge they met three riders, one of them the secretary of a Buffalo, New York, investment company, Mildred Baker. Enthralled by the boaters, she asked Nevills enough questions about a trip in 1940 to send his bruised confidence soaring again. Just as they were returning to the river, an airplane flew over, waggled its wings, and dropped notes. Scrambling around, they retrieved one and discovered that their failure to appear on schedule had caused concern and that photographers and reporters were gathering at Lees Ferry, hoping for a story.

They arrived on the afternoon of July 8. The only problem had been high water, Nevills said, loving the exposure. No one spoke of dissension. Don Harris explained his dropping out of the party by saying truthfully that the USGS had transferred him to a new area. Atkinson talked vaguely of "other commitments." Lois said demurely that of course she was continuing through the Grand Canyon; she was having a marvelous time. One suspects Elzada Clover of orchestrating the responses. "I will not have the trip end here. It is too big a thing," she had written in her diary that morning, and she set about making sure it did go on.

Go how? Norm knew no experienced oarsmen he could employ as substitutes for the defectors, but he had talked about picking up two more men to help with portaging and lining in the Grand Canyon. So Elzie snapped at him, in effect, You brought us through Cataract without experts. If your new men are any good at all, we can finish the same way. Or perhaps Norm's own vanity swung the balance. He was counting as heavily on this trip as she, and he certainly did not want to give up in front of a curious audience. He told the two newsreel photographers who were pestering him for action shots that if they would hang around a little longer, he would put on a show for them at Badger Creek Rapid.

At 10:00 P.M., July 8, Clover, Harris, Atkinson, and Nevills left by car for the roundabout trip through the Navajo Reservation to Mexican Hat. Along the way they stopped at grandiosely named Tuba City and wakened Lorin Bell, a husky young Indian trader, by scratching on his window. "Hey, Lorin! How about going down the river with us?" "Hell, yes! What river?" At 4:30 A.M. they reached the Nevills' lodge. After a few hours sleep Norm and Elzada continued another forty-eight miles over the heart-chilling Comb Ridge road to Blanding and there picked up a second helper, Dell Reid. (Harris and Atkinson went their own ways from Mexican Hat). Personnel thus readjusted, they drove back through the Painted Desert and on to the South Rim to confer with Emery Kolb about the river, about writing an introduction for the book, which was still very much in their minds, and about joining the trip at Bright Angel Creek. They must have been tired on July 12 when they loaded the *Mexican Hat, Botany*, and *WEN* with fresh supplies at Lees Ferry and rowed back onto the chocolate current, the two photographers crowded in with the other passengers.

The filming at Badger went well — afterwards the photographers climbed out through a side canyon — and the party ran Soap without accident, though the new boatmen were scared stiff, as Nevills himself may have been. When it was over he was exultant. "This is a swell gang," he scribbled in his journal. "Lois won't be able to agitate this group." If he didn't like her, Dell Reid did: ". . .a wonderfully good companion, sensible but jolly, and a great tease. . . . For a pal anywhere you could not ask for a better one than she."

In spite of intense heat and Norm's continued tedious examination of rapids, morale lifted noticeably. Though the passengers often carried duffel around the worst rapids so that the lightened boats would be more responsive to the oars, there was not as much lining as there had been in Cataract. Sockdolager, which everyone rode, was a rousing thrill. Later Nevills wrote of it:

"Hey, Lorin! How about going down the river with us?" "Hell, yes! What river?" Bored with what they considered their leader's caution, they ignored his advice and got dumped for their pains — but not chastened.

It is my firm conviction that no one has ever lived until he or she
has had a first view of Sockdolager — looking down into that fury
of water, knowing he has to go through it in a boat — taking off,
pausing on the brink and then, with what seems like express train
speed literally hurtling down into the lashing waves. It's fearful —
quickly changing into a perfectly thrilling exhilaration.

Photographers, reporters, and sightseers were waiting for them at the
suspension bridge near Bright Angel Creek. Leaving Dell Reid in charge of the
boats, the others hiked to the South Rim — except for Elzada, who collapsed
above Indian Gardens and sent for a mule. They gave more enthusiastic
interviews, posed for pictures, and luxuriated in unsilted bath water, and cold
malted milks. When they hiked back down, Emery Kolb was with them and
continued to Lake Mead, enlivening the hours with his yarns and expert
harmonica playing. They were so enthusiastic on reaching Lava Falls that all
except Norm wanted to run it; he said the water was too high and insisted on
lining. On reaching Diamond Creek they invented the Order of Colorado River
Rats and initiated each other into it. The victim crouched on his or her knees,
head pressed against the ground, listened to dire threats, mumbled nonsensical
rhymed responses, was doused with a bucket of water, and received a resounding
whack on the rear with an oar. Much laughter. Much backslapping, embracing,
and, in later years the awarding of a specially designed pin.

The 1938 party was mildly famous now. A Park Service cruiser and a Lake
Mead tour boat with Buzz Holmstrom at its wheel (he had missed Elzada during
his earlier, hurried trip to Lees Ferry) came to the head of the reservoir to meet
them. Lois apparently went to Las Vegas to catch a train east. Elzie could not
tear herself away. She returned with the others to Mexican Hat, pausing en route
to watch an Indian dance and visit Lorin Bell's trading post by daylight. Then
Nevills, who was taking a small, paid party down the San Juan to Lees Ferry,
invited Lorin and her along as guests. She did not leave the Southwest until
mid-November.

The next year she came back to fill out her skimpy cactus collection — but
not by boat. She hiked with Lorin Bell and Bill Belknap past spectacular Havasu
and Mooney falls to the mouth of Havasu Creek, rode a mule down the Kaibab
Trail to the river and a horse around the knife-edge trails of Navajo Mountain to
Rainbow Bridge. She wrote an article, "Danger Can Be Fun," for the *Michigan
Alumni Quarterly Review* and collaborated with Lois Jotter on a scientific paper,
"Cacti of the Canyon of the Colorado River and Tributaries," but the book she
had so eagerly planned with Norman Nevills never materialized.

For Nevills, 1939 might have been anticlimactic — he made only a few
short runs down the San Juan that year — if the promises for 1940 had not kept
his excitement soaring. Mildred Baker, whom he had met at Rainbow Bridge,
was so stirred by the publicity Jotter and Clover had received as the first women
to run unharmed from Green River, Utah, to Lake Mead that she wanted to
outdo them by starting farther north, at Green River, Wyoming. Barry
Goldwater, scion of a prosperous mercantile family, sent in an inquiry. Harry
Aleson, a surveyor for an oil company and known to his fellow members of the
Sierra Club for having climbed the highest peaks in the Cascades, the Sierra, and
Mexico, stopped by to talk in person.

To all who contacted him Nevills outlined expansive schemes. If proper sponsors could be found, the travelers would conduct radio programs from the depths of the canyons. Scientists would discuss the countryside, passengers would describe their adventures, Nevills and others would give readings from historic books about the Southwest. They would also collect minerals and plants, map ancient cliff dwellings, and search for a natural bridge rumored to be larger than Rainbow, all for the modest fee of $650 a person.

Aleson backed out and Goldwater settled for joining the group at Green River, Utah. Nevertheless, five paying guests showed up in Wyoming.[1] By arranging with her mother to care for little Joan, Doris was able to go along and keep an eye on logistics. The men at the oars of the three sadirons were Nevills, Dell Reid, and Hugh Cutler, who was collecting plants for the Missouri Botanical Garden located in St. Louis. When the going was rough, the heaviest passengers rode on the broad decks, stomach down, heels toward the waves — or face forward if they wanted a drenching. The others sat with their feet in the cockpit. Radio broadcasts having proved impractical, messages were entrusted to homing pigeons provided by the Salt Lake City *Tribune* and released at intervals between Green River, Wyoming, and Green River, Utah, where their trip was still enough of a novelty to rate a banquet from the Chamber of Commerce.

It did not stay novel. "Monotony, heat, and the slow going," Doris wrote later in her diary, which was being published in installments in the Grand Junction (Colorado) *Sentinel*, "have all inclined different ones to get on each other's nerves." To these problems she added a mother's worries. At Lees Ferry she borrowed a car and drove as fast as the ill-graded road allowed to Mexican Hat to check on Joan. The child was fine, but Doris' mother, the baby-sitter, had broken an ankle. She was able to hobble, though, and Doris was needed with the boats. Back she went through the night, reaching Lees Ferry in time to help load in fresh supplies for a departure at 1:30 P.M., August 4.

Throughout the canyons they had been encountering piles of driftwood three hundred to four hundred yards long and dozens of feet thick. For years river runners had been setting similar piles afire just to see the spectacular blazes and hear heated rocks explode like cannon shots. The building of Boulder Dam provided a more practical excuse; burning got rid of wood that otherwise would clot into huge jams in Lake Mead, interfering with boat traffic and operations at the dam.[2] The Mexican Hat Expedition of 1940 added a new wrinkle. Anyone who could set a mat afire with a single match became a DWB — Driftwood Burner.

In Boulder Narrows, nineteen miles below Lees Ferry, they halted at the base of a tall rock holding a massive tangle of logs and branches. Passenger Charles Larabee, later to become a well-known boatman, managed to scramble up the red stone and light the pile. That night, as Doris was crawling wearily into bed at the head of North Canyon Rapid, she saw a fantastic spectacle. The driftwood mat had broken apart, and islands of fire were floating down the river, bobbing jerkily and then winking out as they dropped into the rapids.

Biting insects tormented them, and the low water was thick with silt. To clear a bucketful for drinking, they boiled it, skimmed away the scum, and filled their canteens. The taste, Mildred Baker reported, was ghastly. To cool themselves they frequently dropped from the boats into the river and then climbed back onto the deck to let evaporation provide a moment of relief. But

1. There were more shifts in passengers — dropouts and pickups at Green River, Utah, and Bright Angel — than it is useful to follow here.

2. In 1930, while the dam was under construction, Congress named it "Hoover." In 1933 the name was changed by administration action to "Boulder." In 1947, Congress restored the name "Hoover." "Boulder" has continued in popular usage despite the dam's location in Black Canyon.

the drying of the silt on one's skin exacted a penalty. "You picked up a good idea," Goldwater wrote, "of what the inside of a weenie must feel like."

They paused two days at Phantom Ranch beside Bright Angel Creek to luxuriate in the clear swimming pool, shade trees, and cold drinks. Then on again, into sandstorms and more heat. At an unnamed rapids below Hermit Creek, Hugh Cutler's boat tilted immovably against a rock. He threw a line to Goldwater, who was perched on a boulder near shore. Goldwater pulled the rope taut and Mildred Baker and the other passengers came across hand over hand, a whirlpool dragging at their heels. The men then tied more ropes to the lightened derelict's stern and bow, pulled it loose, and let it race, unmanned, downstream. Nevills, waiting in an eddy, darted out and retrieved it.

At Tapeats Creek, Goldwater, Larabee, and Cutler wanted to drop behind to explore. After warning them to study all rapids carefully before risking them, Nevills left for them a boat in which to catch up. Bored with what they considered their leader's caution, they ignored his advice and got dumped for their pains — but not chastened. "We laughed until we almost burst." A few miles farther on, Doris was swept overboard by a wave and so gave her name to a small rapid — Doris Rapid — a little below Deer Creek Falls. At Lava, Nevills studied and studied. A ritual, Goldwater said. Finally Norm ran it, "down a channel he must have seen the first minute he looked at the falls." To which a modern boatman, Roderick Nash, has responded, "The politician's impatience indicated little understanding of the boatman's psychology. Nevills, . . . putting it all on the line, had to be sure."

A mile above Separation Rapid, they saw a branch stuck into a crack in a cliff. Hanging to it were a pair of undershorts. Swinging over, they found a note from Harry Aleson, who was then in the process of completely transforming his life.

Born in Waterville, Iowa, on March 9, 1899, Aleson had been shot down and gassed while a teen-age aviator in World War I. Chronic stomach ailments followed. For long stretches at a time he could eat only canned baby food, yet he seldom slowed down. He left Iowa State College before graduation to begin a series of jobs with geophysical firms exploring for oil in the Southwest. He married in 1928 but was seldom home. His most active tie was his membership in the Sierra Club.

In September 1939, shortly after his first encounter with Norman Nevills, he and his father took a camping trip by motorboat along the shores of Lake Mead. Harry thought the area was the wildest, freest, most wonderful place he had ever seen. Promptly he set out to learn as much about the big lake's many bays and coves as he could. In 1940, he and a Los Angeles friend, Louis West, pushed a rowboat equipped with an outboard motor into the mouth of the Grand Canyon at mile 279. (Miles in the canyon are measured downstream from Lees Ferry. Thus, as one ascends, one's progress is recorded in steadily diminishing numbers.) Almost at once they picked up the Colorado's brown current, flowing relentlessly under the force of the river's own momentum into the blue water of the rising reservoir. They bucked this as far as Separation Rapid at mile 239.5, its lower section already inundated. Aleson's intent was to look around until Nevills' party arrived and then tow them across the shallows to a point where a Park Service cruiser could pick them up.

Near the head of Separation, the two men found the bronze plaque that Dr.

Russell Frazier, Willis Johnson, Julius Stone, then eighty-four, his son, and others had bolted to a granite cliff the previous December after a motorboat run across Lake Mead. It commemorated Powell's defectors, whose names Frazier and Stone felt had been unjustly omitted from the Powell Memorial that stood on the South Rim of the Grand Canyon. The metal letters of the new one read in part,

> Here on August 28
> 1869
> Seneca Howland, O.G. Howland
> and
> William H. Dunn
> Separated from the Original
> Powell Party, Climbed to
> the North Rim and Were
> Killed by the Indians.

All the way to the North Rim! Wanting to learn how the trio had done it, Aleson and West hiked seventeen miles up Separation Canyon to the point where it forked into three stems, chose the wrong one, and ran into an impassable cliff. Lacking time for further exploration, they returned to the river. There they discovered that their boat had floated off into the reservoir. Instead of helping Nevills, they would now have to be helped.

In order to alert the river runners, Harry put on his life jacket and headed upstream along the cliffs. To circumvent places he could not skirt on one bank, he swam the river — this happened twice — and continued up the opposite side. After about a mile he halted, unfurled his underdrawers as a flag, wrote his message, and floated down the stream into and through as much of Separation as had not yet been inundated. That part was fun; in fact, he clambered back to the head of the rapid and bobbed down again, in his life jacket, two or three times before the Nevills group appeared.

With the marooned pair aboard, the travelers coasted on into slack water and then settled doggedly to rowing. Soon the runaway boat was sighted and retrieved. They hitched their hard-used sadirons to it and Harry towed them along until a Park Service cruiser appeared with Goldwater's wife and daughter aboard. By midnight they were in Boulder City. Another record. Two years earlier Elzada Clover and Lois Jotter had been the first women to traverse Cataract and the Grand Canyon. In 1940 Doris Nevills and Mildred Baker topped them by adding Lodore, Desolation, and Gray, a feat that enabled Baker to lecture to several packed audiences in upper New York state the following winter.

Harry Aleson, who was living on a meager disability pension but who had good Sierra Club connections, seemed a potential gold mine to Norm. On November 29, 1940, he wrote Aleson saying that if Harry could round up four other persons for a special trip from Wyoming in 1942 — fare $2,350 each — he could go along free. And that would be just a starter. As the fame of the run spread, the price would rise to $3,000. If Harry continued to be productive, he could join Nevills' firm. Meanwhile, would he meet Norm's small 1941 trip somewhere near Separation and tow it to contact with a Lake Mead tour boat for $30?

Harry agreed to the towing — a piece of cake even at $30. There were only three guests in two boats, plus a folding canvas kayak manned by Alexander ("Zee") Grant. It was the first such craft to run the Grand Canyon.

By that time Aleson had "discovered" Quartermaster Canyon, a tributary that broke through the gigantic, tiered walls of the lower Grand Canyon at mile 260, twenty miles above what had been Pierce Ferry before its inundation by the reservoir. A clear lagoon, fed by water backing up from Lake Mead, filled Quartermaster's throat. In an adjacent cliff of travertine, high enough to to command a fine view of the main canyon and close to an intermittent waterfall a hundred feet high, was a broad-mouthed cave. By glassing the entrance, he told a friend, he could create a modern cliff dwelling seventy feet wide, forty deep, and thirty high — a mere two hundred and fifty miles from the nearest grocery store. He named the place, MY HOME, Arizona — when writing of it he always used capitals — and sent a description to his wife, Thursa, then working as a desk clerk in a Seattle hotel. She responded on November 4, 1941. "Of course I don't have to tell you how I feel about it. To make a success of my life I will have to live in a city. . . . It don't make any difference to you weather [sic] I am in Cal, or Washington . . . I love you a great deal and nothing can change that." And then, as a closing line, "I hope you have a happy birthday," though that event was still four months away. Clearly the ties were cut, although the marriage was not legally dissolved until Thursa's death in 1957. (The cave, it is perhaps unnecessary to say, was never glassed in.)

In the meantime Doris, abetted by Barry Goldwater, had persuaded Norm he would never get his tour business off the ground by being so ambitious. Three thousand dollars for a summer of working like a dog and broiling like a weenie? Guests wanted to be refreshed by vacations, not exhausted by "expeditions." Convinced finally, Norm kept his San Juan trips as they were and shortened those on the main river to the Grand Canyon at a cost of $500 a head. (He did retain the name Nevills Expedition.) Response in 1942 was gratifying — author Neil Wilson, his teen-age son, and a family friend; Egbert Hudson, called Ed, a two-hundred-pound California druggist whose secret dream was to put a motorboat *up* the Grand Canyon; and Otis R. Marston, of Berkeley, California, accompanied by his son Garth.

Though Aleson produced none of these guests, he did contrive to keep attention on himself. He came from MY HOME to Lees Ferry to help push the boats into the water, hurried to Badger to cheer them through that rapid, then drove to the South Rim, hiked to the suspension bridge and shot off rockets as the boats passed underneath. After riding one of them as far as the Hermit Trail, he hiked out, picked up his own boat at Lake Mead, met the travelers on schedule, towed them sixty miles at night under a cloudy sky while they slept as best they could, and hit the dock he was aiming for right on the nose, a remarkable feat of navigation.

Because of the war Nevills took out no trip in 1943. Those of 1944 and 1945 were short runs, one from Mexican Hat to Lees Ferry, the other to the same destination from Moab, Utah. In 1946, Norm trailered his cataract boats to Idaho to run the Snake and Salmon rivers. In 1947, 1948, and 1949 he floated the Grand Canyon. During those later years he was also flying uranium prospectors around the Colorado Plateau, landing on make-do runways that others would not risk and showing off to his river people by flying between the narrow walls of Marble Gorge under Navajo Bridge, zooming up with a shriek of the single engine and diving again.

He had done what he set out to do — open the watery part of the Grand Canyon to tourists. Though volume remained small, the records are significant. Of the first hundred people to traverse the canyon, a figure reached in 1949, nearly one-third went under Nevills' leadership in boats he designed for that purpose. Women became an accepted part of the scene. He trained several boatmen, not the least of whom was Otis Marston, who went with him on at least one trip a year, often more, from 1942 through 1948. At first Marston paid his own way as a dude, accompanied sometimes by his son, twin daughters, or wife, and then, though he was wealthy, as a hired hand earning $10 a day. Eventually a deep animosity separated the two men — they were miles apart in outlook and philosophy — but Norman Nevills was nevertheless the one who wedded Marston to the river, a union that led to Marston's vast, jumbled, and still only partially mined collection of historical documents and photographs.

Like nearly everyone who runs the Grand Canyon, Marston developed a proprietary feeling toward it. He took good movies of it and lectured extensively — he even had an agent make bookings for him — and in so doing brought still more publicity to Nevills. Norm was reaping a great deal of that in those days. He reveled in it — needed it, in fact, to keep his boats filled with paying guests. Part of his appeal was his showmanship. He spun gripping yarns that sometimes skirted the sober bounds of truth and took risks during which, in Marston's opinion, he scared himself half to death just for the sake of the applause he loved.

. . . in Marston's opinion, he scared himself half to death just for the sake of the applause he loved.

His life ended with a bang. On September 19, 1949, following another successful run through the Grand Canyon, Doris and he climbed into his plane at Mexican Hat for a trip. (A bad year for rivermen; Bert Loper, aged seventy-nine, had died in Marble Canyon only a few weeks earlier.) The motor malfunctioned and the plane crashed as the couple's two young daughters stood beside the runway, waving good-bye. Norm was forty-one; Doris, thirty-five.

Preston Walker of the Grand Junction *Sentinel*, who had been one of Nevills' boatmen, and his wife Becky, who had ridden the San Juan several times with Norm, flew down to get the bodies, had them cremated, and scattered the mingled remains over the Grand Canyon. Three of Nevills' boats became memorials to his achievements: one went to the Smithsonian; one is on display in the Utah state capitol building; the third is at the Visitor Center at the Grand Canyon. In 1952 at the suggestion of his good friend, Frank Masland, a handsome plaque dedicated to Doris and him was bolted to the canyon wall underneath the soaring span of Navajo Bridge. In 1969 the United States Board of Geographic Names, overriding Marston's objections, gave the name Nevills Rapid to 75 Mile Rapid. But his truest monument was the work of a set of extraordinary individuals who, even before he died, were developing his river-running techniques in ways he himself never had a chance to try.

Ten

AGAINST THE GRAIN

In 1941 Lake Mead filled for the first time. The rising water finished smoothing out Separation Rapid and crept four miles higher to Bridge Canyon, named for a natural bridge in one of its tributaries. When Harry Aleson rode the rise to Bridge to pick up Norm Nevills' small party for a tow, he took a motion picture camera along. As he filmed the tremendous walls and glistening water, his obsession with the area came to a focus. Why not put a boat all the way up the canyon, past the rage of Lava Falls, past Bright Angel Creek, through Marble Gorge to Lees Ferry, on and on? A name sprang to mind, which, like MY HOME, he always wrote in capitals: THE COLORADO UP RIVER EXPEDITION. If he could find sponsors . . .

After delivering the Nevills group, he went back up the canyon through the stifling heat of August to begin experimenting. With him were five Civilian Conservation Corps youths who had volunteered to spend their short vacations helping. They used three days outfitting in Boulder City and boating the one hundred twenty miles to Bridge Canyon. They'd need two more days to return. That left one day for Harry to figure out how to master a rapid from the bottom up. But at least it was a start.

At the first rapid above Bridge Canyon his helpers tied a five-hundred-foot rope to the bow of the boat and carried the line to the top of the fast water. As Harry rammed the boat into the tail waves, they began heaving. Lesson one: Don't be too eager. He went faster than the lads could pull in the slack and the sagging rope wound around his propeller. They let him drift back into an eddy where he straightened out the tangle, and on the next attempt he made the top.

The next rapid, which they reached as the sun was sinking, was fourteen hundred feet long, nine hundred more than the rope.

The next rapid, which they reached as the sun was sinking, was fourteen hundred feet long, nine hundred more than the rope. Of necessity Harry would

106

have to run as high as he could before swinging into an eddy and hooking up. To lighten the boat he put three of the boys ashore, told the others to hang on, and opened the throttle wide. Wham! — the propeller hit a rock. A pin sheared, and the blades lost their bite.

Grabbing the oars he carried for emergencies, he worked the boat close to the bank and told the two lads with him to jump. Hanging over the transom, he slipped a new pin into place seconds before the current swept him into the rapid up which he had been towed earlier in the day. Swinging around, he slammed back upstream and bucked past his stranded, frightened helpers to a point within two hundred feet of the rapid's boiling top. There, while he was still short of his goal, discretion took over and he veered into an eddy.

Perhaps they could have finished the next morning — he thought so — but that would have made the young men late for their check-in. Amiably, because that was his nature, Harry turned around. He couldn't help thinking, though, that seventy years earlier, in October 1871, a mixed party of boatmen, soldiers, and Mohave Indians under Lieutenant George M. Wheeler of the United States Corps of Topographical Engineers, with no high water to smooth out Lava Cliff and Separation rapids for them, had poled, rowed, and dragged three rowboats as far as Diamond Creek at mile 225.7 — eight miles farther than Aleson had gone. Lesson two: Since he couldn't scare up as many helpers as the Lieutenant had, he'd better get a more powerful motor.

When the United States entered World War II a few months later, he tried to enlist in the Navy. He was rejected because of his stomach ulcers. His conscience free, he took a job piloting a tour boat around the reservoir, hoping to earn enough to buy the equipment he wanted. The work bored him. When the Bureau of Reclamation established a drillers' camp at Bridge Canyon for testing a potential dam site, Harry signed on to bring in supplies by water.

On some of the runs he used a government powerboat. The kick it had tempted him unendurably. After unloading one evening in March 1942, he jumped back in and took off full speed. Later he wrote that when he hit the tongue of the rapid through which the CCC boys had helped drag him, "the boat stood up at possibly twenty degrees . . . and in less than a minute I had run that rapid yelling like a madman." Near the head of the next one he banged into a transverse wave that rolled the boat upside down. Boat, Aleson, stray life jackets, gasoline cans, seat cushions, rags, and old coveralls floated in a swirling mess into the deep, fast pool below the rough water. Thoroughly bruised, Harry caught up with the boat and climbed onto its bottom for a ride through the next rapid.

The drill barge was anchored at its foot. When the men aboard caught sight of Aleson through the dusk, he was standing and waving his yellow shirt. The upset boat was riding so low that he appeared to be walking toward them on the water, an optical illusion that brought him, for awhile, the nickname Jesus. His boss was not amused, however — government property, after all — and that ended his freighting.

Fortunately the Evinrude people decided, at about that time, to lend him a twenty-two-and-one-half horsepower motor, and on May 16, 1942, he took a Bureau of Reclamation surveyor up the river to Diamond Creek, where they ate lunch, and then on to the rapids below Trail Canyon at mile 220. They could have hammered still higher, Harry thought, but the surveyor had to return. Even so, it was a record — nearly six miles farther than Lieutenant Wheeler had gone.

Proudly Harry spelled out the facts with crayon on a driftwood board and left the message for anyone who chanced along.

He supposed he had crossed a hurdle, but not so. Oil companies to which he appealed for free gas to further his scheme waved him aside: didn't he know a war was on? He showed color movies and slides, all entitled "Adventures of the COLORADO UP RIVER EXPEDITION" to every audience he could find, some as far away as Los Angeles and its satellite towns. He advertised in the Boulder City and Las Vegas papers for participants who would actually pay him for the opportunity of struggling up the canyon. More than a year dragged by before he made contact with two young officer candidates in a Naval Training School at Cal Tech, Return Moore and Ward Vickers. They agreed to get him back on the water by sharing the expenses of another upriver run.

Timing was not auspicious. The reservoir level had dropped and the river was low. In places they had to lighten the boat by portaging the cargo. Occasionally they lined it, partly for safety's sake, amid the bristling rock gardens. Often those who were on the shore could advance only by dint of precarious cliff scaling. Even so, they reached mile 217.9, another record by two miles, before the Navy men had to turn around.

Lesson three. They had lost days of valuable time struggling up stretches he had already covered during preceding years. The thing to do was to launch the next attempt from the highest point to which supplies could be brought. That meant Diamond Creek. So they cached the boat and the Evinrude motor near its mouth and hiked twenty-two miles out of the canyon to the bus stop at Peach Springs. Ravenous, Moore and Vickers devoured a huge meal while Harry, his ulcer growling again, celebrated with milk toast.

The following February 1944, the three of them returned for another attempt. Accompanying them were Fred Swenson, a desert prospector, Dr. Hugh Brown of Los Angeles, and Ed Hudson, an overweight druggist from Banning, California, who would shortly move to Paso Robles. Some years earlier, Hudson had built a small motorboat, the *Esmeralda*, for use in the quiet waters below Boulder Dam. Later, in 1942, he had met Aleson when Harry towed a Nevills party sixty miles across Lake Mead to a safe landing in the dead of the night. They got together again in 1943 for short runs in Glen Canyon. From those contacts Hudson developed his own fantasies of pushing a motorboat up the Grand Canyon, a yearning that led him, along with Hugh Brown, to foot most of the bills for the 1944 run. Their dream was to fight through Lava Falls to the egress route at Havasu Canyon, sixty-eight miles above Diamond Creek. There they would cache the boat again until they could return with fresh supplies from the Indian village in the tributary canyon and finish the run.

They took their first batch of equipment and gasoline part way down Peach Springs Canyon by truck and then shifted the loads to mules for the rest of the journey. Orders from the Navy forced Vickers to drop out. Two days of heavy rain pelted the others as they stowed an almost unmanageable amount of gear into the boat they pulled out of its cache. To no avail. While attempting to blast through Granite Springs Rapid, two miles below the previous high point, Hudson and Harry tore up the propeller and its shaft, the rudder and exhaust unit — more damage than they could repair. Disconsolately they dropped back to the mouth of Diamond Creek.

Because fat Ed Hudson doubted his ability to hike the twenty-two steep miles to Peach Springs, they decided to cache the useless motor (Evinrude never did get it back) and row their boat thirty-five miles through rock-studded low water and over silt bars left by the dropping river to Quartermaster Canyon. There they could pick up another of Harry's motorboats for the run across Lake Mead to civilization.

It took them six days to reach MY HOME, and by that time Harry Aleson had faced reality. He did not have and could not get (at least until the war was over) the equipment necessary for climbing the heavy red currents in the canyon. Yet he would not let the idea go. To fill time he turned to related problems that would be less costly to implement but would still keep the name COLORADO UP RIVER EXPEDITION in the public's mind. One of these difficulties had to do with escape. Tourists, he believed, did not sign up for his trips because they feared that if the boat they were in was smashed beyond use, they would be trapped in the canyon bottom. It behooved him, then, to prove they could climb out.

It was not a new idea. In April 1942, shortly after losing his job ferrying supplies to Bridge Canyon, he had clambered up Separation Canyon, probably the first person to do so since Powell's defectors had gone that way in 1869. He found himself in rugged country. Thick growths of oak brush, juniper, and pine twisted among black combs of congealed lava on the slopes of Mt. Dellenbaugh, an extinct volcano rising about six hundred feet above Shivwits Plateau. Running out of water — he had started with three gallons on his back — he gave up trying to force a way around the mountain to the ranching country of the Arizona Strip and dropped back into an unidentified canyon. After restoring himself at a muddy seep he luckily found, he regained the river. There he sat for three days, living on sugared tea until he caught the attention of a passing boat with mirror flashes. So that experiment had been a failure, too, but he was sure that with proper planning he could have gotten through.

While lecturing on the COLORADO UP RIVER EXPEDITION to a Los Angeles Sierra Club group in June 1944, he elaborated on his plans for finding an escape route through that forbidding country. At the conclusion of the talk, he was approached by a small, slim, sad-faced woman who introduced herself as Georgie White. It was a fateful meeting, though of course neither sensed it at the time.

There he sat for three days, living on sugared tea until he caught the attention of a passing boat with mirror flashes.

Georgie de Ross was born in Chicago in 1911. The fatherless family, there were three children, was very poor. The mother, hard-working and self-sufficient, kept the children clean, neatly dressed, and endowed with a strong sense of individual worth. Georgie insists she was born and ever afterwards remained a vegetarian. School held few charms; she preferred swimming in the icy waters of Lake Michigan. When she was sixteen, she married Harold Clark; a year later their daughter, Sommona Rose, was born.

Sommona did not quiet the parents' restlessness. Leaving the child with its grandmother, Harold and his young wife wandered off to Florida and then to New York City, where Georgie landed an office job running a Comptometer. For exercise she took to bicycling in Central Park, a choice that led her and Harold to

109

pedal across the continent during August 1936. They arrived in Los Angles flat broke.

Harold liked nothing about Southern California. Georgie, who soon landed another Comptometer job, thought it a paradise. She persuaded her brother Paul, her sister Marie, and their mother to join her, bringing eight-year-old Sommona Rose with them. The reunited family opened a candy store. Craving physical activity as always, Georgie joined the Sierra Club and spent her free time climbing mountains and hiking on the desert. She also kept up her bicycling, to which she introduced Sommona.

By this time the sexual drives that, according to Georgie, were the only thing holding Harold and her together, lost their insistence. They were divorced, and in time Georgie married James R. White, a powerful, barrel-bodied truck driver fifteen years her senior. Fiercely independent, they went their own ways whenever it suited them. On the outbreak of the war, she took flying lessons and for a time was attached to the WAFS, a Women's Auxiliary Flying Squadron designed to ferry planes from the plants where they were manufactured to the military bases where they were needed.

In June 1944, she obtained leave from the service and as a feature of the vacation started with Sommona on a weekend bicycle trip to Santa Barbara. A passing motorist struck and killed the child. Georgie was devastated, a grief intensified, perhaps, by feelings of guilt over having neglected her daughter over such long periods of time. She did not return to the WAFS and Whitey, her husband, fearful for her sanity, was at his wit's end. Then one day friends prevailed on them to attend a Sierra Club gathering where a man named Harry Aleson was going to show pictures and talk about the Grand Canyon. Something loosened inside Georgie then, and after the lecture she approached Harry to ask if she might go on his next trip.

That was all the push Aleson needed. An announcement in the next Sierra Club newsletter invited participation in a COLORADO UP RIVER EXPEDITION that between August 20 and September 3 would climb from the bottom of the Grand Canyon to the top of Mt. Dellenbaugh before striking one hundred and twenty-five miles across the lonesome Arizona Strip to St. George, Utah. Cost $6 a day.

The only person who signed on in addition to Georgie White was Gerhard Bakker, a young biology instructor at Los Angeles City College. Harry took them by motorboat from Boulder City to MY HOME. After arranging their packs, they put-putted across the river to the mouth of Burnt Spring Canyon. When they finally topped its last rim, their feet were such a mass of blisters that they decided not to climb Dellenbaugh after all but to strike directly through the lava and piñon forests toward St. George. Bakker captured a rare, black-tailed rattlesnake that he decided to take home alive, bound up on top of his pack. This meant keeping it moist, a sore drain on their water supply, but whenever they had to have a drink they found it, twice at cowboy camps they chanced across. Limping around Poverty Mountain, they emerged onto a huge, sunstruck plain. Why hoof across that? When a government hunter named Royal Blake offered them a ride in his pick-up truck they accepted gladly.

On that trip both Harry Aleson and Georgie White found something they needed. Nothing physical, Georgie says, but a kind of mutual sedation for the lonely, restless questing that was eating out their insides. Georgie could not face going home when the trip ended but returned with Harry to Burnt Spring Canyon to recover the boat they had left there. As he was working with the ropes, a scorpion stung his finger. Flashes of pain swept up his arm, followed by partial paralysis. They ran their two boats to the landing at MY HOME and then, with Harry painfully mumbling directions, Georgie piloted the faster one full speed to Boulder City. It was an unnecessary scare, for by the time they arrived he had almost recovered.

Georgie returned home then. Not Harry. In October he made another climb onto Shivwits Plateau with two prospectors looking for an abandoned mine. No luck. At Christmas he visited Georgie and her husband, and they worked out details of a plan that had come to them during the footsore hike around Mt. Dellenbaugh. Climbing was a hard way out of the canyon. Wouldn't a shipwrecked party be better off floating downstream with specially prepared kits? They decided to try during high water at the end of June 1945. To pass the time Harry trailered one of his boats to Glen Canyon and made the first upstream motor run, one hundred and sixty-two miles, from Lees Ferry to Hite. But when he tackled Cataract Canyon — he considered all this part of the COLORADO UP RIVER EXPEDITION — he broke a propeller and had to retreat.

On June 27 Georgie and Harry met at Kingman, Arizona, went by bus to Peach Springs, mailed their city clothes home, and hiked in swimsuits down the ovenlike side canyon to the river. It was moderately high — about forty-eight thousand cubic feet a second according to gauging records preserved at Bright Angel Creek — but Georgie, who had never seen it except where the current was smoothed out by Lake Mead, was stunned. Float these waves, holes, and battering logs of driftwood?

To condition themselves and grow used to the turmoil, they hiked slowly upstream, five miles in two days. At mile 223.5 they found the remnants of a ferryboat draped over some boulders on the left bank. It had broken away from its cable at Lees Ferry seventeen years before, spilling a Model-T Ford into the river and drowning three men. Apparently no one else, not even Aleson on his motorboat runs, had ever sighted the derelict during its long, slow descent. They took movies for the record and camped nearby, dining on supplies, including canned baby food for Harry's ulcer, that he had cached in 1944.

When they were a full sixty miles above the mouth of the canyon, they made ready to enter the river. They wore swimming gear, tennis shoes, and Mae West life jackets, all covered with kapok coats for added buoyancy. On top of that were army backpacks holding watertight tins containing cameras, film, first-aid equipment, and food — dehydrated soup, nuts, candy, more baby food, and some of the first powdered coffee to reach the western markets.

Harry stepped into the current first. He tried to float with his legs forward to absorb the impact of the rocks, but the surging currents spun him out of control until an eddy caught him and he was able to claw up onto the bank. As he was gasping for breath, Georgie bobbed by. He screeched, but she did not hear him over the roar of the water, so he floundered back into the current, took after her, and passed her while she was caught in an eddy. Fortunately she did not see him and stayed put until he could land and walk back to join her.

To prevent further separations they gripped each other hand to wrist and careened on. The water was colder than they had anticipated; they were battered and choked, but only three times during the day were they able to fight their way ashore, rest, and warm up. By dark they had covered about thirteen miles. The next day they traveled about the same distance. As they progressed whirlpools proved to be the greatest hazard. One would suddenly spin them like tops, drag down first one and then the other as they clung desperately with their wrist locks, lungs bursting and blood hammering in their ears.

Eventually they reached water backed up out of Lake Mead, but though the waves ended there, the whirls continued and the current still raced, powered by the steep gradient of the riverbed. On the third day they were whisked along for three hours before they could land and prepare themselves for the six miles that still separated them from the relative comforts of MY HOME.

Enough was enough. They'd finish the run to Pierce Ferry in Harry's boat. But when they arrived, they found it had drifted away from its moorings. Numbly they rested for a day, reentered the river and floated on, slower and slower. They overtook the wandering boat and climbed in, but by then the current was barely moving. They rowed a while, got tangled in a massive log jam, worked their way ashore, and walked four miles to Pierce Ferry. There two government men put them in an automobile and took them to the main highway. They were a bedraggled pair when they boarded the bus for home.

In spite of warning flare-ups from his ulcer — sometimes he would have to lie down and clutch his stomach in agony — Harry went back to Glen Canyon and gave Cataract another try. He got higher than anyone else ever had, which was not very high, and then the pain gripped him so that he went to the veteran's hospital in Salt Lake City for radical surgery. When he was mobile again, he landed a job as night clerk at a hotel in Richfield, Utah.

In the lonely hours before dawn he took to writing Georgie about another test of the lower canyon, the next June, 1946, again on high water. Why not build a raft of driftwood, as the legendary James White (no connection with Georgie's husband) reputedly had done in 1867, and learn whether or not it would be possible for shipwrecked parties to escape from the canyon that way? To make the experiment conclusive, they should increase the amount of rough water they traveled by entering the canyon at Parashant Wash, twenty miles above their previous starting point. She agreed, but chided him for his occasional moments of churlishness. "I do want to learn all things but feel badly when you make me feel silly and helpless if I do not do things right the first time. Remember 35 years is an old goat to be teaching things to." But not too old. Briskly she finished, "Am going to check on flippers [swim fins] today."

On June 17 they met in St. George, Utah, and held a press conference Harry had set up. Royal Blake, the government hunter who had picked them up during their hike in '45, drove them to a ranch at the base of Mt. Dellenbaugh. This time they climbed it, took movies, and afterwards hired a cowboy to pack their gear to a gulch that drained into Parashant Wash. In addition to the same sort of equipment they had used the year before, they carried heavy-duty cord, hatchets, fins, and a lightweight, inflatable rubber raft, three feet wide and six long, a type the air force had developed for fliers who crashed at sea. Because they expected to find water in the gulch bottom, they took only two quarts each with them, though the heat was all but unendurable.

That night they camped dry and woke in misery. Finding a barrel cactus, they chopped it apart and chewed a little evil-tasting dampness out of its white pith. Lime juice made it more palatable, and on they went, carrying their soggy treasure in cups as they eased their way down one ledge to the next. Swarming wasps revealed a wet spot. They fought the angry insects away, dug down, and were able to refill their canteens with a liquid that was half mud.

The ledges grew into cliffs. Again and again they used their ropes to lower their packs and then crawled out onto the sides of the gulch until they found cracks down which they could slither. The chasm narrowed to a corkscrewing slit. A pothole of water appeared. After drinking their fill, Harry wrote later, they decorously separated while they took turns stripping down, wading in, and letting the cool liquid fill their pores.

At the river the next day, where quiet water backed into Parashant, they swam and swam until a sandstorm drove them to cover. The following morning they cut and lashed drift logs into a raft, tore apart an old wooden box they found, shaped its ends into oar blades and used its nails for fastening on handles made of driftwood sticks. Then they discovered they could not force the contraption across the eddy line into the main current. In fact, they did not want to. The river was booming at about forty-eight thousand cubic feet per second, the same level as the year before, and the raft struck them as too light and unstable for such waves. It would be better, they decided, to find a launching spot for their inflatable raft and float along the edges of the stream until they located bigger logs.

Georgie sat in the back, legs dangling in the water. Harry rowed. Balance was the problem. After being tumbled several times by big slaps of water, they began portaging around rough spots. But that was hard work, too, sometimes on high, dizzy ledges, so they took to riding easy stretches in their life jackets, as they had the year before, knowing they could kick free with their swim fins. They built another raft of logs and again failed to get it into the current. But they were learning to keep the inflatable upright and, except for the smothering heat, things went well — until they reached Mile 232, where Glen and Bessie Hyde had disappeared in 1928.

They had intended to portage around those dangerous waters, but they got too near the tongue.

They had intended to portage around those dangerous waters, but they got too near the tongue. The current hurled them down into an exploding wave that tossed the flimsy raft end over end. Both riders landed in the water. Georgie got hold of the raft, but Harry spun down the waves like a chip. He couldn't get out, even with fins. For three miles he gasped and choked in waves and whirlpools before a backwater caught him and let him struggle out onto a hot, black granite wall.

As he clung to the uncomfortable perch, he caught sight of Georgie. She had climbed back into the tiny raft and was roller-coasting downstream with one paddle. She could not stop where he was, but he knew she would turn into the first eddy she could handle. Clambering along the cliffs, he reached her two hours later.

After a night's rest at MY HOME they floated on down the dwindling current. At Emery Falls, four miles above the canyon mouth, they were picked up by a Park Service cruiser loaded with rangers, reporters, and photographers, worried because they were twenty-one hours behind schedule.

Stories of that crazy run were carried by newspapers in thirty-eight states. Irony. Harry had craved publicity, but this wasn't the kind that persuaded either sponsors or paying passengers that the COLORADO UP RIVER EXPEDITION was likely to be a safe investment. Then vandals destroyed MY HOME.

With that gone and nothing left on the lower river to hold them, Georgie and he moved up to Glen Canyon in 1947. They hiked to Rainbow Bridge, prowled through Indian ruins. Each bought a surplus assault raft from the Army, and in one those heavy black craft Georgie made her first orthodox float trips, a glorious one down the Escalante River on high water and an icy run down Cataract in November.

Once they had needed each other, but the inner crises had passed. Harry no longer wrote My Home in capitals or any other kind of letters. Georgie had come, finally, to an acceptance of Sommona's death. They drifted apart, still friends. Harry and Charles Larabee went into business running tourists, especially Boy Scouts, through Glen Canyon and down the San Juan. Harry found a new companion, Lou Fetzner, and with her made his first and only run through the Grand Canyon as an appendage to the 1949 group that took Bert Loper on his last, fatal ride.

Georgie spent her vacations in the same area, running share-the-expense trips with Sierra Club acquaintances. Whitey, her husband, helped shuttle the boats around; her brother Paul sometimes acted as crew member. Her companion on her first Grand Canyon run, in 1952, was Elgin Pierce, with whom she had hiked in the Sierra Nevada before she had ever heard of Harry Aleson. Hance Rapid almost brought the trip to a catastrophic end, but Georgie persisted and, helped over some of the lower portages by Frank Wright and Jim Rigg, Nevills' successors, she became the first woman to handle oars all the way through the Grand Canyon. By then, an old goat of forty-one, she had developed firm opinions on how rivers should be run for the sake of tourists.

So had others. Indeed, from one end of the canyon to the other, it was a time for new and sometimes conflicting directions.

Eleven

THUNDER ON THE WATER

In 1947, while Harry Aleson and Georgie White were looking over the waters of Utah, pharmacist Ed Hudson of Paso Robles, California, returned to his dream of building a powerboat capable of running the Grand Canyon from bottom to top. He hired a Seattle marine architect to design a special hull for an inboard motor craft — he believed an inboard propeller protected by a skag would be less likely to be damaged by rocks — and called on Otis Marston of Berkeley, California, to act as consultant and guide.

The offer came at a propitious time. Marston, then aged fifty-three, had just had an explosive confrontation with his superiors in the San Francisco office of E.F. Hutton & Company and was free, thanks also to the family's extensive real estate holdings, to travel rivers and study river history at will. He was about average in size. In town he wore a small, neat goatee but on trips grew a bristle of whiskers that may account, in the devious way of such things, for the nickname Dock that river runners bestowed on him about that time. His knowledge of engineering — degrees from both the University of California and Cornell — and the practical experience with water hydraulics he was picking up during trips with Norman Nevills enabled him to understand and give valuable suggestions about Hudson's plans. During the first World War he had qualified as a submarine commander; though the conflict ended before he actually took a submarine to sea, residues of the training stayed with him. He was self assured, analytical, methodical, in good physical condition, and inclined to criticize most other rivermen.

Hudson also offered Harry Aleson a place in the boat, the run to take place on high water in June 1948. Harry bristled. *Under* Hudson? By letter he snapped back that the up-river run involved more planning than flying the Atlantic and

116

"could very well become known as one of the important 'FIRSTS' in American history." He had been working on the idea for years and, quite frankly, "there is no one in the world who can make the run ahead of me." He would, however, pilot the *Esmeralda II* for $2,000 and a fat share of any book or movie contracts that resulted.

Hudson replied he couldn't afford the price. When the date for the start rolled around, the crew consisted of Hudson; his sixteen-year-old son, also called Ed; Wilson ("Willie") Taylor, another Californian; and Marston. Aleson, his nose completely out of joint, warned the quartet, in a public letter printed in the Boulder City *News* for June 11, 1948, that "failure in your first attempt is positive" and urged the Park Service to halt the trip for the "boy's" safety.

The river runners ignored the letter, trusting instead to the *Esmeralda II*. It was a sturdy boat, nineteen feet long and six of beam, built of marine plywood over an oak frame and powered by a four-cylinder, seventy-five-horsepower motor. They had arranged for gas deliveries at Diamond Creek and Havasu and would pick up more at Bright Angel Creek, if they got that far. But Harry turned out to be an accurate prophet. At mile 217, a shade above the high point Aleson, Vickers, and Moore had reached in 1943, a lateral wave sent the *Esmeralda II's* stern crashing against one of the very few trees that grow at the water's edge in the canyon. Still, a rock would have been worse, for the tree supplied a convenient branch to which they fastened their block and tackle for lifting the boat's stern, as must be done when repairing an inboard propeller. The patching completed, they limped back to Lake Mead. None of this would have happened, Hudson believed, if they'd had more push, and he ordered a one-hundred-twenty-five-horsepower engine for a high-water run the following year.

Marston believed they needed experience as well as more power. During his last run with Nevills a few weeks later, he studied every hazard along the way, trying to imagine what each would be like during the high water of spring. But that proved unsatisfactory, too. So he proposed to Hudson that they learn what they were up against by first running the *Esmeralda II* down the canyon the following spring. Then they could turn around and, with confidence, blast their way back.

The round trip, he went on, would produce reams of publicity (Ed hoped to make a feature motion picture of the expedition) and would also ease the gasoline problem. Fuel from two depots set up by mule train, one at Bright Angel Creek (mile 87.5) and the other at Whitmore Wash (mile 188) would be enough to carry them down to Pierce Ferry, but they would need much more on the way back. They could provide for this by loading on extra gasoline at Lees Ferry and the other depots on the way down and dropping it off at convenient pick-up points along the way.

For safety's sake, he added, two boats should go together. He also made various technical suggestions about strengthening the *Esmeralda II* and protecting its engine with canvas shields against dousings from big waves sweeping over the bow.

Hudson agreed to everything except the second boat. This was his baby and he did not want to share the glory with another captain. Denied the second craft, Marston invited Bestor Robinson, a former president of the Sierra Club and a skilled mountaineer, to join the *Esmeralda II's* crew, which otherwise was the same as in 1948. Robinson would carry a map of every trail in the vicinity — some far apart, to be sure — and in case of real trouble could scale the cliffs for help. A long shot but better than nothing.

They left Lees Ferry June 12, 1949, on sixty thousand cubic feet a second and, smacking hard against the big waves, ran thirty-three miles through Marble Canyon to a rocky beach a short distance upstream from the vast hollow in the left-bank cliffs known as Redwall Cavern. There they parked the boat and rode a dizzy, swaying cable to a camp the Bureau of Reclamation had established on a bench hundreds of feet above the cavern — the only place big enough to hold the buildings at flood tide. Designed to house engineers and workers examining the area for a dam, the camp was supplied by another cable dropping down from the rim, the handiwork, as was the river cable, of Rod Sanderson, a rugged former All-American football player and one-time employee of King Saud of Saudi Arabia. Though the *Esmeralda II* crew spent the night in this strange eyrie, nothing in their journals indicates that they felt any apprehension about what it might mean to the future of one of America's loveliest gorges, to say nothing of its effect on the kind of adventure that kept drawing them to the river year after year. (Neither had Aleson seemed to worry about a dam at Bridge Canyon.)

From the cavern they raced on toward Bright Angel. In spite of the canvas shields Marston had devised for the motor hatch, waves surging across the bow occasionally caused the ignition to sputter out. But when protection was needed most, in Hance, the device worked. Marston, who took the wheel there, got too far to the right and catapulted into a gaping hole. But the power held and the boat, its cockpit filled almost to the brim, surged up and out.

At Bright Angel they learned that the mules bringing in their gasoline had stampeded for some cause known only to mules and had strewed cans all over the canyon. Did they want to order more? In a passion they said yes, and the load reached them at 6:00 A.M. the next morning. On they roared, the river rising under them. The high water smoothed some rapids, turned others to fury. They camped at Tapeats Creek so Marston could fish for rainbow trout in its crystal water. Two miles farther on they saw lovely Deer Creek Falls dropping a lacy mist directly into the swollen river.

Their trip was attracting attention. John Riffey, long-time ranger in what was then Grand Canyon National Monument (now part of the Park), had clambered with a few friends down the difficult trail from his station near Toroweap to watch them tackle the cauldron at Lava Falls. The gas stop at Whitmore Wash, nine miles farther on, was downright crowded. A barely passable truck road led across the Esplanade to within a mile and a half of the rim. There a trail, which rancher Chet Bundy had said could be used for bringing in gasoline, took over and wound down to a sandy flat beside the river. Thirty-seven people, most of them Bundy relatives, had come along with the mules to watch the performance.

Hurried along by those careful logistics, the river runners reached Pierce Ferry five days and ten minutes after leaving Lees Ferry. The first motor run down the Grand Canyon, but not a fair figure, they decided, because of the delay at Bright Angel. They had actually been on the water only four and a half days, and so they attached that figure to their record. But alas for plans. On the way back, the same current that had sped them downstream halted them short of Diamond Creek.

. . . nothing in their journals indicates that they felt any apprehension about what it might mean to the future of one of America's loveliest gorges.

118

Hudson vowed to try again in 1950, on lower water. Assured he would still be in command of the expedition, he agreed to a second boat, a nineteen-foot Chris-Craft Speedster, inboard motor, purchased by Dock Marston. Marston recruited as its crew Joe Desloge of Missouri and Guy Forcier, an aviator who knew engines. Hudson stuck to his old-timers, his son Ed, Willie Taylor, and, to replace Marston on the *Esmeralda II*, Bill Belknap of Boulder City, Nevada.

The river was fairly low when they started, again on June 12, but rose rapidly. In spite of frequent engine trouble, Hudson put *Esmeralda II* safely through Soap Creek, Hance, Horn, and Hermit. But at relatively mild Boucher, five or six waves, "a hell of a lot bigger than I expected," he wrote later, "really beat the hell out of us." The motor conked out. A "vicious eddy" carried them back upstream and bashed them into a jumble of boulders.

As the Chris-Craft roared by without its occupants seeing the *Esmeralda II*, Hudson managed to start the motor again. It pulled them out, then died once more. They rowed through Crystal, not as formidable in those days as it became in 1966, when a flash flood filled it with mammoth boulders. They almost got through Tuna Creek Rapid as well. Then, just as they saw Marston coming back upstream to learn what had happened to them, Tuna's tail waves threw them into an eddy that swept them toward a pile of boulders on the right bank. As a cushion wave bounced them back, Belknap and young Ed jumped desperately for the boulders with a rope, hoping to snub the *Esmeralda II* before it was swept on into worse trouble. They could not get set in time. The revolving eddy carried the boat around in a wide circle. This time it hit the cliffs with a shuddering crash. Willie Taylor, fortunately wearing his life jacket, was jarred off into the water. As he fell, a trailing bow line somehow came loose and caught in a loop around his neck.

Right while Willie was falling, Belknap and Ed managed to snub the *Esmeralda II* to the boulders. Marston took after Taylor, floating toward another rapid just downstream. One of the crew threw him a rope. It tangled with the one around his neck and he was almost choked to death when Marston, unaware of the problem, slammed around to miss a hole and powered back upstream, dragging Taylor under the water.

They got him out barely in time and then clustered around the stricken *Esmeralda II*. Big Ed Hudson was in despair. The boat was smashed beyond repair, he said. Let it go to an honorable grave. As the others argued with him, he cast off the ropes, and watched the dream craft float away downstream.

Marston ferried the stranded crew from their precarious perches on the boulders to a wide beach on the left bank. There was no possibility, however, that the Chris-Craft could carry all seven of them through the canyon. As the heaviest pair in the group, the Hudsons agreed to drop out. If Ed had been in good condition, he and his son could have climbed out to the South Rim by way of the Tonto and Hermit trails. But he wasn't, and so the others said they would go to Havasu Creek, fifty-eight miles downstream. From there Belknap would walk the dozen miles past the creek's spectacular waterfalls to the Indian village of Supai and telephone for a helicopter.

Off they went, leaving the Hudsons on the beach with their bedrolls and enough food for two days. Ten miles down they passed the *Esmeralda II* bobbing along and listing badly. They did not stop to see how badly she was damaged. As the afternoon waned, Marston decided — on a hunch, he said later — to stop at Tapeats Creek, twenty-five miles short of Havasu, and try the fishing.

Up on the South Rim, meanwhile, Marston's wife Margaret and Hudson's wife were moving from point to point, using binoculars to watch such short stretches of the river as they could see. They knew the expedition's schedule, and when too much time elapsed without a glimpse of the boats at a certain spot, they sensed trouble. Impulsively Margaret drove to the heliport, which had begun service less than a month before with two machines capable of carrying only a single passenger each, and hired a pilot to fly her into the canyon. Glimpsing the *Esmeralda II* in an eddy, they turned upstream, found the Hudsons and learned what had happened. Hurriedly then, to save Belknap his arduous walk, they flew down the canyon, caught the others at Tapeats Creek and spent the night with them.

The next morning Margaret and the pilot flew back to the heliport. Its two machines picked up the stranded father and son, but the motor of the one carrying big Ed — was he a jinx to engines? — failed and it crashed. Though they suffered only a severe shaking up, considerable shuttling was necessary to get everyone out. An expensive ordeal — $3,500 for the *Esmeralda II* (dollars were bigger then than now) and $700 for the helicopter service, plus $9,000 that the company which had insured the wrecked chopper spent lifting the pieces out of the canyon and reassembling them.

There is a sequel. Nevills' successors, Jim Rigg and Frank Wright, came down the river about a month later with three cataract boats and an inboard powerboat. Jim had never handled a motorboat before, but he operated a flying service in Grand Junction, Colorado, and knew engines. He adopted a technique different from Marston's. Dock liked to hit the barrier waves at the top of a rapid full tilt, get the boat to planing, veer toward the bank, and skim over the eddies. Jim, who distrusted eddies, instinctively idled into the tongue as one did with a cataract boat, and used his power just enough to adjust his position in respect to waves, rocks, and holes.

He got himself and his passengers wet that way, but it was fun, and a motor beat rowing the quiet stretches. By the time the little fleet was halfway through the canyon he figured that two or three of them would make a valuable addition to their company. Imagine his joy, then, when he saw the *Esmeralda II* perched on a flat about sixty feet from and ten feet higher than the current water level. Taking off the cylinder head, he found a blown gasket. After he had ingeniously repaired it and had patched the leaks in the hull, the whole party manhandled the derelict into the river. The motor still wasn't running right, but Jim nursed the temperamental craft through the bad water they met and on to the docks at Boulder City.

There the Park Service impounded the boat until the question of title could be determined. Notified of what had occurred, Hudson flew out to claim his property. Bitter arguments followed. Actually, the law of salvage was on Hudson's side; Rigg was entitled only to fair compensation for his work. No one seemed to know that, however, and yet no one was prepared to take the matter to court. In the end the Park Service worked out a compromise. *It* would take the boat over and — a bit of immortality for Hudson — put it on display in the Visitor Center on the South Rim, where it remains. If Rigg got anything — the point is obscure — it came from the Park and amounted to little.

Marston bought a second boat in 1951 and, departing from Lees Ferry once more on June 12, led down a convoy of five motor craft, two of them outboards piloted by Jim Jordan and Rod Sanderson. There were several upsets on the trip, but the outboards got through, the first of their kind to do so. Nearly every year thereafter Marston led another thundering fleet through the gorges, gradually increasing the power of his boats and consistently using outboards. But he made no more attempts to come upstream. Adequate craft did not yet exist, he said.

Not everyone approved of motors in the canyon. Purists complained about the noise and said that such uses of mechanical power ran contrary to the philosophy on which the National Park System had been built. Why not stick to oared craft — either neoprene rafts or wooden boats — that let travelers come into full rapport with the river? Jim Rigg and Frank Wright found themselves in the middle of the controversy. Jim planned to continue using powerboats for those of this customers who wanted this newest form of recreation thrill, but he also loved the wooden cataracts, as did his brother Bob. In the spring of 1951, while attending boat races in Wyoming, the pair came to an impulsive decision. Why not show how fast a cataract boat could go through the Grand Canyon, in comparison to powerboats?

They had to move fast because of other commitments. Bob Rigg spent the night of June 11 trailering the boat toward Lees Ferry, where Jim was waiting, ran out of gas seven miles away and hiked in. An Indian helped them rescue the stalled trailer, and they were on the river, without breakfast, at 5:30 A.M. One rowed while the other, sprawled on the deck, kept shifting position to maintain the boat's balance. They made and ate sandwiches as they traveled. Whenever one rower wearied, they traded places. Toward dusk they collapsed into bed beside Bass Rapid, cold, wet, and supperless, and slept so hard their alarm clock did not waken them as early as intended.

After a breakfast of more sandwiches, they made a late start at 6:15 A.M., hurtled through Lava Falls — the river was at a perfect stage for that — and reached Diamond Creek just at dusk. "From there," Jim reported, "we ran everything by the scant moonlight or the Braille system." Log jams stymied them on the lake. Exhausted, they camped from 12:30 A.M. to sunrise, started out again, and, about a mile from Pierce Ferry, met Bill Belknap and Jim Jordan, who had come up to give them a tow. The two-hundred-eighty-mile run had taken two and a half days. So much for motorboats.

True record seeking and mere stunts — sometimes it was hard to tell the difference. At various times young boatmen and passengers had sought to enliven their trips by floating through single rapids in their life jackets, on air mattresses, or just swimming. And, of course, there were White's and Aleson's wild rides in 1945 and 1946. But it remained for two life insurance salesmen, Bill Beer, twenty-six, and John Daggett, twenty-seven, to decide to spend their vacations floating the full length of the canyon.

They planned carefully, each filling a pair of large, black, watertight rubber boxes with sleeping gear, flashlights, cameras, first-aid kits, and food for twenty-five days. They wore khaki shorts over the bottom half of long-handled underwear, rubber shirts for warmth, Mae West life jackets, and rubber swim fins. They took off from Lees Ferry on Easter Sunday, April 10, 1955. In quiet water they swam and towed their boxes. When rapids loomed, they generally landed, picked out a course among the boulders, walked back into the water,

In the spring of 1951, while attending boat races in Wyoming, the pair came to an impulsive decision.

121

and snugged a box under each arm. The arrangement elevated their upper bodies somewhat, but seldom enough for them to see much of the route they had selected. They stuck their feet out in front, tried to guide themselves by markers on the shore, and changed directions by pivoting on one box or the other.

Waves knocked out their breath, they plunged into holes. Choking under smothers of brown foam, they gasped for air whenever a glimpse of blue sky persuaded them their heads were momentarily clear. They were bruised by rocks and chilled through by the April water. They stayed in the river about five hours a day, then crawled out and hiked to warm up before making camp. Because one of the rubber boxes sprang a leak, they ascended the trail to the South Rim to replenish spoiled supplies — and sleep in good beds. They also spent two days hiking up Havasu Creek to Supai and back. On May 5, they emerged from a transit that, as far as is known, has not been repeated.

The overwhelming part of the adventure, they said, was the unspoiled beauty that engulfed them. Bill Beer was moved enough by it to return the next year for a run in one of three aluminum, thirty-horsepower boats commanded by Dock Marston. Among the passengers was Willie Taylor, who had almost been choked to death in 1950. Three days into Marble Gorge, in an enchanting stretch near Harding Rapid, Willie died of a heart attack. They buried him, says Frank Masland, who offered the prayer for him, high above high water, looking across the river he loved so well.

Georgie White, meanwhile, shrugging aside masculine condescension about a woman trying to handle the Colorado River, was carrying on her own experiments with heavy, black, surplus army assault rafts. Because they were not as stable as she liked, she played safe by requesting the passengers she took with her on share-the-expense arrangements to walk around the most exciting rapids. They complained so bitterly she sought a solution.

Three of the boats tied side by side would keep each other from flipping, she decided. The device would also allow her to add to the number of passengers she took through the canyon on a single trip. As would a thirty-foot "pontoon" boat like those just then being introduced on the Yampa. Their origin was the huge, inflatable cylinders the Army used for building pontoon bridges across rivers. To transform two parallel pontoons into a raft, one simply pulled the ends together to form a shallow, open box, somewhat pointed at the bow, square at the stern. Georgie framed them with wooden braces for rigidity, used transverse planks for seats, and attached stout iron oarlocks for two big, heavy oars.

Her first major experiment with both types came in 1954. After tying three fourteen-foot rafts together side by side she added two sweep oars, one protruding in front, the other in back so that they functioned like the sweeps the Hydes had used on their Idaho scow. Who the first oarsmen were we do not know. Georgie was certainly involved; her husband Whitey, who made his only river trip that year, and her brother Paul probably were also. In spite of upsets, both craft worked well, the pontoon in particular. It wallowed with a heavy rolling motion through big explosion waves, straddled holes, and bounced off rocks that, Georgie believed, would have sunk a wooden boat.

122

Well pleased, she kept elaborating. The three small rafts evolved into the triple rig she used for "thrill rides." Power for hurrying the collection over the canyon's long, smooth stretches came from an outboard motor mounted on the back of the center raft. On approaching a rapid, the boatman swung the three boats sideways to the current and let the rig buck high and unrestrained through the waves, the passengers whooping in delight — and once in awhile in terror. It was not unknown for one raft to fold back over another, creating what the boatmen called a "Georgie sandwich." But she never carried any metal with sharp edges in her boats, and painful injuries were rare.

The next year she tied two twenty-eight foot pontoons on either side of one thirty-three feet long. She cut away the rear part of the middle raft's floor and set a motor in the hole, but water surged through the opening, filling the raft and increasing its weight. To end the problem she simply removed the whole bottom and laid planking on top of the central pontoons. The whole, cinched tight with an intriguing weaving of nylon rope, was called a G-rig, for Georgie — a true tour bus for the river.

A ride on a G-rig could be hair raising, too. Walter Kirschbaum, who, in 1960, apparently took the first rigid kayak through Lava Falls, looked back just in time to see a big G-rig plow into the rapid's topmost hole. One outside pontoon rose to a vertical position, then went on over by forty-five degrees, so that "its passengers were hanging head down over the heads of their companions in the center pontoon for a split second. . . . Then the linking device flung the boat back to its normal position." Kirschbaum could not hear the passengers, but caught himself screaming in fright just watching. Yet no one fell; no one was hurt.

To support herself during those years Georgie sold real estate. Whitey, who never went on another river ride, always helped set up the silver-painted rigs at Lees Ferry — it took two and a half days there to prepare for each trip — painted "The Woman of the River" in red around the perimeter (the name came from a television show in which Georgie had participated), saw each party off, and drove to Temple Bar on Lake Mead to collapse the boats for transportation to the next adventure. "Georgie is his god," wrote one who knew him. He thought she was the greatest river runner of all time, and "his self-appointed mission in life was the upholding and enhancement of her reputation."

She was unique. In 1956, when financial survival was still uncertain, she wrote Aleson, "I know I am right in living TODAY, YESTERDAY IS GONE, TOMORROW MAY NEVER COME." She worked around her boats in a leopard-spotted bathing suit and red-mesh T-shirt. Detractors belittled her pontoons as ugly baloney boats, but ordinary people were fascinated by them. She had opened the canyon to anyone who wanted to go. Having gone, they became not just river rats but Royal River Rats, and were initiated by having an egg broken over their heads. They loved it and flocked back for more.

Others imitated her big pontoon, though few tried the "thrill ride" rig. Motorboats and cataract boats held their own. By mid-1954 the number of people who had gone through the canyon since Powell's run in 1869 had risen to two hundred. Five years later it was above five hundred. Noting the trend, an article in the *National Geographic* predicted that a thousand a year was not beyond possibility. The effect of this on the canyon was not discussed, nor was the possible impact of the high dam rising (1957-1963) in Glen Canyon, fifteen miles above Lees Ferry.[1]

And still no one had gone upstream, a challenge which shone brightly before the eyes of the Indiana Gear Works, manufacturers, under license from the inventors, of what they called "Turbocraft." This highly maneuverable boat was driven not by propellers, which tended to cavitate at low speed, but by a powerful jet of water, a system developed in New Zealand by Bill Hamilton and his son Jon for use on the swift mountain streams of their native country. A traveling Kentuckian, Bill Austin, helped obtain the American rights to the invention for the Indiana Gear Works. Seeking to boost sales, he then conceived the idea of sending a small fleet of Turbocraft thundering up the Grand Canyon.

In the course of furthering the plan, Austin contacted Dock Marston, by then the guru of gasoline. Dock said they'd not make it, and, indeed, a preliminary test in 1959 fell as short as some of Harry Aleson's had. They were so impressive in their failure, however, that when an all-out effort was scheduled for the spring of 1960, Marston agreed to take charge.

They were so impressive in their failure, however, that when an all-out effort was scheduled for the spring of 1960, Marston agreed to take charge.

He followed the routines established with Ed Hudson — a downstream run to familiarize the pilots with the river (because of his age, sixty-six, he did not plan to take a wheel himself) and to cache gasoline between the fuel depots. An immediate return trip would follow. May was to be the month. Since he had started most of his own runs in June, the choice is puzzling, unless predictions of an early snowmelt in the mountains hurried him along.

Two of the boats chosen for the attempt were twenty-four-foot cathedral-hull cruisers with triple bows and square foredecks. Their jet units, designed for ocean racing, were powered by two one-hundred-eighty-five-horsepower motors. They were named *Big Red* and *Big Yellow* and painted accordingly. Their small sisters, the *Wee Red* and *Wee Yellow*, were both eighteen feet long and powered by single one-hundred-eighty-five-horsepower motors. Hulls were of fiberglass. There were no air compartments or styrofoam linings to aid flotation.

Personnel gathered from half the globe. Jon Hamilton, son of the inventor, and Guy Mannering, an expert jetboat pilot, came from New Zealand with their wives Joyce and Margie. Others arrived from Hawaii, California, Indiana, and Washington, DC. The sun-seared beach at Lees Ferry was chaotic with three hundred five-gallon tins of gasoline; packages of food, each marked according to the meal it would provide; cooking and tool kits; life jackets; cameras; and rubber bags stuffed with personal duffel. Thunderous trial runs on the quiet water near the ferry brought some head shakings. The big cruisers did not maneuver well in the narrow confines of the river, a problem that would be intensified by the state of the water — about twenty-two thousand cubic feet per second instead of the forty-five thousand Marston had hoped for.

A little after noon on May 3, 1960, they shoved off. Four miles downstream the *Big Red* crippled herself on a submerged rock. Repairs could be effected as soon as a heavy block and tackle could be brought in from Page, but the impatient rivermen could do nothing to jack up the level of the water. After a night of vacillating they postponed the trip until June 18.

As they were reloading for the second attempt, Georgie and Whitey arrived

1. E.C. LaRue, it will be recalled, had wanted the dam built only four miles above the ferry. It was moved to the higher site in order to obtain more secure footing.

to put their rigs together. After noticing that the river had already peaked at forty-eight thousand cubic feet per second and was falling fast, Georgie predicted that though the motorboats might reach Boulder City in eight days, as the crew planned, they would never, in spite of all that power, get back through the exposed rocks in Lava Falls.

Undeterred, the party set off in high spirits. Three of the boats carried three passengers each. The fourth, the *Big Yellow*, held four — Joyce Hamilton, her husband Jon, Guy Mannering (the New Zealanders called themselves Kiwis), and Jack Reynolds of Tacoma, Washington, in charge of the commissary. The observation party, who would follow progress from the South Rim for as long a distance as possible, consisted of the wives of three of the boat people — Margaret Marston, Margie Mannering, and Fran Belknap, plus Fran and Bill Belknap's sixteen-year-old son, Buzz. The chief pilot was Bill Austin. Marston, who had prepared a written account of the hazards in every major rapid, was chief navigator.

To Joyce the speed was a frustration. In spite of the oppressive heat and gritty winds she wanted time to explore, to soak in the beauty of this canyon so unlike anything she had seen before. There was no gainsaying the excitement, however. They boomed through many of the rapids without pausing to scout them, and, once through, one of the boats often powered back up in order to get the feel of the turbulent water. Convinced by the tests that the twenty-four footers would not be suitable for the return run, they telephoned the Indiana Gear Works from Phantom Ranch to send two eighteen-foot replacements to Boulder City. And because things were going well, they invited Margie Mannering and young Buzz Belknap to hike down the Kaibab Trail and join them for the rest of the downward run.

At Lava Falls the river showed its teeth. Bill Austin plowed into the huge ridge of water at the top of the maelstrom too far to the right, and the *Big Red* took to the air. The impact of the landing broke his right tibia, a compound fracture that exposed four inches of bone. The boat lurched into an eddy. Marston took the wheel, made the rest of the run, and pulled into the first beach, half a mile below the rapid.

As soon as the others had joined them, they gingerly eased Bill out of the boat onto the sand. Quickly the men erected a shelter of canvas and oars and gave him a shot of morphine while a dressing was being applied to the wound. The women made a saline solution of boiled, muddy river water for keeping the cloth and wound moist during the night, until Austin could be moved to a hospital for repairs. Meanwhile Dock and his son Garth in the *Wee Red* and Dick Young in the *Wee Yellow* raced eight miles to the fuel depot at Whitmore Wash. They knew that Chuck Ritchey, Superintendent of Lake Mead Recreation Area, was waiting there to finish the run with them, and hoped a ranger would have accompanied him down the trail — as, indeed, proved to be the case. The ranger hiked back up the zigzags, and by mule, truck, and by telephone a message was relayed to the nearest air force base. Shortly after dawn the next morning a helicopter evacuated the injured man.

On June 28 the others reached Boulder City. Spurred by the dropping river, they worked frantically in the unairconditioned marina to overhaul the *Wee Red* and *Wee Yellow* and to prepare the new eighteen-footers, named on the spot *Kiwi* and *Dock*, for the up-river run. Some crew members dropped out and were replaced. On July 6 the party took to the water again on seventeen thousand cubic feet per second. No women accompanied this group.

The big struggle came, as they knew it would, at Lava Falls. Each boat ran as high as possible between the rough water and the shore. From there the entire group helped portage its cargo over the boulders to the top. Motor roaring, the driver of the lightened craft began his probes, inching higher, looking for an opening he could dart through, getting caught by a surge, floundering, and dropping back, the cockpit filled with water in spite of the tightly laced tarpaulin that covered every inch of space the pilot did not need.

It took Jon Hamilton one day and four attempts to put the *Kiwi* over the top. Guy Mannering tried twice with the *Wee Red* and was slammed twice against the same rock. When Hamilton took over, he was hurled, against reason, against the identical jagged boulder. The impact split part of the deck away from the side and he had to turn and come down fast under power before the *Wee Red* sank. The *Wee Yellow* couldn't make it either, and there was glumness that evening both in the camp and three thousand feet above at Toroweap, where Joyce Hamilton and a friend were watching through binoculars.

The next day began auspiciously. After an hour of digging in against the waves like a football lineman, the *Wee Yellow* broke through and topped the tongue. The *Wee Red*, patched together again, failed, however, and lurched back to hang up on three rocks. They pried the boat loose with driftwood levers, and this time Jon found the right slot and forced the howling jet over the top. Only the *Dock* was left, and Jon took her up, too, in dusk so deep he used the running lights.

Troubles were not over. Crew member Ed I'Anson cracked four ribs in Bedrock. Dubendorff pounded the *Wee Yellow* until the upper deck was torn from the hull two-thirds of the way around the bow — a miserable repair job working with sticky fiberglass in 100° Fahrenheit heat. Still, it was a joy to meet Georgie and her dudes a few miles farther up and tell them what they had accomplished. She believed reluctantly and said, well, they'd never get through the rock garden at precipitous Horn Creek. They did, though, by finding a sort of open gutter between the big waves and the shore.

They reached Phantom Ranch weary but exhilarated, and the next morning thundered happily into Grapevine. Jon Hamilton took the *Kiwi* through without a bobble, but the *Wee Yellow* smacked a wave that tore the repaired deck from the hull. The boat nose-dived and sank, her screeching jet blowing out a farewell plume of water. The two craft waiting below fished out the men and a little equipment as it floated by, but irreplaceable film, tools necessary for the rest of the run, cameras, and many personal possessions were lost.

The party dropped back to Phantom Ranch and ordered replacements rushed in from Flagstaff. Then on again, through Grapevine, Sockdolager, and Hance. On between the high red walls of Marble Gorge, on through the stubborn current of Soap Creek.

So the "impossible" had been done. George Morrison, publicity director of the Indiana Gear Works, said the costly round trip had produced engineering bonanzas: the company had learned more from it than they could have discovered during twenty-five years of normal operations. But the success also presented the Park Service with a dilemma: What should its stance be regarding technological developments that could alter the river and river running forever?

.

Epilogue

AND NOW

W hile Glen Canyon Dam was being built, thousands of people took boat trips through the gorge it was plugging, eager to glimpse for the last time wonders that were about to be lost forever. Inevitably interest carried over into the Grand Canyon. Beginning in 1959, the number of people embarking from Lees Ferry increased at an annual average of fifty-nine percent. Then, in January 1963, the gates of the dam's diversion tunnels were closed so that the reservoir could begin filling. With only one thousand cubic feet per second trickling through to keep fish and aquatic animals alive, boating with standard-sized craft became impossible.

Yet questions arose. What did the bottoms of the once fearsome rapids really look like? What could be learned about scour holes, eddies, and the hydraulics that deposited the sand beaches beloved by campers? Could photographs be taken at frequent intervals for comparison with pictures of high water taken earlier from the same spots?

The National Park Service contracted with photographer Bill Belknap to do the work. He lined up *Argosy* magazine for an article and asked Dock Marston, sixty-nine, if he wanted to go along. The answer was an emphatic "Yes!" and then five more people were recruited: Bill's son Buzz; Mack Miller, a Temple Bar boatman; Cliff Segerblom, his son Tick, and daughter Robin. The last three, however, would have to leave at Bright Angel Creek.

Their main problem was finding craft small, strong, and versatile enough to follow the fast twisting, steeply diving currents. As they pondered, young Buzz Belknap recalled a seven-foot polyethelene dinghy, called a sportyak, he and Tick had seen tied to a big cruiser at the Boulder City marina. Borrowing it, some of the group put it aboard a motorboat, took it to the head of Lake Mead,

128

and played around in Gneiss Canyon's rough water. Everything went fine, and they ordered seven sportyaks from the manufacturers in Detroit, Michigan, — one boat per person.

They were bare-boned craft. They had no splash shields and each occupant had to lace in his duffel sacks as best he could with criss-crossing cords. Within four miles of launching, they discovered that the oarlocks for the little four-and-a-half-foot oars would not do. Halting at Navajo Bridge, where their wives were watching from above, they used their walkie-talkie radios to ask that replacements, bought at Page, be delivered at the head of Jackass Canyon, which enters Marble Gorge at Badger Rapid. As Marston and Belknap were descending the canyon after picking up the material, a sudden flash flood cut them off in a side gully, and considerable roundabout clambering and hiking were necessary before the trip could be resumed.

Other flash floods dumped so much silt into the shrunken river that the water became undrinkable, and the party had to pour bucketfuls of the stuff into one of the sportyaks, where the mud settled out during the night. Lacking splash shields, the little craft quickly filled with water and upset easily. There was little chance to dry out after a spill, for rains were frequent. The four who made the complete run — Marston, Miller, and the two Belknaps — spent twenty-seven days reaching Lake Mead.[1] In spite of the hardships, Belknap remained enamored of the little craft, adapted them to river running, and pioneered sportyak tourist trips on the Colorado's gentler tributaries — the Green, the San Juan, the Dolores.

The Bureau of Reclamation, eager to demonstrate the utilitarian virtues of the Glen Canyon Dam, hoped not to reopen the gates there until enough water had accumulated to allow the huge turbines in the powerhouses to begin generating electricity. Revenues from the sale of that power would eventually pay for irrigation projects in the states of the Upper Colorado River Basin. Runoff from the Rockies had been light, however, and only about half of the necessary water accumulated. Meanwhile, Lake Mead, deprived of its normal inflow, was dropping toward the point at which the production of electricity there would halt. Quarrels immediately erupted between the power users of Southern California, who wanted no lapse in deliveries, and impatient users in the Upper Basin, who wanted no delays in starting.

Seeking a compromise, the Secretary of the Interior, Stewart Udall, ordered a partial reopening. Assured that the flow would continue for some weeks, a party of dedicated Sierra Club members embarked in May 1964, at Lees Ferry on a crusade. The Bureau of Reclamation, they well knew, planned to put three new hydroelectric dams in the Grand Canyon itself — one in Marble Gorge; another at Bridge Canyon; and a tunnel that would divert ninety-one percent of the stream's normal flow between the dams to a generating station in Kanab Canyon, from whence the well-used water would return to the Grand Canyon. Environmentalists were in arms, determined to block the projects, as they had not been able, partly because of their own dilatoriness, to block the canyon-drowning cement plug in Glen Canyon.

Part of their strategy revolved around showing the nation, by words and pictures, how rich and irreplaceable a trip through the Grand Canyon was. Into a book describing the progress of their journey, author François Leydet would

Meanwhile, Lake Mead, deprived of its normal inflow, was dropping toward the point at which the production of electricity there would halt.

1. Two German kayakers also struggled through the canyon that year, bringing the total to six.

weave a summary of the canyon's human and natural history, its stupendous geology, and the spirit of untrammeled wilderness that breathed through it. Accompanying the text would be the finest color photographs available, their message heightened by quotations from authors ranging chronologically from John Wesley Powell and Clarence E. Dutton to Loren Eiseley and Joseph Wood Krutch.

The party consisted of Leydet and his wife Patience; photographer Phillip Hyde and his wife; William Jones, painter and photographer; Dr. Joseph Hall, biologist; boatman Martin Litton, a director of the Sierra Club; and P.T. Reilly, an expert river runner, and his wife Suzie. They traveled in what they called dories, a kind of conservative reaction to the growing popularity of rubber rafts. During the high-water years of the late 1950s, both Litton and Reilly had experimented with versions of the old-style cataract boats first developed by Norman Nevills. They weren't quite satisfied. In fact, Reilly, having lost all his spare oars during the first eighty-five miles of a 1959 trip, decided to halt his journey — and his river career — near Pipe Spring Rapid, where the Bright Angel Trail to the South Rim reaches the river. Filling his boats with rocks, he punched holes in them below the waterline and sank them. Goodbye, Colorado.

Except it wasn't. In 1962, Litton saw some trim boats on the McKenzie River in Oregon he thought could be adapted to the Colorado. The main change would be to make the new ones bigger, with oarlocks placed at the widest part of the beam so the rower could exert maximum pull on long, sixteen-foot oars. An Oregonian, Keith Steele, made and fitted out one such boat for Litton and a hull for Reilly, who did the rest of the work himself.

Litton named his *Portola* after an early Spanish explorer; Reilly called his *Suzie Too* for his wife. Both were sixteen-feet long, pointed at both ends, flatbottomed, brightly painted, and equipped with watertight compartments fore and aft. A rush order to Oregon brought them the third one they needed for the 1964 trip. Named *Lucky Pierre* in the canyon, it was somewhat smaller than its mates and so new there had had been no time to install compartments to help flotation and preclude sinking.

At the start, the weather was cold and rainy. The river was low, the rapids choppy. There was an upset at mile 75 (later Nevills Rapid) and another in Ruby. That, too, was part of what they were looking for: the sense (however illusory) that the river had a will and character of its own. If dams were built, the surge of adrenalin that came from meeting the challenge head-on would never be experienced again.

The illusion of a free, self-willed river soon vanished, for the Colorado now flowed according to human whim. After they had lined their boats through Lava Falls and had coasted on to a camp half a mile below Whitmore Wash, a National Park Service plane flew over, low, and dropped a message. The Upper Basin states, they learned later, had forced an unscheduled closing of the gates at Glen Canyon Dam. The travelers, the message warned, should consider getting out where a trail existed, at Whitmore Wash.

That meant abandoning boats, supplies, and equipment. Defiantly they decided to go ahead on the chance they could keep up with floatable water until they reached Lake Mead and its unsightly deposits of silt. Rowing hard and feeling an intensified bond with the unsuspecting wildlife they passed, they escaped, carrying still more ammunition for their arguments. A living river wiped out so easily! No. Let the nation preserve what it had.

Meanwhile the public's interest in the canyon kept building momentum. Because the reservoir back of Glen Canyon Dam was trapping silt, the stream it released into the canyon was deemed to look as clear as a mountain stream, albeit tinged to a pale, translucent green by microscopic algae growing in Lake Powell. (Side canyons carrying rain water off the plateaus could quickly bring back the familiar stain of red.) Motorboats, pontoon boats, rafts, and dories were being steadily improved. Boatmen were increasing their skills; rescue services were available. By controlling the high water of spring and the low water of fall, the dam, it was believed, made the river safer. But mostly, as Georgie White quickly realized, an increasing number of Americans had become eager to see the unique wildernesses of their country, about which much was written during the decade of the 1960s. She made ready for them, as did about twenty other commercial companies operating under concession from the National Park Service.

In 1969 a hard-hitting coalition of environmentalists, their arguments supplemented by Leydet's eloquent book, *Time and the River Flowing,* and by the new breed of river recreationists, prevailed on Congress to end the immediate threat of dams within the National Park. Later legislation extended the boundaries of the Park to include both Marble Gorge and most of what had been administered as Grand Canyon National Monument. The Lake Mead Recreation Area embraced the lower part of the gorge, so that with the exception of the Hualapai and Havasupai Indian reservations, the entire Grand Canyon was at last federally controlled and protected for public use under the organic laws of the National Park Service.

As interest fed on itself, the influx of humans increased. Five hundred and forty-seven persons went through the canyon in 1965. Among them, in wooden boats, were Senator Barry Goldwater, recent nominee for the presidency of the United States, and his son, Barry, Jr., a California congressman.

By 1970 the number of travelers had jumped above ten thousand a year, and both the Park Service and commercial boaters feared for the quality of the trips. Radical steps followed. Earlier, any qualified applicant could get a permit to run the canyon. After 1970, no additional grants were issued, and counts of "user days" were launched. (One person on the river for any part of a day constitutes, statistically, a user day. Thus one person on a two-week trip adds fourteen user days to the table.) Because preliminary figures for 1971 indicated 106,000 such days, that was the quota set for 1972. A surprise emerged. Though 16,432 people were on the river in 1972, the number of user days amounted to only 89,000 — five and half days per person. The implication was that a lot of people were clipping along at a fast rate aboard big, motorized baloney boats and rafts and were piling up in thick crowds at such popular places as the Indian granaries near Nankoweap, at Elves Chasm, Deer Creek Falls, and Havasu Creek.

Stringent rules followed. The number of annual user days would stay at 89,900, but they would be spread across more months. Limits were placed on the size of parties and on the minimum and maximum time a group could stay in the gorge.

Boats with high horsepower motors were prohibited. Non-commercial users were really crimped. In 1972, forty-four private parties asked for permits and all were granted. In 1976, three hundred and eighty applied; thirty-four were lucky.[2] Other restrictions forbade the building of fires except under special circumstances; they left ugly rings on the beaches, and, besides, no driftwood for fuel got past the dam. Training rules were laid down for boatmen. Cooks were not to spill grease or leave garbage hidden in bushes. By 1977 every party was carrying portable toilets and removing all fecal matter. But no rule could be laid down to prevent the gradual disappearance of the beaches in upper Marble Canyon as the river's normal load of replenishing silt settled out of the water in Lake Powell. Nor did spring floods occur to flush the canyon clean and reduce the increasing salinity of the water.

Another troublesome factor was the daily fluctuation of water levels. As afternoons heated up in central and southern Arizona, tens of thousands of air conditioners started humming. To meet the demand for electricity, water was poured through the generators at Glen Canyon Dam and on into Marble Canyon. At night, demand dropped and so did the flow through the turbines. Boaters well down the river often awoke in the morning to find their rafts high and dry on the sand, or floating at the end of their tie ropes, though they had been securely grounded the evening before.

There was chafing, of course. Where, amid all the fluctuations and regulations was the adventure of the good old days?

Finally a challenge emerged. In June 1980, Lake Powell filled and the authorities decided to test the dam's spillways by letting the reservoir overflow for several days at a rate of about thirty-eight thousand cubic feet per second. Three experienced boatmen — Wally Rist; Kenton Grua, who owned his own dory; and Rudi Petschek — decided to break the Rigg brothers' record of two and a half days for a run through the canyon.

Timing appeared perfect — long summer days and a full moon, according to the calendar. But as they stood on the launching ramp at Lees Ferry, clearing the trip with the ranger, a deluge hit and stayed with them for hours. Mud waterfalls poured over the rims, and when darkness caught them near Redwall Cavern, the obscured moon was of scant help. They rowed on, nevertheless, guiding themselves by the skyline and the feeble gleam of their flashlights. One oarsman worked until weary and then called for a substitute; the other two kept shifting their weight to maintain the boat's exact balance on the water, an important point in fast rowing.

Fearful of hitting Hance Rapid before they could see it, they pulled into an eddy to wait for dawn. Then on again, facing forward when they entered the tongue of a rapid, but swinging around to gain time by rowing backwards at full strength through the tail waves. When another storm caught them in the darkness near Pumpkin Spring, they pulled into an eddy and stretched out on the decks, under tarpaulins, seeking whatever sleep they could get. Six hours later the moon came out, and at 3:15 A.M. they were on their way once more. They reached Grand Wash Cliffs in four minutes less than forty-eight hours after leaving Lees Ferry.

A record — but not as good as they wanted, so when the floods of 1983 sent ninety thousand cubic feet per second through Glen Canyon's spillways, two of the original crew, Kenton Grua and Rudi Petschek, plus Steve Reynolds, set out again. They left Lees Ferry June 26 under a full moon, on seventy-two thousand cfs, far more water than they had experienced before. Sometimes it helped, as

Mud waterfalls poured over the rims, and when darkness caught them near Redwall Cavern, the obscured moon was of scant help.

2. Currently the ratio of commercial to private trips is about seventy to thirty.

floods often do, but when they reached Crystal in midmorning they saw a hole gaping almost beyond imagining and behind it an explosion wave that looked, but probably wasn't, as tall as a three-story building. Moreover, an unexpected new hole blocked the usual run to the right of the heavy water, and when they tried it, the dory whirled upside down. One by one they climbed back onto its bottom, loosened the flip lines that circled the underside of the craft, and, rearing back, tried to pull the boat over. They had reached shallow water and the dory was standing almost at right angles on its side when the flip line broke. All three men went backwards into the river. The boat crashed down, still bottom side up. Then an eddy picked them up, and after a struggle with new lines they righted the boat. Though stern and bow posts had both been damaged, the trouble lay above the water line. Shaking off the demoralization that had followed the episode, they went on.

Whirlpools, boils, and "squirrelly" water below each rapid demanded constant alertness. They were tired when darkness fell; thick darkness, for the moon was behind the walls. But on this trip they had brought along powerful searchlights hooked to car batteries, and they kept running by those strong yellow beams to about mile 203, where exhaustion forced them to pull to the bank and rest awhile. A little after midnight, when the moon rose briefly above the cliff rims, they rowed on. In spite of the rest stop and the upset, they reached Grand Wash Cliffs in thirty-six hours, thirty-eight minutes, and twenty seconds.

A response to a challenge? A stunt? An ego trip? A little of each perhaps. But also a connecting link, however unintentional, with the long story of man's urge to match himself against the canyon, to learn something of himself through learning its ways, and by those means to make it eventually everyone's possession, in imagination if not in direct contact.

There is nothing else quite like it — a deeply entrenched water corridor two hundred and eighty miles long through a desert wilderness of almost overwhelming beauty. No other American river offers, in one unbroken stretch, as great an aggregation of rapids. Contact with nature is direct and powerful. Nor is the encounter limited to water situations. Side canyons, some attainable by trail and some not, offer unexpected plunge pools, waterfalls, banks of ferns, brilliant flowers. One can swim, hike, climb, fish, take pictures, hunt for ancient Indian petroglyphs, study botany or geology in what has been called the world's greatest open textbook, or just sit still, watching small creatures go about their business while the variegated cliffs take on the rich hues of sunset.

Blue haze sinking past purpling walls to mingle with the last streaks of light on the darkening river: it is a good moment to recall those who went before, to heed the Chinese saying, "When drinking the water, remember who dug the well."

133

Acknowledgments

I would like to begin this statement of gratitude for help generously given with a nod toward the ghosts of those who collected the bins of material I raided so eagerly — Otis Marston, Harry Aleson, Emery Kolb, Frederick Dellenbaugh — and then to those who helped me find my way through those treasure troves: Mrs. Virginia Rust and Dr. William Frank of the Huntington Library, home of the complexly arranged three hundred ninety-six big, green file boxes of the Marston Collection (and home also of the E.C. LaRue Collection); to Louise Hinchliffe of the Park library in the Visitor Center on the South Rim of the Grand Canyon; to William Mullane, head of Special Collections, University of Northern Arizona, where the Kolb Collection resides; to Gary Topping of the Utah Historical Society, holders of the Aleson Collection; and to the staff of the Arizona Historical Society, site of the Dellenbaugh Collection.

Bill and Fran Belknap, Amos Burg, F.E. Masland, Jr., Joan Nevills Staveley, Becky Walker Tucker, and Georgie White talked with me or wrote to me about their own experiences back in the pre-dam days. The many Dales — O'Connor, Roberta, Regan, and Otie — Brad Dimock, Martin Litton, Roderick Nash, John Olson, Rudi Petschek, and Kenly Weills added their valuable bits about more modern times. Also special mention for Randy Tate and Marilyn Rivas-Tate, who did so much to teach my wife and me what river running is all about. Martin Litton and the Stanford University Alumni Association enabled me to go through the canyon in the summer of 1983 for another look.

The manuscript was read in its entirety by Bill and Fran Belknap; Cort Conley, who also lent me some original Burg-Holmstrom correspondence; Brad Dimock, and Robert Euler. Frank Masland covered it in part. In a few instances I went my own way in spite of this formidable array of talent, and of course must

134

bear the responsibility for whatever errors may have resulted from the stubbornness.

The fact that the manuscript was finished at all is due primarily to my wife, Mildred, her sharp, proofreader's eyes, trusty typewriter, and steady encouragement.

Bibliography

All of the unpublished material listed below is from the Marston Collection, Huntington Library, San Marino, California, unless otherwise noted. Material cited as Aleson Collection is at the Utah Historical Society. Copies of some material, especially diaries, repose in various institutions; for instance, there are two volumes of transcripts, *Colorado River Journals and Diaries* at the Grand Canyon National Park Library. Wherever I used such duplicates, generally as a matter of convenience, I have noted the location in the following compilation.

Primary Sources

Published and unpublished diaries, reminiscences, correspondence.
ALESON, HARRY. Biographical sketch, Aleson Collection, B-157.
———. Citing individual items among the mass of correspondence, trial manuscripts, journals, etc., is not feasible here. However, see box 2, appropriate folders, for Harry's early up-river attempts, his 1944 hike with White and Bakker, his 1945 swim with White; and box 29 (mislabeled box 25) for his 1946 raft-swim adventure with Georgie White.
BARBER, DEVERGNE. Diary 1927. Pathé-Bray trip. Marston and Grand Canyon collections.
BARTL, ROBERT. Diary 1927. Eddy trip. Grand Canyon Library.
BISHOP, FRANK. Diary 1871-72. *Utah Historical Quarterly*, combined volumes 1948-49. Powell's second trip.
BRADLEY, GEORGE. Diary 1869. *Utah Historical Quarterly*, Volume 15. Powell's first trip.
BRENNAN, JACK. Diary 1949. Loper's last trip.
BROWN, FRANK. Diary 1889. Stanton's first trip.
BURG, AMOS. 1938 progress reports written on postcards to A.W. Mendenhall, Director, USGS.

CAMPBELL, IAN. Diary 1937. The Cal Tech-Carnegie Tech trip.

CLEMENT, LESLIE. Interview, Marston, December 12, 1947. See also under Russell.

CLOVER, ELZADA. Marston's notes from her diary of 1938 trip with Nevills and Marston's interview with her, August 1950.

COGSWELL, RAYMOND A. Diary 1909. Julius Stone trip.

DUBENDORFF, SEYMOUR S. Diary 1909. Stone trip.

EDDY, CLYDE. Diary 1927.

———. Diary 1934.

FLAVELL, GEORGE. Data in Stanton's unpublished "The River and the Canyon." Also Marston files.

FREEMAN, LEWIS R. Diary 1923. USGS survey.

GALLOWAY, NATHANIEL. Diary 1909. Marston files; copy in Aleson Collection.

HALL, JOSEPH. Diary 1964. Leydet trip. Grand Canyon Library.

HARRIS, DON. Diary 1949. Loper's death. Grand Canyon Library.

HATCH, ALTON. Diary 1934. Frazier-Eddy trip.

HILLERS, J.K. *"Photographed All the Best Scenery": J.K. Hiller's Diary.* (Dan D. Fowler, ed.) Salt Lake City: University of Utah Press, 1977. Powell's second trip.

HOLMSTROM, BUZZ. Diary 1937, said to have been edited by his mother. Several copies around. I used one loaned me by Brad Dimock. See also correspondence, Marston files.

HUDSON, E.H. Correspondence about his 1944-50 boat runs in both Aleson and Marston.

HYDE, BESSIE and GLEN. Quantities of miscellany, Marston Box 86, HY-JC and chronology file 1924-28.

JOHNSON, WILLIS. Diary 1938. Burg-Holmstrom Trip. Copy loaned me by Cort Conley.

JONES, STEPHEN V. Diary 1871-72 in combined volumes 1948-49, *Utah Historical Quarterly.* Powell's second trip.

KOLB, E.L. "River-Running, 1921: The Diary of E.L. Kolb," edited by W.L. Rusho. *Utah Historical Quarterly,* Spring 1950. Contains material about E.C. LaRue.

KOLB, EMERY. Correspondence with Col. Birdseye, USGS, and with his family concerning 1923 USGS Survey. Kolb Collection, University of Northern Arizona.

LARUE, E.C. Diaries 1921, 1923. USGS surveys.

LOPER, ALBERT. Diary Winter 1911-12. Copy, Aleson Collection.

MARSTON, OTIS. Taped interview, May 28, 1976, with Jay Hammond and John Hoffman about river people and episodes. Transcript. Aleson Collection.

MASLAND, F.E. JR. Reminiscences, 1948-49, 1954-56. Copy sent me by the author.

NEVILLS, DORIS. Diary 1940. Published in installments, Grand Junction (Colo.) *Daily Sentinel,* June 15, 1940 et. seq.

NEVILLS, NORMAN. Log and Notebook, 1938.

NIMS, FRANKLIN A. *The Photographer and the River, 1889-90.* (ed. Dwight Smith) Santa Fe; Stagecoach Press, 1950. Stanton trips.

PATHÉ-BRAY, miscellaneous documents. Marston chronological file, 1924-28.

POWELL, WALTER CLEMENT. Diary, 1871-72. *Utah Historical Quarterly,* combined volumes 1948-49. Powell's second trip.

REID, DEL. Diary and unpublished manuscript, 1938. Nevills-Clover trip.

RICHMOND, WILLIAM CHESLEY. Reminiscences of trip with Galloway, 1895-96.

RIGG, JAMES P. Correspondence with Marston concerning the salvage of the *Esmeralda II,* 1950, and the record run of 1951.

RUSSELL, CHARLES SILVER. His adventures with Edwin Monett, Bert Loper, A.J. Tadje, Goddard Quist, and Leslie Clement, intermittently 1907-1915, in Marston's subject files MIT-MORD, RUS-RY and chronological files 1897-1907, 1912-1913. There are also a few pertinent Russell and Loper letters in the Kolb Collection, Northern Arizona University.

SANGER, ARTHUR R. Fragmentary diary. Hum Woolley trip, 1903.

STANTON, ROBERT BREWSTER. Unpublished manuscript. "The River and the
Canyon." (Both Smith's edition of *Down the Colorado* and Belknap's edition of
Colorado River Controversies are drawn from "The River and the Canyon.") In
describing the river trip, Stanton drew on his diary. (I used the copy of the diary in
the Dellenbaugh Collection, Arizona Historical Society.) The diary is much more
explicit than the manuscript about such things as mining near Bright Angel Creek
and the quarrel with McDonald.
STEWARD, JOHN W. Diary, 1871-72. *Utah Historical Quarterly*, combined volumes
1948-49. Powell's second trip.
SUMNER, JACK. Diary, 1869. *Utah Historical Quarterly*, volume 1947. Powell's first trip.
TADJE, AUGUST. Interview with Marston, December 4, 1947. See also under Russell.
THOMPSON, ALMON H. Diary, 1871-75. *Utah Historical Quarterly* 1939. Powell's
second expedition.
UNITED STATES GEOLOGICAL SURVEYS, Colorado River surveys, 1921-23.
Manuscript material in Marston chronological files.
WHITE, GEORGIE. Notes written to Harry Aleson concerning her first (1952) trip
through Grand Canyon. Aleson Collection, Box 28, Folder 15.

Books

BAKER, PEARL. *Trail on the Water.* Boulder, Colorado: Pruett Press, 1970. (Biography of
Bert Loper.)
BELKNAP, BUZZ. *Grand Canyon River Guide.* Salt Lake City: Canyonlands Press, 1969.
BUTCHART, HARVEY. *Grand Canyon Treks.* Los Angeles: La Siesta Press, 1976. Traces
climbs out of the canyon by Stanton, Harry McDonald, August Tadje, and others.
CLARK, GEORGIE WHITE with Duane Newcomb. *Georgie Clark: Thirty Years of River
Running.* San Francisco: Chronicle Books, 1977.
COLLINS, ROBERT O. and RODERICK NASH. *The Big Drops: Ten Legendary Rapids.*
Sierra Club Books: San Francisco, 1978.
DUTTON, CLARENCE E. *Tertiary History of the Grand Canyon District.* Layton, Utah:
Peregrine Smith, 1977.
EDDY, CLYDE. *Down the World's Most Dangerous River.* New York: Frederick A. Stokes,
1929. Eddy's 1927 run.
FEWKES, J. WALTER. "The Snake Ceremonial at Walpi," in volume 4, *Journal of
American Ethnology and Archaeology.* Cambridge: Massachusetts. Houghton Mifflin
Co., 1894. Tiyo legend.
FREEMAN, LEWIS R. *The Colorado River, Yesterday, Today, and Tomorrow.* New York:
Dodd Mead & Co., 1923.
————. *Down the Grand Canyon.* New York: Dodd Mead & Co., 1924. Mostly the 1923
USGS survey trip.
GASKILL, DAVID L. and GEORGE SIMMONS. *Marble Gorge and the Grand Canyon.*
Flagstaff: Northland Press, 1969. Geology for river runners.
GOLDWATER, BARRY. *Delightful Journey Down the Green and Colorado Rivers.* Tempe,
Arizona: Arizona Historical Foundation, 1970. Contains a section on geology by
Carlton Moore and a letter from Emery Kolb concerning the disappearance of the
Hydes.
HAMILTON, JOYCE. *White Water.* Christchurch, New Zealand: Caxton Press, 1963.
The 1960 up-river jet boat expedition.
HOFFMAN, JOHN. *National Parkways: The Grand Canyon* . . . Casper, Wyoming:
World-Wide Research & Publishing Co., 1977.
HUGHES, J. DONALD. *In the House of Stone and Light.* Grand Canyon: Grand Canyon
Natural History Association, 1977. The story of man at the Grand Canyon.
JAEGER, OSCAR R. *The Great Grand Canyon Adventure.* Dubuque, Iowa: Published by
Jaeger, 1932. Jaeger joined the 1927 Eddy expedition at Lees Ferry.
KOLB, ELLSWORTH. *Through the Grand Canyon from Wyoming to Mexico.* New York:
The Macmillan Co., 1920.
KRUTCH, JOSEPH W. *Grand Canyon, Today and All Its Yesterdays.* New York: W. Sloane
Associates, 1958.

LARUE, E.C. *Water Power and Flood Control of the Colorado River below Green River, Utah.* USGS Professional Paper 550. Washington, DC, 1925.

LEYDET, FRANÇOIS. *Time and the River Flowing: Grand Canyon.* San Francisco: Sierra Club, 1964.

MASLAND, F.E., Jr. *By the Rim of Time.* Privately printed.

MCPHEE, JOHN. *Encounters with the Archdruid.* New York: Farrar, Straus, and Giraux, 1971.

POWELL, JOHN WESLEY. *The Exploration of the Colorado River and Its Canyons.* New York: Dover Publications, Inc., 1961.

RUSHO, W.L., and C. GREGORY CRAMPTON. *Desert River Crossing: Historic Lees Ferry on the Colorado.* Salt Lake City: Peregrine Smith, 1975.

STANTON, ROBERT BREWSTER. *Colorado River Controversies.* Boulder City, Nevada; Westwater Books, 1982. Discusses James White's alleged traverse of the canyon in 1967 and the "desertion" of three of Powell's men at Separation Rapid.

———. *Down the Colorado.* (ed. by Dwight L. Smith). Norman: University of Oklahoma Press, 1965.

STAVELEY, GAYLORD. *Broken Waters Sing.* Boston: Little Brown, 1971.

STEGNER, WALLACE. *Beyond the Hundredth Meridian: John Wesley Powell and the Second Opening of the West.* Boston: Houghton Mifflin Co., 1954.

STEVENS, LARRY. *The Colorado River in Grand Canyon.* Flagstaff, Arizona. Red Lake Books, 1983.

UDALL, STEWART. *The Quiet Crisis.* New York: Holt, Rinehart & Winston, 1963.

WALLACE, ROBERT. *The Grand Canyon.* New York: Time-Life Books, 1972.

WATKINS, T.H., *et al. The Grand Colorado: The Story of a River and Its Canyons.* Palo Alto, California. American West Publishing Company, 1969.

WHEELER, GEORGE. *A Report upon United States Geographical Surveys West of the 100th Meridian.* Washington, DC: Government Printing Office, 1889.

Articles

ALESON, HARRY. "Colorado River Raft Drift." *Southern Sierran,* August 1946.

———. "Swim Trip with Georgie White." *Boulder City News,* July 6, 1945.

ALLEN, DAVID. "A Daring Voyage Down the Colorado." *The Wide World Magazine,* November 1908. Exaggerated account of Russell-Monett trip.

BEER, BILL. "Tragedy, Close Calls, and Thrills Mark River Trip." *Los Angeles Times,* July 1, 1956. Willie Taylor's death.

———. "We Swam the Colorado." *Collier's Magazine,* August 5, 1955. Trip with John Daggett without boats.

BELKNAP, WILLIAM, JR. "Shooting the Rapids in Reverse." *National Geographic Magazine,* April 1962. Up-river jet boats, 1960.

[BIRDSEYE, CLAUDE E.] "Daring Scientists Conquer Grand Canyon." *New York Times,* November 11, 1923. USGS Survey, 1923.

BIRDSEYE, CLAUDE E. and RAYMOND MOORE. "A Boat Voyage Through the Grand Canyon of the Colorado." *The Geographical Review,* April 1924. USGS, 1923.

BURG, AMOS. "Grand Canyon Adventure" in *Hell and High Water.* New York: Robert M. McBride, 1945.

CLOVER, ELZADA U. "Danger Can Be Fun." *Michigan Alumni Quarterly Review,* Winter 1939. 1938 trip with Nevills.

EULER, ROBERT. "Willow Figurines from Arizona." *Natural History,* March 1966.

———. "The Canyon Dwellers." *American West,* May 1967.

FREEMAN, LEWIS R. "Surveying the Grand Canyon of the Colorado." *National Geographic Magazine,* May 1924. The 1923 USGS expedition.

HUDSON, ED. "Hudson Expedition," *Sea,* December 1948.

IVES, RONALD L. "Bert Loper — the Last Chapter." *Journal of Arizona History,* Spring 1970. Finding Loper's remains.

KIRSCHBAUM, WALTER. "Grand Adventure." *American Whitewater,* November 1960.

KOLB, ELLSWORTH, and EMERY KOLB. "Experiences in the Grand Canyon." *National Geographic Magazine,* August 1914.

LAVENDER, DAVID. "James White: First Through the Grand Canyon?" *American West*, November/December 1982. See bibliographic note for literature on the controversy.
LEOPOLD, LUNA B. "The Rapids and the Pools — Grand Canyon" in *The Colorado River Region and John Wesley Powell*. Geological Survey Professional Paper 669. Washington, DC: Government Printing Office 1969.
LOS ANGELES *HERALD EXPRESS*. "Angelenos Swim Down Grand Canyon." July 9, 1945. Aleson and Georgie White.
MARSTON, OTIS. "River Runners: Fast Water Navigation." *Utah Historical Quarterly*, July 1960.
———. "Separation Marks." *Journal of Arizona History*, Spring 1976. Early parties at Separation Rapid.
———. "With Powell on the Colorado." Brand Book II, San Diego Corral, Westerners, 1971.
MORRISON, GEORGE. "Up the Colorado by Jet Boat." *Power Boat*, May 1961.
PEDERSON, SARAH. "Emery Kolb" in *Discovery Series 7*, Flagstaff: Northern Arizona University, 1980.
REILLY, P.T. Woolley-Sanger trip of 1903, title unavailable. *Desert Magazine*, December 1962.
SAYRE, JOEL. "Georgie's Roaring River. " *Sports Illustrated*, June 6 and 23, 1958.
SEGERBLOM, GENE. "Shooting the Grand Canyon in a Power Boat." *Popular Mechanics*, April 1950.
SMITH, DWIGHT L. "The Engineer and the Canyon." *Utah Historical Quarterly*, June 1960.
SPEARMAN, RUPERT. "Expedition Including Women Safely Navigates Colorado River." *Reclamation Era*. September 1938. Clover-Jotter-Nevills trip.
SPIERS, JACK. "The Conquest of the Colorado." *Sports Afield*, Spring 1952. Powerboat trips, 1949-50.
STRUTIN, MICHELE. "The White Water Queen and the River Rats." *New West*, August 27, 1979.
VOTH, HENRY R. "The Oraibi Snake Ceremony." Field Columbian Museum Publication 38, November 1903. Tiyo legend.

Index

A

Adger, Gordon, 67, 70
Aleson, Harry, 55, 100, 101,
    123; escape ideas of, 109-14;
    upstream attempt by, 106-9;
    with Hudson, 116; with
    West, 102-4; with White,
    109-14
airplanes, 72, 81, 98, 104-5,
    120, 125, 130
animals, 67, 68, 69, 70, 71, 74
Arizona, the, 45
Army Corps of Engineers, 20
artists, 19, 30, 97, 130
Ashley, William H., 36
Atkinson, Eugene, 97, 98, 99
Austin, Bill, 124, 125

B

Badger Creek, 52
Badger Creek Rapids, 23, 35,
    39, 61, 69, 89, 99
Baker, Charles, 9
Baker, Mildred, 98, 100, 101,
    102, 103
Bakker, Gerhard, 110
Barber, Devergne, 71, 73, 74
Bartl, Robert, 68, 69, 70
Bass, William, 54
Bass Camp, 50
Bass Rapid, 121
Bass Trail, 50, 63, 82
Beaman, E.O., 19
Beer, Bill, 121, 122
Belknap, Bill, 100, 119, 121,
    125, 128, 129
Belknap, Buzz, 125, 128
Bell, Lorin, 99, 100
Best, James, 31
Big Red, the, 124, 125
Big Yellow, the, 124
Birdseye, Claude H., 59,
    60-63, 95
Birdseye, Roger, 61, 62, 63,
    64, 65
Blackwell, Frank, 67, 70
Blake, H.E., 60, 61, 65
Blake, Royal, 110, 112
Blossom, Rose, 73, 74
boat descriptions: aluminum,
    122; cataract, 120, 121;
    motored, 107, 116, 117, 119,
    120, 121, 122, 124, 125,
    131; plywood, 55; pontoon,
    122; sportyak, 128; steel,
    44, 51, 53, 60, 61;
    turbocraft, 124, 125;
    wooden, 13, 18, 22, 25, 34,
    36, 37, 38, 40, 48, 55, 67,
    71, 75, 76, 79, 86, 94, 97,
    105, 122, 123, 128, 130. *See
    also* kayaks; rafts
boils, 7
Boles, John, 73, 74
Bolster, Charles, 39, 40
Bonelli, Daniel, 37
Bonnie Jean, the, 25, 29
Botany, the, 97 98
Boucher, Louis, 46
Boucher Canyon, 46
Boucher Rapid, 119
Boucher Trail, 53, 54
Boulder Dam, 92, 101
Boulder Narrows, 101
Boulder Rapid, 62
boulders and boulder fans, 5,
    46, 53, 119
Boulder, the, 61, 64
Bradley, George, 13, 15, 16,
    17, 18
Bray, J.R., 66, 72
Bridge Canyon, 107
Bright Angel Creek, 16, 20, 29,
    48, 73, 90, 100, 117
Bright Angel Trail, 42, 45, 69,
    80, 130
Brooks, Jim, 82, 83
Brown, Frank M., 22, 23, 24
Brown, Hugh, 108
Bundy, Chet, 118
Bureau of Reclamation, 51, 59,
    66, 107, 118, 129
Burg, Amos, 93, 94, 95
Butchart, Harvey, 53

C

cairns, 38
Cal Tech-Carnegie Tech, 87,
    89, 92
Campbell, Ian, 89
Cañonita, the, 19
Canyon Country, 42
Canyonlands National Park, 51
Carey, Mr., 70
Case, Robert Ormond, 93
Cataract Canyon, 5, 23, 31, 35,
    41, 45, 48, 51, 67, 71, 72,
    78, 88, 98, 111, 114
Cave Springs, 73
Chalfant, James, 75
Charlie, the, 94
Clark, Harold, 109, 110
Clark, Owen, 71, 74, 80, 86
Clark the Trapper, 34
Clegg, Mrs., 95
Clement, Leslie, 53, 54
Clover, Elzada U., 96-100
Cogswell, Raymond, 40-42
Colorado River: body-floating
    down, 103, 111-13, 121;
    firsts on the, 42, 62, 95;
    high water of, 19, 64, 69,
    118, 125, 132; low water of,
    41, 76, 82; stream flow of,
    58, 80, 132; upstream runs
    on, 20, 45, 102, 106, 116-19,
    124-26; USGS survey along,
    59; user days rules for, 131
Colorado River Commission,
    58
Colorado River Compact, 59
Colorado River Controversies, 16,
    75
*Colorado River Yesterday, Today,
    and Tomorrow, The*, 59
Columbia River, 59
Coronado, the, 67
Crystal Creek, 29, 30
Crystal Rapid, 53, 54, 119
Cutler, Hugh, 101, 102

D

Daggett, John, 121
Daily, Dean, 73
dam site exploration, 51, 55,
    58, 65, 95, 107, 118, 131
Davis, Arthur Powell, 59
death list, 83
Deer Creek Falls, 91, 102, 118
Defiance, the, 48, 49, 50
Dellenbaugh, Frederick, 19,
    20
Dellenbaugh, the, 67, 70
Desloge, Joe, 119
Diamond Creek, 20, 30, 50,
    81-83, 92, 100, 108, 121
Disaster Falls, 14
Dock, the, 125, 126
Dodge, Frank, 59, 60-63, 65,
    71, 73, 74, 86, 87, 89
Doll House, 51
Doris Rapid, 102
Down the Colorado, 65
Driftwood Burner (DWB), 101
Dubendorff, Seymour Sylvester,
    41, 42
Dubendorff Rapid, 70, 91
Dunn, William (Bill), 13, 16,
    17, 18, 75
Dutton, Clarence E., 130

E

Eddy, Clyde, 66-70, 72-74, 75,
    76, 91
Edith, the, 48, 49, 50, 58
Edwards, William H., 31
Eiseley, Loren, 130

Index

Emery Falls, 113
Emma Dean, the, 13, 15, 17, 18
Escalante, Silvestre Velez de, 93
Escalante River, 114
Esmeralda, the, 108
Esmeralda II, the, 117, 119, 120
Examiner, the, 34
Explorers Club, 93

F

Fahrni, Bill, 76
Fetzner, Louise, 55, 114
Fewkes, J. Walter, 8
Flagstaff, Arizona, 39, 89
Flaming Gorge Reservoir, 36
Flavell, George, 34-36, 38, 95
Forcier, Guy, 119
Francy, Bob, 81, 82, 83
Frazier, Russel G., 75, 76, 93, 103
Freeman, Lewis R., 59, 60, 61, 63, 65
funding, 13, 18, 22, 25, 39, 44, 67, 93, 97, 108

G

Gable, Gilbert, 71, 72, 73
Galloway, Nathaniel (Than), 35, 36-38, 40-43
Galloway, Parley, 36, 37, 67, 69 70, 75
Galloway Canyon, 42
Gannon, Pat, 71
Garfield, James, 20
Gaskill, David, 5
Georgie sandwich, the, 123
Gibson, George, 23, 24
Gibson, William, 97
Gilliland, Mrs., 62
Glen Canyon, 19, 23, 25, 35, 38, 41, 45, 55, 59, 66, 71, 89, 93, 111, 124
Glen Canyon Dam, 128, 131
Glen, the, 61, 64, 65
Gneiss Canyon, 129
Goldwater, Barry, 100-102, 104, 131
Goodfellow, Joe, 8
Goodman, Frank, 14
Grand Canyon: egress from, 16, 20, 24, 29, 45, 50, 52, 53, 62, 82, 108, 109, 111-12, 118, 119; number of people through the, 123, 131; number o rapids in the, 7. *See also* Colorado River

Grand Canyon, the, 55
Grande Ronde River, 95
Grand River, 9
Grand, the, 60, 64, 65
Grandstedt, Greta, 79
Grand Wash Cliffs, 7, 18, 31, 35
Granite Falls, 42, 91
Granite Park, 92
Granite Springs Rapid, 108
Grant, Alexander (Zee), 104
Grapevinve (rapid), 73, 126
Green River, 13, 14, 94
G-rig, 123
Grua, Kenton, 132
Guleke, Harry, 79

H

Hall, Andy, 14, 18
Hall, Joseph, 130
Hamilton, Bill, 124
Hamilton, Jon, 124, 125, 126
Hance, John, 28, 35
Hance Rapid, 28, 35, 49, 62, 73
Hansbrough, Peter, 24, 27, 62, 73
Harbin, Jack, 82, 83
Harding, President, 61
Harding Rapid, 62, 122
Harris, Don (Laphene), 55, 97-99
Hatch, Alton, 75
Hatch, Bus, 75, 76, 88
Havasu Canyon, 108
Havasu Creek, 63, 83, 119
Havasupai, the, 131
Hawkins, Billy, 13, 17, 18
Hell's Half Mile, 88
Hemlick, Earl, 78
Henry's Fork, 36
Hermit Creek Rapids, 42, 46, 72, 74, 91, 102
Hermit Trail, 66
Herrick, Vernon T., 71, 72
Hillers, Jack, 19
Hislop, John, 23-26, 29, 30, 31
holes, 6
Holmstrom, Haldane (Buzz), 86-95, 100
Holt, Ed, 68, 69
homing pigeons, 101
Hoover, Herbert, 58
Hoover Dam, 76
Hopi, the, 7-8
Horn Creek Rapid, 29, 42, 91, 126
Howland, Oramel, 13, 16 17, 18, 75
Howland, Seneca, 13, 16, 18, 75

Hualapai, the, 83, 131
Hudson, Egbert (Ed), 104, 108, 116-20, 124
Hyde, Bessie, 78-84
Hyde, Glen, 79, 80
Hyde, Phillip, 130

I

I'Anson, Ed, 126
ice, 52

J

Jackass Canyon, 129
Jaeger, Oscar, 69, 70
Jayne, Fred, 76
Jeffs, Jake, 52
Johnson, Jeremiah, 80
Johnson, Warren M., 23, 26, 27
Johnson, Willis (Bill), 94, 95, 103
Jones, William, 130
Jordan, Jim, 121
Jotter, Lois, 97-100
Julius F., the, 94

K

Kaibab Trail, 125
Kanab Canyon, 20
Kanab Creek, 20, 91
Kanab, Utah, 19, 68
Kane, Elmer, 29, 30, 31
kayaks, 104, 123
Kerschner, Glen, 71, 75
King, John, 39
Kirschbaum, Walter, 123
Kiwi, the, 125, 126
Kolb, Blanche, 63
Kolb, Earnest, 50
Kolb, Edith, 62
Kolb, Ellsworth, 46-50, 52, 58, 73, 82, 87
Kolb, Emery, 46-50, 52, 58, 60-64, 69, 79, 80, 81-83, 86, 87, 91, 99, 100
Kominsky, Felix, 63
Krutch, Joseph Wood, 130

L

Lake Mead, 92, 95, 100, 101, 102, 106, 129
Lake Powell, 131, 132

143

Lantier, Felix, 28, 30
Larabee, Charles, 101, 114
LaRue, Eugene Clyde, 59, 62, 63, 65, 66, 71, 72
Lauzon, Bert, 50
Lava Cliff Rapids, 18, 20, 31, 35, 42, 65, 83, 92, 95
Lava Falls, 35, 50, 64, 83, 91, 92, 95, 121, 123, 125, 126
Lee, John D., 19
Lees Ferry, 7, 12, 15, 23, 26, 35, 37, 41, 45, 59, 68, 71, 80, 99, 102
Lehnert, Sonny, 91
Leland, Frank, 36
Leydet, François, 129, 130, 131
life jackets, 35, 46, 62, 69, 79, 80, 103, 111, 119, 121
lining, 14, 35, 42, 106
Lint, Leigh, 60, 62, 63, 64
Litton, Martin, 130
Lodore Canyon, 14, 35, 36, 37, 48, 76, 88, 94
Loper, Albert, 44, 45, 51, 52, 54-56, 58, 87, 105, 114
Lucky Pierre, the, 130

M

Mannering, Guy, 124, 125, 126
Mannering, Margie, 125
Marble Canyon, 6, 23, 55, 61, 69, 87, 132
Marble Gorge, 5, 15, 37, 41, 105, 122, 131
Marble Platform, 27
Marble, the, 61, 63, 64
Marston, Garth, 104, 125
Marston, Otis R. (Dock), 19, 75, 104, 105, 116-22, 124, 128, 129
McDonald, Harry, 23-29, 31, 32
McGregory, Mr., 67, 69
McKee, Edwin, 92
McKenzie River, 130
Mexican Hat, Utah, 96
Mexican Hat, the, 97, 98
Mile 25 Rapid, 24
Mile 75 Rapid, 105, 130
Mile 232 Rapid, 82, 83, 113
Mile Zero, 59
Miller, Mack, 128
Mohave, the, 20
Mojave, the, 60
Monett, Edwin R., 44-47
Montéz, Ramón, 34, 35
Moon, Karl, 45, 46, 47
Moore, Frank, 86
Moore, Raymond C., 61, 65

Moore, Return, 108
Moran, Thomas, 30
Morrison, George, 126
Mowrey, Royce, 75, 76, 88
MY HOME, Arizona, 104, 114

N

Nash, Roderick, 102
National Park Service, 131
Navajo Bridge, 80, 89, 105, 129
Nelson, John, 82, 83
Nevada, the, 45
Nevills, Doris, 97, 101, 102, 103
Nevills, Norman, 94, 96-105, 114, 116
Nevills Rapid, 105, 130
Nevills, W.E., 97
Nichol, Wayne, 55
Nims, Franklin A., 22, 25, 26, 27
No Name, the, 14, 17
North Canyon Rapid, 90, 101
North Rim, 29
notation for rapids, 80

O

Order of Colorado River Rats, 100

P

Pahl, Catherine, 60
Paiute, the, 20, 37
Panthon, the, 35
Parashant Wash, 112
Paria (creek), 15, 19
Paria Riffle, 37
Pathé-Bray Company, 66, 71-75
Patraw, P.P., 81, 82
Peach Springs, 30, 50, 82, 108
Petschek, Rudi, 132
Phantom RAnch, 48, 72, 102, 125
photographers: early still-camera, 19, 22, 26, 40, 44; later, including movie filming, 47-50, 51-54, 55, 60, 63, 66-70, 71-75, 76, 80, 95, 99, 105, 106, 128
Pierce, Elgin, 114
Pipe Spring Rapid, 63, 130
plaques, 75, 93, 102-3, 105

portage, 14, 50
Portola, the, 130
Potter, C.E., 23
Powell, John Wesley, 5, 9, 12-21, 75, 130
Powell, the, 67, 70
Powell, Walter, 13, 18
President Harding Rapid, 62, 122

Q

Quartermaster Canyon, 104
Quartzite, Arizona, 38
Quist, Goddard, 52

R

radios, 61, 63, 71, 72, 73, 90, 101, 129
rafts, 7, 9, 55, 93-94, 112, 114, 122, 130
Rainbow Bridge, 98
Red Creek Rapid, 88
Red Wall Canyon, 118
Reeder, Bill, 51, 52, 79
reflex waves, 6
Reid, Dell, 99, 100, 101
Reilly, P.T., 40, 83, 130
rescue. *See* search and rescue
Reynolds, Jack, 125
Reynolds, Steve, 132
Richards, Henry, 23, 24, 73
Richmond, William, 35, 36-38
Rider, Roy, 41
Rider Canyon, 26
Riffey, John, 118
Rigg, Bob, 121
Rigg, Jim, 114, 120, 121
Rist, Wally, 132
Ritchey, Chuck, 125
River of No Return, 79, 87
Robinson, Bestor, 117
Rogue River, 87
Ross Wheeler, the, 51, 52, 53, 54
Royal River Rats, 123
Russell, Charles Silver, 44-47, 50-54
Rust, Dave, 48

S

Salmon River, 79, 87
Samoff, Nick, 73, 74
Sanderson, Rod, 118, 121
Sanger, Arthur, 39, 40
San Juan River, 9

Schell, Madame, 38, 39, 40
search and rescue, 38, 71,
    81-83, 120
Segerblom, Cliff, 128
Separation Canyon, 109
Separation Rapid, 17, 20, 31,
    37, 46, 65, 69, 75, 76, 83,
    92, 95, 102, 106
Serpentine Rapid, 20, 91
Sharp, C.C., 40, 41
shear line, 6
Sheer Wall, 73
Shivwits, the, 18, 20
Sierra Club, 100, 110, 114,
    117, 129
Silver Creek, 16
Simmons, George, 5
Slate Canyon, 53
Smith, Leigh, 71, 72, 74
Smithsonian Institution, 13,
    105
Soap Creek Rapids, 23, 35, 39,
    49, 61, 69, 73, 90
Sockdolager Rapid, 28, 39, 69,
    73, 80, 99, 100
South Canyon, 24
South Rim, 44, 48
Spencer, M.F., 86
Spencer Canyon, 18, 82, 83
Staker, Sadie, 37
standing waves, 6
Stanton, Robert Brewster, 6,
    16, 17, 22-32, 38, 40, 75
Stanton's Cave, 25
Staveley, Joan, 97
Steele, Keith, 130
Stone, Julius F., 38, 40-43, 47,
    75, 76, 93, 103
Stone Canyon, 42
Strole, George, 9
Sumner, Jack, 13, 16, 17, 18,
    19, 26
Supai, the, 83, 119
Suzie Too, the, 130
Swain, Frank, 75, 76, 88
Sweet Marie, the, 25, 28
Swenson, Fred, 108

T

Tadje August, 51-54
Talbot, Hayden, 45, 47
Tanner, Seth, 28
Tapeats Creek, 102, 118, 120
Taylor, Wilson (Willie), 117,
    119, 122
techniques, 35, 36, 39, 47, 69,
    76, 80, 87, 92, 101, 111-13,
    120, 122-23, 124, 125, 132
Thompson, Almon, 12, 19
Through the Grand Canyon from

Wyoming to Mexico, 87
Time and the River Flowing, 131
Titanic II, the, 52, 53
Tonto Platform, 29, 46, 53
Trail Canyon, 107
transport power, 6
Travertine Canyon, 92
Truxton Springs, 20
Tuna Creek Rapid, 119

U

Udall, Stewart, 129
United States Board of
    Geographic Names, 105
United States Geological
    Survey, 5, 42, 55, 58, 59-63,
    95, 97
Upper Granite Gorge, 5, 16,
    28, 39, 45, 48, 73
Upset Rapid, 63
Utah, the, 45, 46

V

Vasey, George, 25
Vaseys Paradise, 25
Vickers, Ward, 108
Virgin River, 18, 37

W

Walker, Preston, 105
Waltenberg, John, 54
Waltenberg Rapid, 50, 63, 70,
    91
Ward, the cook, 63
Water Lily, the, 25, 29
waves, 6
Wee Red, the, 124, 125, 126
Wee Yellow, the, 124, 125, 126
WEN, the, 97, 98
West, Louis, 102
Wheeler, George M., 20, 107
White, Georgie, 109-14, 122,
    126, 131
White, James, 8-9, 75
White, James R. (Whitey),
    110, 114, 122, 123
White, Paul, 122
Whitmore Wash, 117, 125, 130
Widstoe, John A., 59
Wilson, Neil, 104
women on rivers, 62, 78, 94,
    100, 103, 105, 114
Woolley, Elias Benjamin
    (Hum), 38-40

Wright, Barton, 56
Wright, Frank, 114, 120, 121

Y

Young, Dick, 125

Z

Zoroaster Rapid, 73

Photography Credits

1. Photo copied from the original in the library collections of the Arizona Historical Society
2. Reproduction from the collections of the Library of Congress
3. Photo owned by Charles G. Sumner
4. Copied from the original in the library collections of the Arizona Historical Society
5. Credited by Marston to Stanton Collection
6. Copy of print owned by Mamie Hall Laughlin
7. Reproduction from the collections of the Library of Congress. Photograph by E.O. Beaman
8. Photograph by J.K. Hillers, US Colorado River Expedition
9. McCormick photo
10. Photo by Central Photo Parlors, Denver
11. Photo owned by Mrs. Mary Raworth Ward Brown Gillman
12. Nims photo, National Archives
13. Photo from collection of Anne Stanton Burchard
14. Print owned by Mrs. Richmond
15. Photo by Raymond Austin Cogswell
16. Copy of print in Sanger Album
17. No credit available
18. Print owned by Edward A. Dubendorff
19. No credit available
20. Copied from print in Stanton Collection
21. Kolb photo courtesy of Northern Arizona University Special Collections Library
22. Photo owned by Goddard Quist
23. Photo by Bill Belknap
24. Copy of print from National Archives
25. Photo owned by Mrs. Nellie Miller
26. No credit available
27. Blake photo
28. Kershner photo
29. Kershner photo
30. Kolb photo courtesy of Northern Arizona University Special Collections Library
31. No credit available
32. USGS photo
33. No credit available
34. Freeman photo
35. Kolb photo courtesy of Northern Arizona University Special Collections Library
36. Copied from small print in Chenoweth album
37. Eddy photo
38. Weatherhead photo
39. Eddy photo
40. No credit available
41. Weatherhead photo
42-46. Kershner photo
47. Ted Hatch collection, courtesy Belknap Photographic Services

48. Photo by Adolf G. Sutro
49. Photo by Bill Belknap
50. Marston Photo, Marston Collection, Huntington Library, San Marino
51. Photo by Amos Burg
52. Marston Photo, Marston Collection, Huntington Library, San Marino
53. Photo by Bill Belknap
54. Photo by Elzada Clover
55. National Park Service photo
56. Barry Goldwater photo
57. Barry Goldwater photo
58. Marston Photo, Marston Collection, Huntington Library, San Marino
59. Photo by Bill Belknap
60. Hudson photo
61. No credit available
62. Marston Photo, Marston Collection, Huntington Library, San Marino
63. Photo by Fran Belknap
64-70. Photo by Bill Belknap
71.   Marston Photo, Marston Collection, Huntington Library, San Marino
72-75. Photo by Bill Belknap

Note: Many of the photographs used in this volume were located in the massive collection of Otis "Dock" Marston. Valiant attempts were made to locate the owners of the photos. Some of the attempts were successful, some not. We asked Bill Belknap if he could tell us where to find several people to whom Marston had credited photos. Bill's reply: "All of them I knew anything about 'ran the last rapid' as Dock used to say." We sincerely apologize to anyone we missed.